THE INTERNATIONAL CENTER FOR ECONOMIC GROWTH is a non-profit research institute founded in 1985 to stimulate international discussions on economic policy, economic growth, and human welfare. The Center sponsors research, publications, and conferences in cooperation with an international network of correspondent institututes, which distribute publications of both the Center and other network members to policy audiences around the world. The Center's research and publications program is organized around five series: Sector Studies; Country Studies; Studies in Human Development and Social Welfare; Occasional Papers; and a Reprint Series.

The Center is affiliated with the Institute for Contemporary Studies, and has headquarters in Panama and a home office in San Francisco, California.

Publication signifies that the Center believes a work to be a competent treatment worthy of public consideration. The findings, interpretations, and conclusions of a work are entirely those of the author and should not be attributed to ICEG, its affiliated organizations, its board of overseers, or organizations that support ICEG.

For further information, please contact the International Center for Economic Growth, 243 Kearny Street, San Francisco, California, 94108, USA. Phone (415) 981-5353; Fax (415) 986-4878.

ICEG Board of Overseers

MODELS OF DEVELOPMENT

MODELS OF

DEVELOPMENT

A COMPARATIVE STUDY OF ECONOMIC GROWTH IN SOUTH KOREA AND TAIWAN

Revised and Expanded Edition

**Edited by
LAWRENCE J. LAU**

An International Center for Economic Growth Publication

ICS PRESS
San Francisco, California

© 1990 by the Institute for Contemporary Studies.

Publication signifies that the center believes a work to be a competent treatment worthy of public consideration. The findings, interpretations, and conclusions of a work are entirely those of the authors and should not be attributed to ICEG, its affiliated organizations, its board of overseers, or organizations that support ICEG.

Inquiries, book orders, and catalog requests should be addressed to ICS Press, 243 Kearny Street, San Francisco, CA 94108, USA. Telephone: (415) 981-5353; Fax: (415) 986-4878; book orders within the continental United States: (800) 326-0263.

The cover was designed by Melissa Bay Mathis.

The index was prepared by Shirley Kessel.

Library of Congress Cataloging-in-Publication Data

Models of development: a comparative study of economic growth in South
    Korea and Taiwan / edited by Lawrence J. Lau. — Rev. and expanded ed.
          p.   cm.
    "An International Center for Economic Growth Publication"
    ISBN 1-55815-102-8. — ISBN 1-55815-005-6 (pbk.)
    1. Korea (South) — Economic policy — 1960–   2. Taiwan —
Economic policy — 1945–   3. Korea (South) — Economic conditions —
1960–   4. Taiwan — Economic conditions — 1945–   I. Lau,
Lawrence J., 1944–
HC467.M64   1990   90-32765
338.9519'5 — dc20   CIP

Contents

     OF PASSAGES
     Lawrence J. Lau

6   THE ECONOMY OF SOUTH KOREA, 1980–1987   217
     Sung Yeung Kwack

7   CONCLUSION   237
     Lawrence J. Lau

     APPENDIX—Profiles of Policymakers   245

     NOTES   251

     CONTRIBUTORS   261

     INDEX   263

List of Tables and Figures

Chapter 4

Chapter 5

Chapter 6

MODELS OF DEVELOPMENT

Foreword

South Korea and Taiwan have continued to make unusual economic progress since the original publication of this study, and the favorable comments that I made in the foreword to the first edition have not changed in a fundamental way. These two economies are outstanding in the sense that they are very promising cases for elevation from developing-country status to developed-country status. In fact, many people who are familiar with the use of the concepts "developing" and "developed" already assume that these two economies are, in fact, developed.

There are some interesting pieces of information that lead one to this conclusion, apart from observation of such achievements as high output/income levels, strong international trade accounts, and the excellent quality of their manufactured goods. Both countries are selling world-class goods in sophisticated lines in international markets.

Their strong positions in world trade were formerly associated with favorable currency exchange rates, which were essentially pegged to the U.S. dollar. During the past few years, both the New Taiwan dollar and the South Korean won have been allowed to appreciate, just as the currencies of "members of the club" would have done in similar circumstances. It is true that the respective central banks and treasuries moved very cautiously toward currency appreciation, and it is also true that they were talked into this action by the United States; nevertheless the currencies did appreciate, and both countries continue to enjoy healthy export-led growth. Both took the requisite steps and realized substantial rises in the value of their currencies against the U.S. dollar— approximately 40 percent in the case of the New Taiwan dollar and 25 percent in the case of the South Korean won. Both countries have performed better with appreciating currencies than their leaders thought was possible.

In the face of increased competitiveness from the United States, Western Europe, Japan, and Australia, as well as from the other newly industrialized economies, both countries continue to realize significant trade surpluses, service their debts, show strong real growth, and hold domestic prices to steady trend paths. These achievements exhibit a kind of economic maturity. They will find it ever harder to grow through exporting alone.

Although their prices are rising along a moderately increasing growth path, it does not appear that Taiwan and South Korea are approaching a condition of accelerating inflation. But times have changed. Work forces in these countries put in a very strong effort at low wages in order to gain a foothold in international commerce through competitive pricing. It is only natural that workers now demand much better wages so that they can better enjoy the fruits of their labor. Wage increases are now higher, and the only way that prices can be kept at competitive levels is to have strong productivity gains. There is, therefore, a real challenge to worker effort and ingenuity, together with entrepreneurial guidance, to overcome the rising exchange value of their currencies and continue to sell manufactured goods in world markets. During the first few years of meeting the challenge under the new conditions, these two countries have been wonderfully successful, and there is every reason to believe that success will continue.

Taiwan and South Korea have been pressured by the United States to liberalize trading policies, to import more U.S. goods, and to look more than in the past toward domestic economic expansion. South Korea attained a measure of high international economic status through its sponsorship of the Asian Games in 1986 and the Olympics in 1988. Taiwan has repeatedly been called upon by the United States to contribute, along with other "advanced" countries, toward the resolution of the LDC debt problem. South Korea has been paying off its foreign debt ahead of schedule. It is their mature responses to these extraordinary requests and pressures that, more than anything else, place these two economies in the most advanced international classification.

Taiwan and South Korea are following the Japanese economic route in many respects, and the similarities are also striking in the case of education. We educators have come to appreciate the high level of achievement of the scholars from Taiwan and South Korea; both countries operate impressive educational establishments domestically. The performance of their students in international competition and in absolute levels of scholarly achievement is quite impressive. Scholarly achievement played a very positive role in elevating Japan to the world's highest economic status, and I can perceive the same forces at work in Taiwan and South Korea. In many respects, the student flow that I personally encounter at the higher education level in American universities reminds me of the similar performance of Japanese students during the 1950s and 1960s.

The fact that a second edition of this book is called for is indicative of the point that world readers in the field of economics are deeply interested in the two success stories being analyzed in the present study. There is a great desire to know as much as possible, in subtle detail, of the factors that made possible the economic achievements of Taiwan and South Korea. Many third world and centrally planned economies want to emulate these two cases.

Lawrence R. Klein
Nobel Laureate in Economics

Preface

We are very pleased to publish a revised and expanded edition of the well-received *Models of Development*. In South Korea, Taiwan, and throughout the world, significant changes have occurred since the first edition was published in 1986 that make this an important publication.

In the past four decades, Pacific Basin countries have compiled extraordinary records of economic performance. The experience of the "four tigers"—Hong Kong, Singapore, South Korea, and Taiwan—provides a sharp contrast to the stagnation or decline experienced in many other developing countries. Of the four, South Korea and Taiwan have political, demographic, and geographic qualities that are more representative of third world countries in general and thus provide better examples for other developing countries. The particular focus of this book is on economic policies that can be adopted in other social and political settings.

We are confident that this edition will have the same broad appeal of the first edition and that the experiences of South Korea and Taiwan will be of interest in many other countries. Indeed, the first edition has been translated into Spanish and into Chinese in both the People's Republic of China and the Republic of China on Taiwan.

Nicolás Ardito-Barletta
General Director
International Center for Economic Growth

Panama City, Panama
August 1990

Editor's Preface

This second edition of *Models of Development* has been motivated by two factors. First, although there continues to be a strong demand for the original edition, published in 1986, it has been out of print for quite some time. Second, since the preparation of the first edition, significant changes have occurred in the two economies and in the world at large: For Taiwan and South Korea, the 1980s have been sufficiently different from the preceding two decades to deserve some in-depth examination. In particular, both economies face all the political, social, and economic problems that the transition from developing- to developed-country status entails. How the two economies deal with this transition will determine whether or not they finally achieve developed-country status. Thus, this is an attempt to bring the book up-to-date.

In this edition, the original chapters prepared by Ramon H. Myers, Sung Yeung Kwack, and Tibor Scitovsky have been left unaltered. New chapters analyzing developments in Taiwan and South Korea in the 1980s, prepared by Lawrence J. Lau and Sung Yeung Kwack respectively, as well as a short concluding chapter, have been added. Revisions have been made in the introductory chapter to reflect the changes in the contents of the second edition. Finally, Professor Lawrence R. Klein has very kindly written a new foreword for the second edition.

L. J. L.

Acknowledgments

A volume such as this one is always the collective effort of many people; however, one person, Dr. S. W. Kung, is particularly instrumental in making this volume possible. Without his active encouragement and support, this volume would never have been written. Lawrence Chickering provided help and encouragement in the preparation of both editions. I would also like to thank Professor Lawrence R. Klein and the other contributors to this volume.

Professor Jau-Huey Chen, Dr. Jeanne J. Fleming, Rex Jones, and Y. T. Lin deserve thanks for their advice and assistance during various phases of putting the first edition together. Robert Davis, David Givens, and Emanuel Rapoport of the Institute for Contemporary Studies were most helpful during the editorial and production phases of the first edition. And Susan Furrier deserves credit for the preparation of that manuscript.

On the occasion of the publication of the second edition, I would like to thank Becky McGovern and Ysbrand van der Werf for their excellent editorial work, Paul S. Lau for his invaluable research assistance, and Deborah Johnston for her expert preparation of the final drafts of the manuscripts. Last but not least, I would like to thank my wife, Tamara, for her tender, loving care throughout the preparation of both editions.

L. J. L.

1

LAWRENCE J. LAU

Introduction

In any international comparison of economic performance during the past quarter century, four countries—Hong Kong, Singapore, Taiwan, and South Korea—invariably stand out. While their economies still lag behind Japan and the industrialized West in real income and real consumption per capita, in terms of other dynamic indicators they rank far ahead of all economies—including Japan and the industrialized West. All four excel in growth rates of real income and real consumption per capita, in low inflation and unemployment rates, and in most non-economic, social welfare indicators such as life expectancy and literacy. In fact, Hong Kong, Singapore, Taiwan, and South Korea have done so well in the past two decades they are often collectively referred to as the "four tigers," "four little dragons," or the "gang of four."

Why are they so successful when other developing countries are still struggling to maintain bare subsistence? With growth rates ranging between 8 and 10 percent per year over the past quarter century, luck alone cannot have been responsible for their *high and sustained* rates of economic growth. It is obvious that Hong Kong, Singapore, Taiwan, and South Korea must all be doing something right. Of course, each of the four countries has a unique history; faces a unique constellation of economic, political, social, and environmental forces; and has a unique set of resources at its command. Identifying the factors important in their success and weighing each component's relative contribution is a complicated task.

An analysis of each country individually, however, does not go far enough. One major reason to analyze the factors that have contributed to the economic successes of Hong Kong, Singapore, Taiwan, and South Korea is our desire to see what factors they have *in common*. Were initial conditions in the four countries comparable? Are their economic policies similar? Are their institutional environments alike? And most important, what successful policies, if any, may be found in all of them?

The ultimate purpose is to ascertain whether any general principles can be induced from the successful experiences of these four countries. Are some factors more important and others less so? To what extent have certain economic policies been the engines of growth? Which policies have been most pivotal in the development process? Are certain institutional environments more conducive to economic growth?

Even if these general principles can be found, however, the problem of transferability remains. Will the same strategies work in other developing countries? If similar economic policies are adopted elsewhere, will the same success follow? Or are the policies unique in their benefits to these economies? These questions are difficult but crucial.

The experiences of the city-states of Hong Kong and Singapore, which are substantially dependent on unique geographies and histories, are largely irrelevant for the majority of developing countries. By contrast, both Taiwan and South Korea had initial conditions similar to those of most other developing countries, and their natural resources and endowments were even poorer than most. Their experiences are thus likely to be more relevant for other countries than the experiences of Hong Kong and Singapore. In Chapter 2, Ramon H. Myers analyzes the rate and pattern of economic growth in Taiwan between 1965 and 1981 and the factors underlying Taiwan's superior performance. He concludes that the critical element in Taiwan's economic transformation was a change from a development strategy of import-substitution—domestic production of commodities that substitute for imports, often behind protective trade barriers—to one of export-promotion. In Chapter 3, Sung Yeung Kwack analyzes the same issues in the South Korean experience during the same period. Again, a switch from import substitution to export promotion is found to have played a central role. In Chapter 4, Tibor Scitovsky compares and contrasts the two development experiences that led to both economies' being classified as "newly industrialized" in the early 1980s.

For both Taiwan and South Korea, the 1980s have been a particularly crucial period, not only because of the changes in the international economic environment, but also because of significant changes in their domestic political climates. Both countries undertook what are for them giant steps of democratization, with enormous implications for the directions of economic policies and social welfare. In Chapter 5, Lawrence J. Lau examines developments in the economy of Taiwan in the 1980s. During this period, the economy of Taiwan continued to prosper. Nevertheless, a new and different set of economic problems—chronic trade and balance-of-payments surpluses resulting in a high growth rate of money supply and rapid appreciation of the domestic currency, low aggregate demand (both consumption and investment) at home, protectionism abroad, environmental and labor issues—began to come to the fore. At the same time, the Republic of China on Taiwan boldly initiated the process of an epochal political transition to a democracy. No easy solutions exist for many of the economic problems, especially since they are frequently intertwined with political ones. Nevertheless, government leaders of Taiwan, in their best pragmatic tradition, have generally been effective in maintaining reasonably smooth economic growth. In Chapter 6, Sung Yeung Kwack examines the Korean economy in the 1980s. He shows how it is adjusting to the new domestic and international circumstances and identifies the most important economic issues facing South Korea in the future.

In Chapter 7, Lawrence J. Lau summarizes and compares the current economic conditions in Taiwan and South Korea and speculates on their prospects for continued growth. He ends on an optimistic note, based partly on the experience of postwar Japanese economic development and partly on the tremendous stock of human capital that has been accumulated in both economies. In the long run, human capital is what counts most.

Taiwan's Success Story, 1965–1981

In Chapter 2, Ramon H. Myers describes and analyzes Taiwan's economic growth between 1965 and 1981. Among other issues, he discusses the development of Taiwan's financial institutions, the country's economic planning structure and strategies, the stability of the economy, and changes in income distribution. Taiwan's economy averaged 9.4 percent real growth per year in gross national product (GNP) between 1965 and 1981. Many factors contributed to this remarkable growth: Partly as a legacy of the Japanese occupation from 1895 to 1945, Taiwan had a relatively modern infrastructure in the form of roads, railways, harbors, and the like to build on. Throughout the 1950s and early 1960s, Taiwan also received substantial economic and military aid from the United States, which helped create the stable economic and political conditions that enabled the economy to thrive. Even after direct U.S. aid ceased in 1965, the United States continued to contribute to the Taiwanese economy through trade, direct investment, technology transfer, and the education and training of advanced students. Taiwan was also fortunate enough to enter the world market at a time of rapid trade expansion. By all accounts, however, two economic policies, which were innovative at the time, played a decisive role in transforming Taiwan from an agrarian backwater to a thriving industrial society. These two policies were promotion of exports and liberalization of interest rates.

In the 1950s and early 1960s the prevailing wisdom was that, in order to grow, developing countries needed to adopt an import-substitution strategy, that is, to produce domestically (under protection if necessary) goods that had been imported. But instead, Taiwan's economic planners chose to promote exports, setting an exchange rate close to the market-clearing rate and reducing or removing import tariffs and quotas on producer goods. As a result, Taiwan's exports soared—from US$449.7 million in 1965 to US$22,611.2 million in 1981, a phenomenal increase. With it the economy prospered.

Again defying the conventional wisdom of the day, Taiwan's economic planners in the early 1960s set interest rates at close to market-clearing rates, which, moreover, yielded a positive real rate of return to savings depositors. As a result, the ensuing two decades in Taiwan saw a huge increase in the ratio of savings to income. For example, gross national savings as a percentage of GNP went from roughly 20 percent in 1965 to 35 percent in 1973, dropping slightly to 31 percent in 1981. As the 1965 figure suggests, the people of Taiwan seemingly have a cultural predilection for saving, so the rate of savings has always been relatively high once a minimum threshold level of per capita real income has been reached. But the country's realistic interest-rate policies pushed the rate of savings up even further. In fact, domestic savings alone was able to provide virtually all of the huge pool of investable funds that was so crucial to Taiwan's capital accumulation and growth.

These twin strategies of export promotion and realistic interest rates caused not only dramatic economic growth in Taiwan, but also a tremendous improvement in the living standards of the average citizen. The people of Taiwan became much better fed, better educated, and better housed. They also enjoyed, contrary to the predictions of most economic development theories, an income distribution that was among the most equitable in the world. The degree of income inequality among households in Taiwan decreased as the country's economic growth soared.

Myers cites a number of factors that contributed to this surprising trend. First, land reform in the late 1940s and early 1950s promoted income growth among rural households by improving land distribution and encouraging increased productivity. Second, the high rate of employment between 1965 and 1981 increased labor's share of income and narrowed the gap between the wages of skilled and unskilled labor. Third, the increasing average level of education in Taiwan helped reduce income inequality. Myers reports, for example, that the proportion of students enrolled in post–high school educational institutions grew from 4.5 percent to 20.1 percent of all students over the fifteen-year span from the mid-1960s to the early 1980s. This trend brought about a corresponding increase in labor's share of income.

Fourth, Myers notes that Taiwan's government implemented a number of taxation policies aimed at redistribution. For example, it levied higher excise taxes and tariffs on luxury goods and instituted estate and gift tax laws. Fifth, the government designed its social welfare, health care, and education expenditures principally to benefit lower-income groups. Finally, the small average size of businesses in Taiwan made it easier for entrepreneurs to get started and put a ceiling on the profits of any single enterprise. Both phenomena had the effect of reducing the concentration of income.

South Korea's Success Story, 1965–1981

In Chapter 3, Sung Yeung Kwack addresses many of the same topics discussed by Myers, but in relation to South Korea. He examines in detail prices, exchange rates and monetary policy, the development of financial markets, investment, savings and rates of return, South Korea's foreign economic relations, and the country's income distribution. In a number of respects, South Korea's success story strongly resembles Taiwan's. South Korea began the 1960s in a very underdeveloped condition. The country was poor and politically unstable and had few apparent resources. South Korea's economic planners also opted to pursue export promotion, rather than import substitution. Like Taiwan, the country had the benefit of entering the world market at an auspicious time, enjoyed a legacy of Japanese-built roads and harbors (but also suffered the destructions of the Korean War), and was the recipient of substantial economic and military aid from the United States. South Korea's economy also grew very rapidly, averaging 8.7 percent real growth per year in GNP between 1965 and 1981.

Like their counterparts in Taiwan, South Korean economic planners also aimed to mobilize domestic savings by setting realistic interest rates and maintaining positive real rates of return for savers. Although successful, South Korea was not as successful as Taiwan in this regard; foreign capital provided a very important source of investable funds for the country, especially in the late 1960s and again in the late 1970s and early 1980s. The proportion of foreign capital in total capital formation remained high. In 1979 it was 21.6 percent; in 1980, 32.4 percent; and in 1981, 30.4 percent. Kwack highlights two factors responsible for this high ratio: interest payments and oil prices.

First, interest payments on foreign debts—including remittances of profits to foreign investors—grew rapidly over the period. Amounts skyrocketed during the 1970s (from US$75 million in 1970 to US$3,689 million in 1981). Second, oil prices rose sharply in the 1970s, and oil imports increased at the same time, resulting in huge import bills.

The rate of domestic savings in South Korea vacillated between the late 1960s and early 1980s. On the whole it rose, but it never quite matched Taiwan's rate. The proportion of private-sector savings to total savings was 38.1 percent in 1965 and 47.1 percent in 1971; it reached a high of 71.6 percent in 1977. Corporations played a more significant role than households in the formation of private savings. Kwack reviews in detail the structure of domestic savings in South Korea in Chapter 3.

Economic growth in South Korea produced significant improvements in the living standards of South Koreans. They ate better and lived longer and more comfortably in the 1980s than they did in the 1960s. Unlike Taiwan, however, income inequality did not improve—by some measures it even worsened slightly.

Comparison of Taiwan and South Korea, 1965–1981

In their chapters, Myers and Kwack reveal additional similarities between Taiwan and South Korea. First, both countries, on the eve of their economic takeoffs, had similar initial conditions and endowments. Both countries experienced successful land reforms. Both economies were and still are poor in natural resources. Both faced military threats from aggressive adversaries—across the Taiwan Strait in one case and across the thirty-eighth parallel in the other—and thus had to devote a large fraction of their national budgets to defense. Second, both economies had institutional environments conducive to economic growth. Both Taiwan and South Korea enjoyed considerable political and social stability, at least most of the time, coupled with economic mobility. Their governments were also strongly committed to economic development as a national goal. And there were effective and efficient mechanisms for social decision making. The combination of these factors meant that over long periods of time consistent and continuous policies were maintained to provide a favorable and low-risk climate for investments, both domestic and foreign.

Third, Taiwan and South Korea had broadly similar economic policies. We have already identified the replacement of import substitution with export promotion and the maintenance of a realistic interest rate as central policies both shared. Other common policies include the maintenance of a realistic exchange rate and fiscal budget surpluses (most of the time). Through these policies, the two economies were able to exploit their comparative advantages by developing labor-intensive manufacturing industries oriented toward the world market. These industries were established with the investable funds provided by the high volume of private savings generated by a realistic nominal rate of interest and, by developing country standards, a relatively low inflation rate.

Despite their similarities in both performance and policy, the economies of Taiwan and South Korea also had some important differences. The most striking difference, as noted above, was in income distribution. In South Korea, income became quite concentrated—as most development theories predict. Taiwan, however, provided an important counterexample: despite the very high rates of growth and capital formation, income distribution became much more equal between 1965 and 1981. In other words, lower-income groups in Taiwan have received disproportionate benefits from economic growth. As a result, the improvement in their standard of living, as reflected in the rate of growth of their per capita real consumption, was greater than that of comparable lower-income groups in South Korea. Indeed, Taiwan's experience has been constantly used as an example for developing countries of how to achieve *both* growth and equity. Taiwan's success in this regard was undoubtedly due at least partly to the fact that the nation's leaders explicitly aimed to enhance the "people's livelihood," that is, the standard of living of the average citizen, under their ideology of the "Three Principles of the People."

A second major difference between Taiwan and South Korea had to do with the stability of the growth rates of real gross domestic product (GDP) and inflation. Despite comparable average growth rates, Taiwan's growth between 1965 and 1981 was on average more stable than South Korea's. Because of differences in the monetary policies pursued by their respective central banks, Taiwan also performed consistently better than South Korea in maintaining price stability.

A third major difference between Taiwan and South Korea had to do with the management of their respective international financial positions. South Korea had to devalue its currency several times between the mid-1960s and the early 1980s, while Taiwan was able to maintain its exchange rate within a narrow band of approximately 10 percent during the same years. Moreover, despite the existence of similar foreign-exchange regulations in both countries, Taiwan's official exchange rate was very close to the equilibrium rate most of the time. The black market exchange rate in Taiwan was virtually the same as the official rate. These factors produced much more stability in Taiwan in sectors of the economy affected by international financial transactions.

It is noteworthy that South Korea relied heavily on international borrowing to finance its investments, while Taiwan used international borrowing only sparingly, relying principally on domestic savings. Taiwan, as a result, had a much lower foreign debt burden than South Korea. As with price stability, the difference in the international financial positions of the two economies can be attributed to differences in the objectives pursued and policies adopted by their respective central banks.

A fourth major difference between Taiwan and South Korea lay in the degree of industrial concentration in each country. By the early 1980s the South Korean economy became dominated by the large conglomerates, known as *chaebols*, patterned after the *zaibatsus* of Japan. The ten largest industrial groups in South Korea produced 75 percent of the country's GDP. By contrast, Taiwan had literally hundreds of thousands of independent enterprises, all competing with one another. The largest industrial enterprises in Taiwan did not come close to the size of those in South Korea. It is debatable whether a high degree of concentration is advantageous for economic growth. It is easy to see, however, that industrial concentration must have contributed to the considerably greater income inequality in South Korea.

The difference in industrial concentration resulted partly from efforts by South Korea's economic planners to achieve economies of scale. The South Korean government also took a very active role in controlling market forces. The government of Taiwan, in contrast, tended to rely relatively more on the workings of the free market. The difference, however, is only a matter of degree: by the standards of the advanced industrialized western economies, both governments may be regarded as interventionist.

In Chapter 4, Tibor Scitovsky provides a detailed comparison of how the two economies developed. He discusses at some length the philosophies behind Taiwan's and South Korea's economic development, relating these philosophies to the average size of businesses and the degree of income inequality in each country. As discussed earlier, Taiwan and South Korea pursued quite similar economic development strategies. The philosophies guiding the strategies were different in some important ways, however, and their outcomes have been unique.

The fundamental difference between Taiwanese and South Koreans development philosophies, Scitovsky argues, lies in their views on the role government should play. Specifically, the government's efforts to control private enterprise were more considerable in South Korea than in Taiwan. Taiwan certainly implemented a variety of economic controls, but these tended to be more selective and less intrusive than in South Korea. Where South Korea tended to vigorously enforce an elaborate roster of economic "dos and don'ts," Taiwan aimed instead to create an economic environment conducive to growth.

The result of this stance in Taiwan was to foster the proliferation of small businesses and to keep the businesses relatively small. Taiwan's monetary policy, for example, had some important indirect effects on the development of small businesses. Because the credit market was relatively open, it was relatively easy for a small business to obtain financing and so to get started. Moreover, realistic interest rates limited the profits of business enterprises, resulting in slower rates of growth of individual firms and thus helping to keep very large firms from crowding out small ones.

The presence of many small firms was also encouraged by factors such as Taiwan's public ownership of monopoly-prone industries (electric power for example), and the establishment of industrial parks and districts, which provided a variety of advantages for start-up firms. But the most important factor in the preservation of many small businesses in Taiwan was the absence of policies encouraging the growth of large enterprises and the government's willingness to let market forces take their course once conditions conducive to economic growth were obtained.

The advantages of having a large number of small businesses are many. Scitovsky emphasizes that small firms are more adaptable to changing conditions than big ones. Moreover, small businesses help to keep the market competitive and the entrepreneurial spirit alive. Most important, though, the plethora of small businesses in Taiwan played a very significant role in reducing income inequality in the country.

South Korea's story is very different in this regard from Taiwan's. South Korea tended to have far fewer small businesses, and a considerably less equitable income distribution. Government influence over economic affairs was much more overt and detailed in South Korea than in Taiwan, with the economic planning structure larger, more centralized, and more elaborate. The factors that encouraged small businesses in Taiwan did not operate in South Korea. First, credit was much less "naturally" allocated through the open market, but was instead more "rationed." The criterion qualifying borrowers for low-cost credit was much more precisely defined in South Korea. The concessionary or subsidy component of the cost of credit was, in addition, several percentage points higher in South Korea than in Taiwan. Borrowing from abroad was prohibited unless expressly authorized by the government. Moreover, firms that did not "go along" with government strictures in South Korea reportedly had a very difficult time getting loans. This was an especially harsh sanction given the extent to which businesses relied on bank loans in South Korea.

The same philosophy dominated in the area of tax incentives. For example, South Korea provided lower rates of profit taxes and substantial depreciation and wastage allowances in order to promote export and investment in targeted industries. On the disincentive side, the tax returns of wayward firms tended to be very carefully scrutinized.

These policies helped to give rise to larger-sized firms in South Korea than in Taiwan. Firms that "went along," Scitovsky notes, made huge profits and expanded accordingly. Start-ups had a difficult time competing with the large, government-favored firms, and many simply died aborning for lack of credit. In turn, the lower number of firms in South Korea made government control of business easier, reinforcing the process. These factors tended to work against income equality, and accounted for some of the gap between Taiwan and South Korea in this important measure of social welfare.

The Economy of Taiwan in the 1980s

1981 marked a critical turning point for the world economy. The price of oil finally stopped its once seemingly inexorable rise and began a steep decline in both nominal and real terms over the next several years. In the earlier part of this decade, however, many of the advanced industrial countries were still just beginning to come out of their recessions. Most developing countries, especially those in Latin America, were burdened by their external debts, and the once promising economic prospects of Argentina, Brazil, and Mexico turned into nightmares. Against this backdrop, the growth of world trade slowed and protectionist sentiments rose worldwide.

Nevertheless, Taiwan was able to continue remarkable economic growth during this period. The effects of the second oil shock were allowed to pass through to the economy immediately, resulting in a one-time increase in the price level, which then stabilized. Inflation remained at a low level through the rest of the 1980s. Exports continued to grow rapidly, and Taiwan began to run a string of large trade surpluses. By the end of the 1980s, Taiwan amassed official foreign- exchange reserves of US$75 billion, ranking behind only Japan.[1] The currency was pegged to the U.S. dollar in the early 1980s, but, persistent large trade surpluses and pressure from trading partners, especially the United States, led to a steady appreciation of the New Taiwan dollar beginning in late 1985. By 1989, the New Taiwan dollar has appreciated more than 40 percent against the U.S. dollar (approximately from 40 NT$ per US$ to 25 NT$ per US$). Despite the massive increases in foreign-exchange reserves, and consequently in the domestic money supply, the central bank was successful in holding the rate of inflation to a very low level.

The 1980s also saw a sea change in the political landscape of Taiwan, with potentially important ramifications on the economy: martial law was lifted, bans on new political parties and newspapers were removed, and citizens were allowed to visit mainland China for the first time in forty years. With increasing democratization amidst a relaxed political atmosphere, demands by labor and other interest groups became far more numerous and vociferous. Work stoppages, strikes, and demonstrations became commonplace: Taiwan has yet to develop an effective and orderly mechanism for resolving socially divisive issues without resorting to the streets.

Liberalization of the economy, especially in international trade and financial markets, has been proceeding apace since the mid-1980s.

Restrictions on imports are now minimal, with the exception of agricultural products. Tariff rates have been drastically reduced. Capital flows, both inward and outward, have also been liberalized. Plans for the privatization of the government-owned banks have been approved, but privatization and deregulation of financial institutions without the corresponding financial discipline can be disastrous. Taiwan must be careful to avoid repeating the costly savings and loan association debacle of the United States.

All in all, Lawrence J. Lau concludes that the prospects for continued economic growth are bright. This does not mean, however, that there will be no problems, or that they can be easily solved; it only means that the government leaders of Taiwan have demonstrated the ability to make the necessary changes that conditions demand. The environmental and labor strife will eventually pass with the evolution of a social consensus on how to deal with them. If there is a dark cloud on the horizon, it would be the rampant speculation on the Taiwan stock exchange. The price level of the stock market has risen to unsustainable heights, with price-to-earnings ratios exceeding 200 for some shares: it is a bubble waiting to burst. When it does, it is hoped that the whole economy will not be brought down with it.

The Economy of South Korea in the 1980s

The 1980s also saw major changes in the direction of the South Korean economy. The recovery from the recession and inflation of 1980 and 1981 was achieved through a combination of tight fiscal and monetary policies. As a result, the rate of inflation declined from the more than 20 percent per year of 1980 and 1981 to the low single-digit levels of the mid-1980s. Despite the tight fiscal and monetary policies, economic growth during this period remained robust. Part of the reason for continued growth lay with the continual devaluation of the South Korean won in real terms in the early 1980s. The lower world price of oil and international interest rates also helped. Moreover, beginning in the mid-1980s, the significant appreciation of the Japanese yen vis-à-vis the U.S. dollar and the South Korean won helped divert demand from Japan to South Korea and was partially responsible for the strong performance of the South Korean economy.

In the 1980s, the "Big is Beautiful" philosophy was reevaluated by the South Korean government and gradually supplanted. Greater efforts were made to ease entry in various industries in order to promote competition in both domestic and export markets by South Korean firms. The commercial banks, which played such an important role in financing the growth of the large South Korean conglomerates, were denationalized and the financial market was gradually deregulated. Imports were liberalized through the elimination of restrictions and the reduction of tariffs. Income distribution and social welfare assumed greater importance as objectives of government policy, especially under President Roh Tae Woo.

In the mid-1980s two important milestone events occurred. First, the South Korean current account turned from a chronic deficit position into a surplus position. Second, the domestic savings rate rose significantly and for the first time since the Korean War exceeded the investment rate. The process of transformation from a net international debtor to a net creditor has thus begun for South Korea.

With the increasing democratization of South Korea, however, labor has become much more restive and demanding. Industrial strikes became increasingly common and bitter in the late 1980s. In addition, Sung Yeung Kwack identifies three other major economic issues facing the South Korean economy today: How to counter protectionist sentiments abroad so as to maintain the continued growth of exports. How to further increase competition at home and thereby improve the distribution of income as well as economic efficiency. And finally, how to reduce the debt-to-equity ratio of South Korean firms and thereby increase their long-term viability and competitiveness.

Concluding Remarks

Looking back at the past quarter century, can one identify the reasons behind the success of Taiwan and South Korea? Lawrence J. Lau examines this important question in the final chapter and finds that there was significant saving, capital accumulation, and growth of the labor force in both economies. In other countries, however, similarly high rates of investment did not lead the economies to take off. Thus one has to look elsewhere for the cause. The replacement of import substitution with export promotion, together with the maintenance of realistic interest rates, deserves a great deal of credit (South Korea was not as faithful as Taiwan in adhering to the latter policy). Nevertheless, many other countries, such as Brazil and Mexico, also tried export promotion, and some succeeded for a while, but most failed to take off into sustained growth. There have also been claims that the authoritarian nature of the governments of Taiwan and South Korea was responsible for their successes.[2] There is doubtless a considerable advantage in having a government that can make effective decisions for society in an expeditious manner, but the world's economic "basket cases" are often governed by authoritarian regimes.

Lau identifies the three essential factors common to the success of both Taiwan and South Korea as, first, reliance on private enterprise; second, establishment of the rule of law in the economic sphere; and third, the existence of domestic and international competition. Moreover, all three factors must be present simultaneously. Private enterprise without competition will result in private monopolies with possibly far worse consequences for allocative efficiency than public monopolies. It is only because of real or potential competition that private entrepreneurs must strive for efficiency in order to make a profit. The rule of law then guarantees that the fruits of their efficiency will not be arbitrarily taken away from them, either directly by the government or indirectly by other enterprises with special privileges or good government connections.[3]

What are the prospects for future growth in Taiwan and South Korea? Despite the many current problems, such as the environment, labor, and the even bigger issues of working out an orderly mechanism for resolving social conflicts and achieving a consensus on social policies, Lau remains optimistic. Most of the people in Taiwan and South Korea are pragmatists. They will soon realize that confrontation and noncooperation work against everyone's interests and that accommodation and cooperation are "positive-sum" strategies. In this regard the Japanese development experience provides hope. Although the Japanese management–labor relationship is widely admired today, industrial peace is actually a relatively recent phenomenon in Japan. As late as the early 1960s, the Japanese industrial scene was marked by long and frequently bitter strikes, not unlike those now seen in the two economies, especially in South Korea. Today, however, they all seem distant and largely forgotten.

In addition, the high level of human capital in both economies will help raise their technological levels—Taiwan and South Korea have the highest postsecondary school enrollment rates in the world. Both will be upgrading their industries as labor costs and exchange rates keep climbing. Already, labor costs in Taiwan are no longer low compared with other newly industrialized economies (NIEs) and would-be NIEs, and they are creeping higher in South Korea. Major restructuring of the industries has already begun, especially in Taiwan.

In many other aspects, the two economies remain different. Taiwan continues to have better control over inflation than South Korea. The New Taiwan dollar has been allowed to appreciate much more than the South Korean won. South Korea is once again looking at a devaluation of the won as a way of maintaining international competitiveness. At the same time, there also seems to be some convergence in their economic policies. South Korea has begun to pay more attention to income distribution and social welfare, and Taiwan has begun to pursue a more active industrial policy through government funding of major R&D projects.

Where can Taiwan and South Korea go from here? The two economies should attempt to find their own ways that take into account their respective histories and cultures. The social welfare states of Western Europe, such as the Scandinavian countries, West Germany, and the United Kingdom, do not provide a good model for emulation. When workers have no incentive to work, consumers have no incentive to save, entrepreneurs have no incentive to be efficient, and investors have no incentive to invest, and more generally, when people do not have the incentive to take responsibility for their own well-being, the economy and the society will be in serious trouble. Japan does not provide a good model either. Although there is no question that as measured in U.S. dollars, Japan has a higher per capita income than the United States, most Japanese people will readily acknowledge that their standard of living has a long way to go to achieve parity with that of the Americans. This situation has been brought about by severe distortions in the allocation of resources in the Japanese economy; distortions that cannot be easily corrected because of the vested interests built up over so many years. These distortions are manifested in prices of food, housing, and other consumer goods that are extremely high relative to prices in the rest of the world. It is important for Taiwan and South Korea to avoid the same distortions. A real danger is that they will end up like today's Japan, with a high per capita nominal income but a low real standard of living for the average citizen.

2

RAMON H. MYERS

The Economic Development of the Republic of China on Taiwan, 1965–1981

Known for its rugged terrain and the majestic beauty of its mountain ranges, the island of Taiwan is separated from the mainland of China by the Taiwan Strait, eighty miles wide at its narrowest point. Since 1949 it has been the bastion of the Nationalist government of China. Today its 13,803 square miles are home to a population of over 18 million.

The period 1965–1981 was a true turning point for the economic fortunes of this island republic. From a largely agricultural economy plagued by underemployment and economic dualism, Taiwan, in the company of South Korea, has emerged as a model that inspires other developing nations. How was this economic miracle achieved?

The answer is complex, but must begin with some understanding of Taiwan's peculiar historical development. Colonized by the Chinese for over three centuries, by the late nineteenth century it had become a prosperous agricultural and commercial region within the great Ch'ing empire. In 1895 it passed to imperial Japan, a rich prize for the victor of the first Sino-Japanese War (1894–95). In the next fifty years, the colonial rulers oversaw a "green revolution," promoted public health improvements that reduced the mortality rate by more than one-half, and built a modern infrastructure of finance, transport, and education that facilitated commercialization and rapid export growth.[1] But the spread effects of these developments were limited. Urbanization and industrialization made little headway in what remained a largely agrarian society.

Taiwan reverted to the Republic of China after the defeat of the Japanese in 1945. During the next few years, living standards declined, runaway inflation consumed existing wealth, unemployment worsened, and an invasion from the mainland by the Chinese Communists seemed imminent. But between 1949 and 1953 the Nationalist government was able to reverse these trends with the help of U.S. economic aid. It sold considerable public property to private enterprise and initiated a program of agrarian land reform. As a result, by 1952–53, production and distribution reached pre-war levels.

By 1954 there was cause for both optimism and concern over the economic future of Taiwan. On the one hand, agricultural output had increased and the small manufacturing and services sectors had greatly expanded their productive capacity. On the other hand, the Nationalist government relied upon considerable U.S. economic aid, which provided the country with much-needed raw materials for agricultural and industrial production. Of the US$1,482 million in aid which would eventually come from the United States by 1968, roughly 75 percent, or US$1,100.3 million, went to this non-project type of assistance. In addition, the government allocated almost half of its budget to support the large military establishment.

Yet on the whole, the future seemed bright, largely because the policy of import substitution had so far been successful. Import substitution called for strict controls to overvalue the Taiwan dollar, to ration foreign exchange to preferred importers, and to regulate all foreign trade under quotas and tariffs. It protected fledgling domestic industries from foreign competition. Yet although Taiwan's economic growth indicators in the early 1950s were impressive, there were no tangible signs that economic dualism had begun to disappear. Agriculture still contributed a larger share to GNP than did manufacturing, generated the highest value of exports, and employed at least half of the labor force. The pace of urban growth remained very weak, while the population continued to explode at the rate of 3.5 percent per year.

In the second half of the decade certain warning signs appeared. Between 1955 and 1959 manufacturing and services failed to generate enough new employment to reduce the serious underemployment that existed, domestic demand did not expand rapidly enough to buy goods and services at prices that enabled firms to remain at full capacity and cover costs, and inventories began to rise. The government adamantly refused to reflate the economy through deficit financing lest inflation be rekindled. Instead, it opted for a different course.

In 1958–59 the government initiated new policies that reversed the import substitution strategy, reoriented the economy to the world market, and pegged the national currency, the new Taiwan dollar (NT$), to a value equivalent to its real international market value. These reforms laid the groundwork for the transformation of Taiwan's economy.

The sections below describe the salient economic characteristics of that transformation, examine the growth mechanism underlying it, and describe government policies and the activities of the private sector that made this economic transformation possible.

The Transformation: 1965–1981

The period 1965–1981 was a crucial turning point in Taiwan's economic history. Resources were reallocated at an accelerated rate from low to higher value-added activities, while the economy was restructured based on the widespread usage of modern technology. Of course, this change had no sharply defined beginning. In fact, several important economic indicators showed important new trends in the early 1960s. However, for purposes of convenience and comparison, we will refer to the period 1965–1981 as the transformation.

The first indicator of change was an accelerated expansion of real GNP and output per capita. As figure 2.1 shows, the annual growth rate of real GNP fell sharply in the late 1950s but took an abrupt upturn in the early 1960s and essentially remained at this elevated level throughout the transformation. The growth of real GNP per capita mirrors this trend.

Gross capital formation, a second indicator, rose even earlier than GNP and GNP per capita as shown in figure 2.1. Much of the capital accumulation of the late 1950s was in the form of excess manufacturing capacity and unplanned inventories. However, during the transformation high rates of growth of capital accumulation were sustained generally without incurring excess capacity.

A sudden rise in the rate of savings complemented the accelerated rate of capital formation. Figure 2.2 illustrates that the ratio of savings to GNP rose dramatically to a peak of 31.4 percent in 1981—a remarkable feat for a country with a per capita income of only US$2,500 and that spent close to 10 percent of GNP for defense. Moreover, this represented mostly voluntary savings by firms and households.

Figure 2.1   Annual Growth Rates of Key Economic Indicators, 1952–1981
                (1976 Prices)

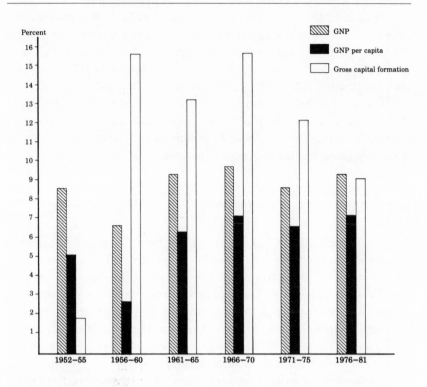

Source: Council for Economic Planning and Development, Executive Yuan, Republic of
China, Directorate-General of the Budget, Accounting, and Statistics, *Taiwan Statistical Data
Book 1983*, p. 23.

In Taiwan, households played a significant role in total capital formation. Household savings supplied from 36.02 percent of total capital formation in 1975 to a high of 47.19 percent in 1977, leveling off to 36.11 percent
in 1981. The average savings propensity of households was high, ranging
from 11 percent to 24 percent during 1965–1981. This is particularly impressive when compared with household savings in other developed
countries. For example, in 1981 the ratio of savings to disposable personal
income in the United States was only 6.7 percent, in the United Kingdom
13.5 percent, in West Germany 14.9 percent, and in Japan 19.7 percent.

By comparison, from 1975 to 1981, corporate savings supplied
between 28.65 percent and 44.46 percent of total capital formation. Because the major form of corporate savings was provisions for fixed cap-

Figure 2.2   Savings as a Percentage of GNP, 1952–1981

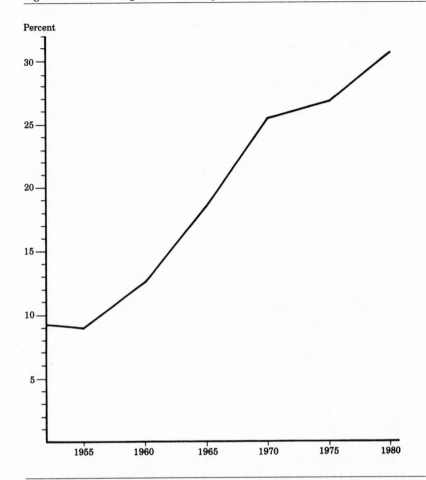

Percent

Source: Council for Economic Planning and Development, Executive Yuan, Republic of China, Directorate-General of the Budget, Accounting, and Statistics, *Taiwan Statistical Data Book 1983*, p. 49. Calculated on the basis of GDP at current prices.

ital consumption, net savings were much less important. Provisions for fixed capital consumption contributed from 22.94 percent in 1975 to a high of 33.38 percent in 1979, and later stabilized at 25.03 percent in 1981. The government's share of the total followed a similar pattern, from 22.84 percent in 1975, increasing to 30.66 percent in 1978, and leveling off to 24.66 percent in 1981.

How did Taiwan achieve such a high rate of savings? The two central strategies were to insure positive real rates of return on savings deposits and to offer attractive tax incentives. These will be discussed in greater detail in later sections, but here some mention should be made of a factor quite independent of government policies: a cultural proclivity to save, perhaps reflecting a greater concern for future security than present consumption.

In addition to an acceleration of the rate of growth of GNP and rate of savings, a third distinctive feature of the transformation was a change in the composition of net domestic product originating from the agricultural, manufacturing, and services sector (figure 2.3). Throughout the 1950s agriculture (which includes forestry and fishing) contributed over 30 percent of net domestic product, and services accounted for well over 40 percent. Though rising, the contribution of manufacturing remained below 25 percent. A change in this pattern occurred in 1965 when manufacturing's share overtook that of agriculture, which continued to fall. By 1981 manufacturing accounted for 45 percent of net domestic product, while agriculture's share had dropped to less than 10 percent.

Behind the changes in these economic indicators lay important new developments in the way the populace lived and worked. For example, as the relative shares contributed to net domestic product by agriculture and manufacturing shifted, a huge reallocation of manpower took place (figure 2.4). The manufacturing sector had absorbed 42.4 percent of the labor force by 1981, compared with only 22.3 percent in 1965 and 16.9 percent in 1953. Agriculture, which had employed over half of the work force prior to 1965, accounted for less than one-third of all jobs by 1981. Employment in the services sector had also risen during the transformation.

Rapid urbanization accompanied industrialization. For decades the countryside had harbored a large reservoir of chronically underemployed labor. Although between 1965 and 1981 many of these workers found jobs in rural industries, most migrated to the cities. In 1950 roughly four-fifths of the population resided in villages and small towns of less than several thousand people; in 1981 the comparable figure was less than one-quarter. Between 1964 and 1973, at the height of the migration, the population in the five largest cities rose 48 percent while increasing only 3 percent elsewhere.[2] In the 1970s half of the annual population growth in Taipei came from immigration.[3] This huge population shift never produced the urban blight and poverty seen in many other developing nations. As quickly as new immigrants arrived from the country, jobs in urban manufacturing and services were created for them in the private sector. Unemployment declined steadily throughout the period (figure 2.5).

Figure 2.3   Contributions to Net Domestic Product by Economic Sector,
1952–1981

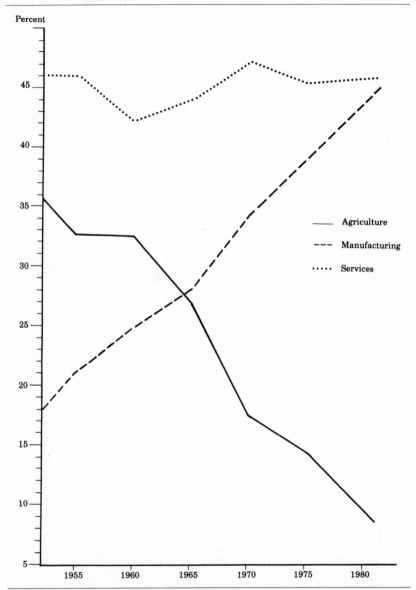

Source: Council for Economic Planning and Development, Executive Yuan, Republic of
China, Directorate-General of the Budget, Accounting, and Statistics, *Taiwan Statistical Data
Book 1983*, p. 33. Calculated at 1976 prices.

Figure 2.4   Distribution of Manpower by Economic Sector, 1952–1981

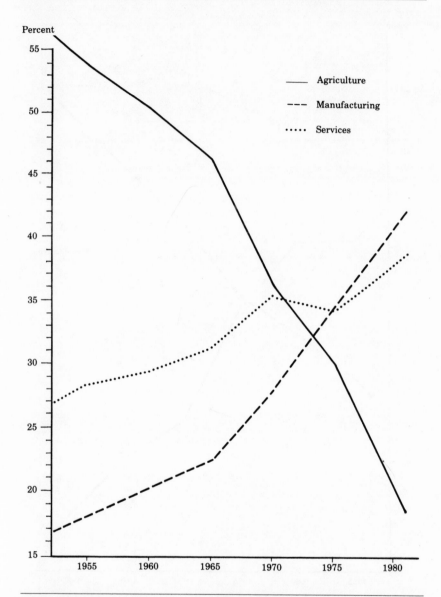

Source: Council for Economic Planning and Development, Executive Yuan, Republic of China, Directorate-General of Budget, Accounting, and Statistics, *Taiwan Statistical Data Book 1983*, p. 16.

Figure 2.5   Unemployment, 1952–1981

Source: Directorate-General of Budget, Accounting, and Statistics, Executive Yuan, Republic of China, *Quarterly National Economic Trends, Taiwan Area, The Republic of China* 24, February 1984.

The rise in GNP reflected not only higher levels of employment but also gains in worker productivity. As confirmed by numerous studies, factor productivity has increased for the past three decades. Capital accumulation and the restructuring of the economy have facilitated this trend.

Contrary to the experience of many developing countries, not only were more people employed more productively in the creation of national income, but that income was also distributed among them more equally. The first step had been the agrarian land reforms of the early 1950s. The ratio of the income of the top 20 percent of households to the bottom 20 percent had already fallen from 20.47 in 1953 to 11.56 in 1961 (figure 2.6). This ratio fell still further to 4.17 in 1980.

As incomes rose, both consumption and savings increased. More will be said of savings later, but a few interesting and important points regarding consumption should be noted here. In 1964 households still spent nearly 60 percent of their outlays on food, beverages, and tobacco (table 2.1). This pattern approximated that for developing countries of very low per capita income as well as that for Mainland China itself in the 1920s and 1930s.[4] But in 1981 households spent only 39 percent of their outlays on food, beverage, and tobacco, bringing Taiwanese consumption patterns more in line with those of other developed industrial nations. At the same time, households found they expended more for rent, fuel, and power, and could afford more for education and recreation.

By any measure, the quality of life had improved immensely. Consumption of protein and vitamins in the diet rose (table 2.2) as better-quality vegetables and fruits and more pork, fish, chicken, duck, and even beef found their way into the pantries and onto the tables of more Taiwanese families. Private clinics and physicians as well as public health services increased in quantity and quality. Better diet and medical care led to a vast improvement in the overall health of the population.

Thus the Republic of China on Taiwan had experienced a true transformation. GNP in absolute terms and on a per capita basis had risen; sustained capital formation had been achieved; the nation had become industrialized and urbanized; unemployment had fallen while productivity had risen; income distribution had become more equal; and the population had more discretionary income and enjoyed an improved health status. This was a miracle indeed for an economy and society that a few decades earlier had been beset with underemployment and uncontrolled inflation. How had Taiwan achieved this remarkable turnaround?

Figure 2.6   Income Distribution among Households Divided into Five Groups of Equal Size, 1953–1980

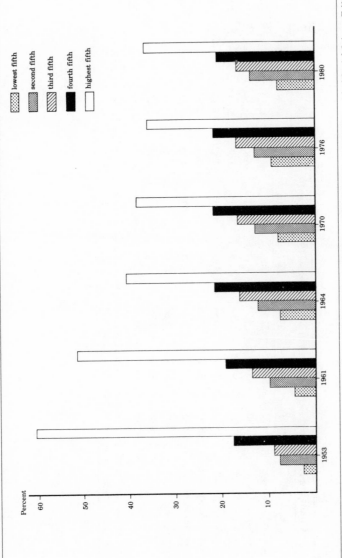

Source: Data for 1953 from Kowie Chang, "An Estimate of Taiwan Personal Income Distributed in 1953," *Journal of Social Science* 7 (1956), p. 260. Data for 1961 from Kowie Chaig, "Report on Pilot Study of Personal Income and Consumption in Taiwan," (prepared under the sponsorship of a working group on national income statistics, Directorate-General of Budget, Accounting, and Statistics, Executive Yuan) p. 23, table A. Data for 1964–1981 from Directorate-General of Budget, Accounting, and Statistics, Republic of China, *Taiwan Statistical Data Book 1983*, p. 54.

Table 2.1   Changing Household Expenditures in Taiwan, 1964–1981 (percent)

	1964	1968	1970	1972	1974	1976	1978	1979	1980	1981
Food, beverage, and tobacco	59.70	51.75	52.46	47.81	49.40	46.38	42.93	41.03	40.35	39.44
Clothing and footwear	6.30	5.84	5.79	6.47	6.15	6.83	6.66	7.41	7.03	6.80
Rent, fuel, and power	17.20	19.01	18.19	20.78	20.71	21.45	22.64	22.91	23.65	24.13
Family furniture & equipment	3.40	4.66	3.96	3.95	3.79	3.87	4.13	4.64	4.57	4.58
Medical care & health expenses	5.30	5.54	5.95	3.89	3.92	4.61	4.74	4.62	4.20	4.50
Transport & communications	2.00	2.70	3.00	3.53	3.99	4.99	5.67	6.12	6.68	6.89
Education & recreation	1.20	1.65	2.66	7.06	6.06	6.38	7.50	7.63	8.18	8.30
Others	4.90	8.85	7.99	6.51	5.98	5.49	5.43	5.64	5.34	5.36
Total	100.00	100.00	100.00	100.00	100.00	100.00	100.00	100.00	100.00	100.00

Source: Council for Economic Planning and Development, Executive Yuan, Republic of China, Report on the Survey of Personal Income Distribution in Taiwan Area, Taiwan Statistical Data Book 1983, p. 54, Table 3–16.

Table 2.2   Food Intake and Nutrition per Capita per Day

Year	Energy (kcal.)	Protein (gm.)	Vitamin A (I.U.)	Vitamin D (mg.)	Vitamin C (mg.)
1952	2078.2	49.0	4310.4	0.47	91.3
1956	2262.0	53.9	4356.3	0.50	90.4
1960	2390.0	57.1	4548.7	0.54	95.2
1965	2410.6	61.2	3728.6	0.58	79.6
1970	2661.7	72.2	4261.5	0.74	93.7
1975	2721.7	74.7	4695.8	0.80	116.1
1981	2728.6	75.3	6408.0	0.90	128.8

Source: Council for Economic Planning and Development, Executive Yuan, Republic of China, Council for Agricultural Planning and Development, *Taiwan Statistical Data Book 1983*, p. 269, Table 14–6.

Achieving the Transformation

New economic policies initiated in the very late 1950s liberalized Taiwan's economy, redeployed resources to higher value-added manufacturing and services, and redirected much of that output to the international market. These policies encouraged private enterprise to establish more factories and service establishments, increase output and employment, and direct more of that output to overseas markets. These forces, then, produced a remarkable concatenation of economic activities unprecedented in Taiwan's economic history: rising market demand, primarily of foreign origin; and rapid producer response to supply more to the expanding market. Let us examine these trends in demand and supply in more detail.

The world market produced the major source of new demand. Taiwan's export growth represented that new supply response to a broadly expanding international market. In 1952 and 1960 exports in constant price terms still accounted only for 9 and 10 percent, respectively, of GNP. In 1965, however, exports already had risen to 17 percent; in 1970 exports accounted for 29 percent; and by 1981 exports had risen to an incredible 53 percent of GNP.[5] Exports had risen far more rapidly during the transformation phase than in the preceding period.

More complex economic analysis confirms this simple finding. A recent input-output analysis showed that the export growth after 1965 had accounted for an increasing share of the economy's total output growth (table 2.3). By the mid-1970s roughly two-thirds of the economy's output growth came from the expansion of exports.

Table 2.3   The Contribution of Exports to Output Growth (percent)

Period	Output expansion due to domestic expansion	Output expansion due to export expansion	Output expansion due to import substitution
1965–61	61.6	22.5	7.7
1961–66	63.2	35.0	0.5
1966–71	51.4	45.9	5.7
1971–76	34.7	67.7	−2.4

Source: Kuo, Shirley W., *The Taiwan Economy in Transition* (Boulder, Colo.: Westview Press, 1983), p. 149, Table 7.6.

What category of exports played such a critical role in the rapid spurt of export growth? When exports are divided into agricultural, processed agricultural, and industrial products, we observe that in 1965 industrial products made up less than half of the total value of exports (46 percent) but rose to 78 percent in 1970 and continued to climb, reaching 92 percent by 1981.[6] In other words, the huge expansion of exports was largely fueled by the accelerated growth of manufacturing that was taking place.

Why had exports expanded so rapidly? The reasons owe much to the new financial incentives for manufacturers that originated in the reform of the foreign exchange system and the sweeping liberalization of trade controls between 1958 and 1966. These reforms simply had made it enormously profitable for suppliers of manufactured goods to sell abroad rather than at home. Taiwan producers rushed to enter the export market. During the 1960s and 1970s the demand for manufactured goods in Japan and the West rapidly expanded. The demand is highly income-elastic. Therefore, for every one percent rise in per capita income in Japan and the West, there was an even larger percentage increase in demand for Taiwan's manufactured goods. Because so many Taiwanese goods were inexpensive and their quality was improving, demand accelerated. Between 1965 and 1981 Taiwan's manufactured exports to the United States rose from US$95 million to US$8,100 million as the United States soon became its leading foreign market. In 1965 Taiwan's most important buyer, Japan, was taking 30 percent of all exports, compared to 21 percent from the United States. But by 1981 their roles had reversed: the United States purchased 36 percent of Taiwan's exports and Japan took only 11 percent.[7]

In employment, the textile industries led the way in growth, followed by basic metal products, chemicals and plastics, and food processing. Moreover, manufacturing firms increased their capital investment so that the capital input rose more rapidly than the labor input: between 1966 and 1971 total capital assets nearly tripled (NT$87 billion to NT$238 billion), but employment only roughly doubled. Finally, in spite of the fact that more industries substituted capital for labor, wages rose in the 1960s, so that the share of labor income in value added rose more rapidly than the share of capital during this same period. This development also contributed to greater income equality.

What kind of manufacturing firms did entrepreneurs create between 1961 and 1971? For the nine categories of manufacturing industries, there were a total of 44,054 establishments in 1971. Of this total 68 percent were small-scale firms employing fewer than twenty workers, with another 23 percent of medium size employing up to fifty workers. The distinctive feature of rapid manufacturing development after 1961, then, was the tremendous growth of small and medium-sized firms. Small firms, in particular, predominated in the manufacturing of textiles, apparel, leather goods, wood and bamboo products, basic metals, metal products, machinery equipment, and miscellaneous industrial products. More large firms could be found in the industries producing food, beverage, tobacco, paper, printing, chemicals, and nonmetallic mineral products.

Although urban manufacturing growth outpaced that of the countryside, a great many of these small and medium-sized firms took root near villages and small towns. Rural employment in manufacturing rose quickly during the transformation: 13.5 percent for 1966–71 and 12.1 percent for 1971–76, as compared to 16.9 and 8 percent, respectively, for urban manufacturing employment. The fact that rural manufacturing employment grew more rapidly than urban manufacturing employment in the 1970s is most impressive. In rural manufacturing, establishments producing rubber products, leather and fur, electronics and their equipment, and metal products led the way in having the highest growth rates for employment.

The economic impact of expanding rural employment was considerable. Nonfarm income for rural households greatly increased, rising from 79 percent of household income in 1966 to 89 percent in 1976. Of this nonfarm income earned by rural households, industrial employment generated about 60 percent in 1966 and 66 percent in 1976.

Meanwhile, family farms were gradually purchasing more machinery and equipment that in turn allowed more labor to be released from farming. But as Taiwan farms became more capital-intensive and

Table 2.4   Growth Rates of Value Added by Sector, 1952–1981 (percent)

Period	Net domestic product	Agriculture	Industry	Services
1952–56	7.4	3.8	13.2	7.6
1956–61	6.3	3.9	8.0	6.9
1964–66	9.8	5.6	12.9	10.4
1966–71	10.8	1.1	16.8	10.5
1971–81	9.0	1.8	11.3	8.9

Source: Kuo, Shirley W., *The Taiwan Economy in Transition*, p. 245.

their productivity rose, their demand for labor also increased during planting and harvesting periods, so that agriculture also generated more employment during the transformation phase. More machines extended multiple cropping throughout the year, and that development became an important source for expanded agricultural employment.

While our discussion has focused upon the export-led development that initiated a major manufacturing spurt in both the rural and urban areas, services also played a most important role in generating more employment and income. In table 2.4 we observe that the rate of growth of value added in services greatly exceeded that for agriculture, and was not far behind manufacturing.

Among service categories, finance, banking, insurance, and real estate led the way in generating increased value added.[8] This explosion of services along with the spurt in manufacturing helped to employ 3 million additional persons between 1961 and 1981, and to bring about full employment in 1971. The services sector alone absorbed 193,000 persons in 1961–66, 486,000 in 1966–71, and another 418,000 persons in 1971–76 to account for 51 percent, 47 percent, and 45 percent of the incremental employment growth for Taiwan's economy in each period.[9] Meanwhile, labor productivity rose progressively in the services sector over these periods.

Service establishments were typically small and medium-sized operations employing fewer than twenty and fifty persons, respectively. Therefore, we now have an important clue as to why supply responded so readily to match both rising foreign and domestic demand during the transformation period. Countless entrepreneurs came forward to create new establishments, and older ones merged with others to grow even larger. Even so, Taiwan's economy today is notable for its predominance of small and medium-sized firms. What made it possible for so much new entry into the marketplace? Every day, of course, business firms failed, but their ranks were filled by new enterprises. Taiwan's factor markets deserve special attention, for it was obviously the successful functioning of the factor markets that enabled this tremendous new growth of enterprises to take place.

Let us examine, then, the markets for financial capital and labor. By better understanding how these markets facilitated the increase in supply during the transformation, we will at last have come full circle in analyzing the growth mechanism that made Taiwan's transformation possible.

The Financial Capital Market. Since Taiwan reverted to Nationalist rule there have been three principal sectors in the financial capital market: the first consists of relatives and friends who privately advance financial capital to kinsmen in business; the second comprises private moneylenders who make loans, usually short-term, to businessmen; finally, there are formal credit institutions of national and private banks and other large-scale lending institutions that make loans to and discount notes for businesses. We do not know what proportion of the total credit supplied in any period originated from these three groups of lenders. But in the early 1950s the formal credit suppliers probably provided the smallest share of financial capital to all businesses in Taiwan.

Because the statistical evidence does not cover the first and second financial sectors, we must focus upon the formal credit market that became increasingly important over the period. There is little doubt that this source of credit supply has rapidly increased over the past thirty-five years, especially during the transformation phase. We can observe from the selected data presented in table 2.5 that the rate of growth for total loans grew rapidly over the period, particularly after the mid-1960s.

Moreover, if we separate these loans and discounts by their length of maturity we note that formal credit institutions increasingly made long-term loans. That development began to take place after 1959 and continued to the present. By 1981 nearly one third of all bank loans were for more than three years maturity. Although we cannot conclude for certain from this information that formal credit suppliers truly dominate the financial capital market in the 1980s, there is every reason to suspect that during the transformation phase formal credit institutions supplied an ever larger share of Taiwan's capital, and these modern

Table 2.5   Loans and Discounts of All Banks by Their Maturity (percent)

Period	Total loans (NT$ million)	Annual rate of growth	Up to 1 year maturity	1–3 years maturity	Over 3 years maturity
11/59	3,846	—	76	13	11
12/60	9,326	142.28	73	17	10
12/65	26,096	22.87	72	12	16
11/70	70,420	21.98	73	12	15
11/75	306,991	34.49	68	20	12
12/78	470,186	15.23	67	9	14
12/81	760,369	17.45	59	11	30

Source: Bank of Taiwan, *T'ai-wan chin-jung t'ung-chi yueh-pao* (Taiwan Financial Statistics Monthly): Nov. 1955, p. 36; Dec. 1960, p. 38; Dec. 1965, p. 44; Dec. 1970, p. 46; Dec. 1975, p. 46; June 1984, p. 80.

institutions are important determinants of the amount and cost of credit for businesses.

It is clear that formal credit institutions have expanded the proportion of their total loans to the private sector compared to the government and public enterprises. In 1953 the total loans and discounts supplied by all banks amounted to nearly NT$2 billion, with 25 and 5 percent, respectively, being furnished to business firms and individuals, 65 percent to public enterprises and 5 percent to government.[10] By 1955 loans had risen to NT$3.6 billion, with 38 percent and 5 percent, respectively, going to private enterprise and individuals.[11] Financial conditions quickly changed thereafter: bank loans skyrocketed to NT$26 billion, with 59 and 12 percent, respectively, being loaned to private enterprise and individuals.[12] By 1975 total bank loans had climbed to over NT$300 billion, with 68 percent and 10 percent, respectively, going to private firms and individuals.[13] By 1981 bank loans had risen to NT$760 billion, with 50 percent and 22 percent, respectively, being loaned to private enterprise and individuals.[14] Beginning with the transformation phase, then, bank loans increasingly moved to the private enterprise sector, and by the end of the 1970s around three-quarters of all bank loans and discounts flowed to that sector.

Businesses always drew upon these three sources of credit, but obtaining loans from the banks proved very difficult for those without collateral. Having little choice, borrowers had to negotiate credit from the higher premium-charging private moneylenders. As economic growth promoted a larger pool of loanable funds from savings, all three sources of credit cited above provided an increasing supply of financial capital to businessmen to establish new firms and obtain their working capital. Costs for that credit naturally varied, being highest in the private moneylending sector of the credit market. In the twenty-five years between 1956 and 1981, the formal credit market changed greatly.

In 1981, there were twenty-four modern banks with 714 branches throughout the island, along with trust and investment companies, credit cooperatives, credit departments for the farmer and fishery associations, bill finance companies, security finance companies, and insurance companies. Of the total number of banks operating, only three were privately owned. All commercial banks are now subject to government regulations pertaining to the assets they can produce, their credit and reserve ratio, and their liquidity ratio. Bank funds originate from different deposits, especially customer demand deposits. Banks then use their funds to acquire income-earning assets like loans, overdrafts, discount bills, government bonds, treasury bills, and corporate debt instruments. According to official data for December 1981, banks accounted for more than 70 percent of the assets, deposits, loans, and investments held by financial institutions in Taiwan.

As early as spring 1950 the Bank of Taiwan had begun to raise interest rates on its deposits. By attracting loanable funds for demand and time deposits, the Bank of Taiwan hoped to augment savings and limit spending, thus breaking the back of the postwar inflation. This policy proved to be very successful, and bank deposits ballooned during the next three years, while at the same time the rate of price increase greatly declined. But complaints then began to arise that credit costs were too high to undertake new investment and expansion. The government then began to lower its loan rates but continued to charge higher monthly interest rates for businesses and individuals than for public enterprises.

Interest rates charged by private moneylenders remained nearly double those of monthly loan rates on unsecured loans offered by banks to businesses.[15] Between 1955 and 1965 bank interest rates slowly drifted downward as did private money lending rates, and then they leveled off until the oil crisis of 1973, when all rates again moved upward.[16] But by the mid-1970s interest rates again fell, only to rise in 1979–80 because of the worldwide inflation.

Lowering bank loan rates alone could not have financed the spurt in manufacturing exports during the mid-1960s. Other sources of credit also had become available. In July 1957 the Bank of Taiwan began supplying low-cost export loans to manufacturers on the provision that they would undertake the development of markets abroad. These short-term loans were offered at 6 percent per annum for those repayable in foreign currencies and at 11.88 percent per year for loans repayable in local currency. These rates were very much lower than the 19.8 percent for secured and 22.32 percent for unsecured loans then available to private enterprises.[17] Loans for manufacturers of exports rapidly expanded in the late 1960s and 1970s.

Financial capital markets in Taiwan, then, not only greatly increased the supply of credit for private enterprise, but these markets also allocated credit to those branches of industry and services that were rapidly expanding and in great need of credit. Rapid economic growth, of course, generated even more savings, so that more firms were able to reinvest earnings and supplement their financial requirements by short-term borrowing from the banks or private moneylenders.

The Labor Market. Taiwan's labor market consists of complex informal markets in which suppliers of different labor and occupational skills sell their services to bidders for those various skills. These markets are highly competitive and open. Organized labor never has been an intervening element in the marketplace. Entry into labor markets always has been easy, and informal personal networks provided information of job and occupational opportunities for job seekers.

Demand for labor for fishing, forestry, and agriculture came principally from family farms that hired labor at planting and harvesting periods. These brief intervals of intense labor demand became more frequent as multiple cropping spread. The proliferation of small and medium-sized manufacturing firms and services establishments also greatly increased the demand for more semi- and fully skilled labor in the 1960s and after. Labor markets readily allocated more labor to meet that demand. Furthermore, those markets seemed to have generated the correct signals about job opportunities so that specific labor scarcities never worsened for any long period. As soon as potential workers learned of these opportunities, they acquired the vocational skills and advanced professional degrees to fill those openings.

In the early 1950s the highly protected manufacturing sector required more semi-skilled workers, and because those shortages still persisted the real monthly wage rate grew. But in the late 1950s the slowdown in manufacturing and the absence of such shortages greatly reduced the rate of real wage expansion. Then in the 1960s the great acceleration of manufacturing increased labor demand. The growth rate for real monthly wages spurted, only to slow down again in the early 1970s as the world oil crisis hit Taiwan severely, rekindling inflation and forcing some cutbacks in industrial activity. The combination of these two factors raised the consumer price index and slowed labor demand in different branches of manufacturing. But in the late 1970s real monthly wages again jumped because the labor market became extremely tight: unemployment dropped to an all-time low and manufacturing demand for labor continued expanding. We note that labor productivity more than kept pace with the expansion of real wages except in the late 1970s when the economy began to experience some price inflation.

Participation in the workforce was roughly as high in 1975 as in 1953, although the trend had been downward until the mid-1960s and then moved upward. Meanwhile the total labor force had nearly doubled.[18] The reason for this high participation rate during the transformation was the rapid entry of females into the labor force at the same time males remained in school for longer periods and entered the labor force at an older age than was the case in the very early 1950s, when many more young teens were working.

Just as participation in the workforce remained high, the quality of manpower greatly improved over these three decades, especially during the transformation, when many more people entered vocational schools as well as junior and senior high school. Between 1952–53 and 1964–65 the total number of persons passing through vocational schools rose from 40,092 to 106,811, and that number shot up more than three-fold to 348,169 in 1980– 81.[19] Primary school lasting six years had been declared mandatory for all children as early as 1952–53, but only 21,046 and 71,900 students, respectively, were in senior and junior high schools in those years. But their numbers had risen to 100,611 and 381,969, respectively, in 1964–65 and then skyrocketed to nearly 180,800 and over 1 million, respectively, in 1980–81.[20] Even more impressive was the fact that in 1980–81 about 96 percent of all graduates from primary school were enrolled in junior high school and roughly two-thirds of all junior high school students were able to enter high school. The tremendous expansion of the educational system naturally contributed to upgrading the skills of workers who could virtually all read and write and even possessed considerable quantitative skills.

If financial capital and labor markets worked smoothly and effectively to allocate scarce resources to their highest value-added uses, what of the money supply, prices, and variability of economic activity during the transformation? If Taiwan's economic transformation took place with minimal economic fluctuation and inflation, then domestic factor and product markets were not only well-integrated into the world market but efficiently responded to changes in world market demand without producing high economic costs at home.

Variations in Economic Activity, Prices, and Money Supply. As the Republic of China became more enmeshed in the international economy after 1965, the island's economy began to experience greater economic fluctuations in prices, money supply, and the output of goods and services. External shocks to the island economy occurred, due to fluctuating petroleum prices and cyclical economic activity in Japan and the United States. How serious were these developments? Let us examine foreign trade first.

If we examine the balance of payments for the sixteen years 1965–1981, we note that exports grew 497 percent or at a growth rate of 11.8 percent per year, and imports by 395 percent or a growth rate of 10.5 percent, to net the economy a whopping surplus in the trade account of over US$8 billion. But for services there accrued an overall deficit of over US$5.8 billion because of expanding payments for freight, insurance, other transport services, tourism, and payments of investment earning to foreign investors.

For the capital account around US$5.7 billion flowed into the Republic of China between 1965 and 1981, largely in long-term investment. Except for the years 1965, 1968, 1974–75, and 1980, capital inflows more than offset deficits in the current account throughout the transformation period. The general picture, then, was that on both current and capital accounts large surpluses accrued.

But meanwhile trade dependency, measured as the sum of exports plus imports divided by gross domestic product, had registered over 100 percent in 1979 and remained over 100 percent except in 1982.[21] In 1976 for each U.S. dollar's worth of fixed capital formation, US$0.4283 was spent on imported goods, and for each U.S. dollar's worth of exports, there were US$0.3407 worth of imports.[22] In order to reduce the high import-content ratio, it will be necessary to develop a more advanced machinery industry because machinery still accounts for about half of all fixed capital formation.

Because foreign trade has now become so important as a motive force for Taiwan's economic growth, any slowing or sudden decline in export earnings would cause a contraction of the economy. But during the transformation period this difficulty never occurred, even though oil prices jumped in 1973 and 1979. Perhaps because markets worked so well to facilitate a vigorous supply response to changing demand and international trade conditions, and because public policies also worked well to help reallocate resources, the adverse effects of oil price increases in the 1970s merely caused a severe short-term economic downturn without any serious recession. A survey of economic activity during the transformation phase certainly does show that a rapid transmission of international market fluctuations into Taiwan's economy took place, but that overall economic variations were not really any different from those of the 1950s, when the economy had been more insulated from international market fluctuations (see figure 2.7, panels 1, 2, and 3; the GDP index in panel 1 is in 1952 prices). This finding is rather astonishing because domestic markets rapidly transmitted international fluctuations.

The exceptional event was the quadrupling of oil prices in November 1973 and another spurt in oil prices in 1979. The consumer price index (CPI), which averaged an increase of only 8.5 percent between 1965 and 1981, surged upward in 1973 and again in 1979. Because the government-owned China Petroleum and Taiwan Power companies absorbed most of the high petroleum prices, it was higher-priced imports that accounted for roughly half of the price change in 1973–84.[23] In other words, both higher-priced imports and higher-cost energy compelled firms to raise their prices and pass their costs on to consumers. The variations in money supply, CPI, and output certainly move together.

Yet the annual growth rate change for money supply was very large during the 1970s. Export surpluses and the sale of foreign exchange by exporters to the Central Bank have accounted for much of these large annual surges in the money supply. In 1972–73 and 1977–78 changes in net foreign assets were highly correlated with an increase in the money supply—as much as 30 percent.[24] The high trade surpluses of those four years brought a vast pool of additional money to the Taiwan economy. Some of these funds were spent domestically, but other funds flowed outward as capital to foreign countries. These large trade surpluses had naturally originated from Taiwan's highly competitive export prices. During the 1970s foreign prices rose more rapidly than domestic prices, and therefore exporters would expand their sales more rapidly than would otherwise have been the case. Taiwan's increasing trade

Figure 2.7 Change in GDP Index

Change in CPI Index

(Figure continued on next page)

Figure 2.7 (continued)   Change in Money Supply

Index
(Percent)

KEY
1953–65 ----
1965–81 ——

dependency made it more vulnerable to economic fluctuations. Why? Because sudden changes in the economic conditions of Taiwan's major trading partners (Japan and the United States) produced unpredictable changes that led to large fluctuations in the money supply.

The Economic Growth Mechanism Reviewed. An expanding international market during the 1960s provided the initial demand impetus for Taiwan to accelerate its economic growth. More producers began marketing for export; resources increasingly shifted to new manufacturing and services. The financial capital and labor markets effectively facilitated the redeployment of resources. Small and medium-sized firms led the way, locating in both the countryside and cities, hiring more workers—especially women—and buying new machines, equipment, and tools. An enormous construction boom also occurred.

Rising employment and new capital investment generated greater spending and income at home. Taiwan's labor-intensive commodities were inexpensive and improving in quality; they found rapid acceptance among foreign buyers, and so export proceeds rose rapidly. From this new income source higher savings could be realized. To be sure, the favorable financial climate on the island attracted a large flow of foreign investment. Between 1965 and 1981 about US$1.9 billion of foreign capital entered Taiwan, compared to only around US$91 million between 1954 and 1964.[25] As of December 31, 1982, the Republic of China had only US$1.8 billion worth of foreign loans outstanding.[26] The Republic of China had financed its growth during the transformation phase without relying heavily upon foreign credits. Economic growth had been self-sustaining and virtually self-financed.

The real, if simple, explanation for this achievement lies in the rate of national savings discussed earlier. Comparison with the historical experience of South Korea can be used to support this assertion. At the end of 1984, Korea's external debt totaled the equivalent of US$43 billion, 53 percent of its GNP. By contrast, Taiwan's total debt was just under US$12 billion, or 21 percent of GNP. Between 1960 and 1983, Taiwan managed to save, in gross terms, nearly 25 percent of GNP, while the corresponding figure for South Korea was 17 percent.[27]

As resource re-deployment continued, the capital-labor ratio began to rise, more rapidly in urban firms than in those located in the countryside.[28] The bulk of output produced by these firms went into exports as industrial consumer goods, such as apparel and plywood, for the markets of the high-income developed countries. The growth of intermediate and capital goods exports from the more capital-intensive firms, such as petroleum and chemical products, went to the markets of developing countries, mostly located in the Pacific Basin region.[29] These trade trends show that Taiwan adhered to its comparative advantage by producing the low-cost, high-quality goods that its most abundant resource, labor, favored. Moreover, the small and medium-sized firms that specialized along these lines could do so by combining an easily learned and adaptable technology with abundant low-cost and highly skilled labor. The step-by-step progression in manufacturing that had marked the 1960s continued throughout the 1970s. More firms began switching to electronics assembly, especially for export to developed countries, and producing machine tools and equipment.

The rate of export growth greatly exceeded the growth rate of money wages, therefore leaving an ever larger surplus for exporting firms to finance their expansion of plant and facilities. An expanding financial capital market, more formal and more fine-tuned to finance manufacturing for exports, also proved helpful. Highly competitive product and factor markets permitted rapid readjustments of supply and demand. Most notably, remarkable price stability characterized the 1963–72 period: wholesale prices rose at only 1.8 percent per year. Even between 1973 and 1982, when wholesale prices rose at 10.3 percent per year, Taiwan's inflation remained well below that of the developed countries.

Our story is still incomplete without mentioning those specific government policies that modulated the economic growth mechanism just discussed. Furthermore, we also must say something about how private enterprise and public firms responded to these policies and why they did so in the manner they did.

The State and the Private Sector

A strong tradition of state interference in the management of economic activity has always existed in Chinese history. This tradition certainly had not changed. Government policies significantly shaped the pattern of economic development on Taiwan. First, the state insisted upon retaining control over most critical industrial production and services like energy and water in the early 1950s. By 1960 little had changed and still about 48 percent of that output value originated from publicly owned and managed enterprises. Between 1965 and 1981, however, the share of output value for privately owned enterprises rose much more rapidly than public-sector enterprises. By 1981 about four-fifths of all such production originated from the private sector. This great shift attests to the expansion and vitality of the private sector, but it also represents the willingness of the ruling elite to permit the state to recede from the economy instead of extending greater control. Looking at this striking shift in another way, we can observe that the annual growth rate of private industrial production greatly exceeded that of publicly managed firms. This trend, in particular, materialized during the early years of the transformation phase.

But if state control over property rights and its share of industrial production rapidly declined, government expenditures as a percentage of GNP rose as did the tax burden. The reasons for this are complex and have little to do with greater state efforts to regulate economic activity. Taiwan's leadership became especially concerned about national security in the 1970s and made vigorous efforts to upgrade the defense establishment. At the same time the government spent more for expanding the country's infrastructure (transport, harbors, etc.) and increasing services (education, public health, public administration, etc.). Greater government promotion of these activities necessitated a higher tax burden, and indeed that burden did begin to rise during the 1970s. Between 1961 and 1981 government spending as a proportion of GNP rose from 21.4 to 27.5 percent and the tax and monopoly revenues as a share of GNP for the same period rose from 14.5 to 20.0 percent. Between 1965 and 1981 the government always realized a budget surplus. Even when state spending exceeded tax revenues (as in 1981) income from monopolies, public enterprises and utilities, and loans for construction proved sufficient to prevent a deficit.[30]

Although the level of government spending has risen and society now pays a higher tax burden, prudent fiscal policy continued through all decades. Between 1952 and 1963 the government ran a budget deficit in only seven years, but it did not rely upon long-term deficit financing because those annual deficits were not large and were made up by surpluses generated in subsequent years.[31] From 1964 to 1981, however, revenues exceeded expenditures and surpluses accumulated in all years. Only in 1982 did the government run a modest NT$3 billion deficit because the worldwide recession had engulfed Taiwan and tax revenues did not rise as rapidly as expenditures. Therefore, during the transformation years government policies to promote economic growth were entirely financed through balanced budgets. Furthermore, the increase in government spending and taxation remained modest compared with other economies during their transformation phase.

Economic Doctrine and Policies. Sun Yat-sen's ideas have served as a beacon for policymakers.[32] One principle, that there must be planning within the context of a free economy, is undoubtedly the source from which so many specific policy recommendations flow.[33] The state must nurture the private sector, but it should also allow free markets to function and permit the existence of private property. Such a mixture of concerns required the achievement of four objectives.

First, most resources should be privately owned and managed except for those resources and activities that government deems necessary to manage on behalf of society: defense, communications, social services, etc. Second, policies should produce sustained, high economic growth rates but under conditions of stability. Third, new wealth should not be created at the expense of others, but all groups should be able to share the flow of benefits from development. Finally, economic growth should not be associated with distortions that lead to scarcities of resources or goods and services.

In order to realize these objectives, various kinds of policies must be initiated, refined, and abandoned as conditions dictate. If we review the policies that played such a critical role in launching Taiwan's export-led growth phase, we can refer to three broad categories: policies to restructure economic incentives; policies to induce more competition, channel the flow of economic activity in new ways, and facilitate the role of markets; and policies to achieve equilibrium within the economic system. The following examples relate to the policies that contributed so impressively to promoting Taiwan's transformation.

Probably the most important initial policy for restructuring incentives was the land reform that began in January 1949 and continued until 1955. This reform entailed reducing tenant rents, selling public lands to farmers and tenants, and limiting landholdings to roughly 1.7 acres of paddy and 7.2 acres of dry land, while redistributing all land held above that size to other rural households.[34] The government compensated landowners with bonds that could be cashed and their proceeds used to develop urban industry and services. The new farming class received government loans to purchase their land and could repay these loans over a fifteen-year period at low interest rates. The land reform proved very successful in directing rural landlords into urban businesses and giving tenants and small farmers the opportunity to purchase property of their own. Both groups had an enormous incentive to use their financial and physical resources efficiently because of the new opportunities now available to them. Land reform greatly improved the distribution of income, and it helped to promote better management of the land and to raise productivity.

The reform of the foreign exchange system that commenced in 1958 also restructured economic incentives in important ways. In spite of an initially mixed public reception, the reform was eventually implemented, largely due to the foresight and perseverance of K.Y. Yin, the leading technocrat of the 1950s. Yin argued that the exchange rate that over-valued the local currency had lowered the cost of imported goods tremendously. Because imports were so restricted and scarce in supply, there was a large discrepancy between the domestic market price of imported goods and their actual cost to importers. Windfall profits were earned by those lucky enough to obtain their quota of foreign exchange, but entrepreneurs engaged in production and dependent upon imported raw materials or intermediate goods were penalized.

The system that flourished from 1949 to 1958 set a favorable exchange rate for importing goods essential for economic development, applied a general exchange rate to bulk exports of the government and highly profitable private exports, and applied a still more favorable exchange rate to other exports. This control system was both "supply restrictive" and "cost restrictive" respectively for exporters and importers, so that the fixed multiple exchange rates favored different parties, particularly the government. The system worked reasonably well in the early 1950s to reduce imports, transfer excessive trade profits to the government, promote the growth of government-protected industries, and stabilize a minimum level of living for the people. Managing this system only required that government periodically adjust the dual rates as internal prices changed.

And so the system brought economic profits to importers, revenue gains for the government, and profits for the protected industries. But by 1955–56 the distortive effects had become more glaring. After a hard-fought battle between reformers and those who favored the status quo, a three-stage reform began on April 12, 1958, and was completed on August 10, 1959, when the basic exchange rate was merged with the exchange certificate rate to form a new basic exchange rate of NT$36.38 per US$. Taiwan at long last had moved to a single exchange-rate system.

By moving to the single exchange rate, the government was effectively devaluing the NT$ and making imports more expensive. Higher-priced imports might have generated some price inflation. Other events also threatened to make price inflation worse: an offshore gun duel with Communist China in August 1958 and a giant typhoon that destroyed much of the 1959 crop endangered the economic home front. In order to prevent current spending from pulling up prices, the government raised surtaxes, and the monetary authorities quickly elevated interest rates. Indebtedness of firms jumped in 1960, and many business failures occurred. For example, the Tang Eng Iron Works already had incurred loans of NT$245 million that it could not repay, and went under.[35] But demand deposits shot up from NT$925 million in 1960 to NT$2,800 million in 1961 due to higher interest rates paid on savings. In 1961–62 banks began making more loans and cutting their interest rates. Inflation had been defeated, and economic activity resumed.

At the same time, the government began expanding the list of allowed imports and reducing tariffs. Between 1957 and 1970 a total of 1,471 items that had been on the restricted import list were removed.[36] The government also helped exporters by remitting their taxes and conferring upon them special import duty reductions for commodities they vitally needed to manufacture for exports. Between 1963 and 1968 a total of NT$15.8 billion of taxes and duties was remitted to Taiwan exporters.[37] Banks also began offering more loans for promoting exports.

These government policies just outlined for the years 1958 through 1961 completed the reform of the foreign trade control system that had enveloped Taiwan in the previous ten years. The economy had begun to experience a very different kind of takeoff: export-led growth was now a reality. In order to keep the economy on the new course, the state began to introduce incentives to promote greater domestic saving and investment and to attract more foreign investment.

But why did this development only begin to take place at this time? Perhaps a major reason was the phasing out of U.S. economic aid in 1965 just as the new export-led development pattern was also beginning to take form. Between 1951 and 1968 the Republic of China had received nearly US$1.5 billion in aid from the United States. That program officially ended in 1965 even though materials already in the pipeline continued to arrive as late as 1968. About 25 percent of that aid had been used in the Republic of China for special projects to produce more electrical power, improve transport, enhance farm production, and modernize the military. The remainder of that aid went to import capital, raw materials, and consumer goods that the country could not afford to import because it lacked foreign exchange. Thus, U.S. economic aid financed about 95 percent of the trade deficit on current account of balance of payments. These imported goods greatly helped to stabilize domestic prices in the 1950s. Therefore, as U.S. economic aid was to end in 1965, the government recognized the need to increase savings and attract more foreign investment in order to develop export industries and finance more capital formation.

As already pointed out above (figure 2.2), savings rapidly increased during the transformation period. How did policymakers encourage a high rate of savings by households, private enterprises, and public enterprises? One strategy already used in the early 1950s and repeated later was to raise interest rates for time deposits in banks. The average rate of return for one-year time deposits (deflated for price change) ranged from 1.18 to 10. 15 percent between 1965 and 1981, except for the years 1974, 1980, and 1981.[38]

A second strategy was to introduce new tax incentives. In September 1960 the government exempted recipients of interest earned from time deposits of two years or longer from paying any income tax. Then in January 1971 the government passed legislation exempting recipients from paying any tax on interest income from the following sources: trust funds in accounts for two or more years; monthly savings deposits or postal savings in accounts for a year or longer less than NT$1,200 a month; savings deposits for tax payments; and construction savings debentures maturing after three years. Again on January 1, 1981, the government made it possible for recipients of interest from other kinds of income sources to be exempt from paying tax: postal passbook savings and short-term commercial paper; income from trust funds that constituted a real savings fund; and dividends accruable on registered share certificates publicly issued and listed by company, if total amount of deduction for a year came to less than NT$360,000.

The government also created new incentives for businesses to invest. In September 1960 the government had passed legislation designed to encourage greater investment. Such tax benefits included the following: five-year tax exemptions or accelerated depreciation of fixed assets; investment credits ranging from 10 to 15 percent; preferential rates on firms' income taxes ranging from 22 to 25 percent; and reduction of up to 15 percent of money paid for acquiring share certificates in the consolidated income tax in any current year. As already mentioned, exporters also began receiving tax incentives when purchasing raw materials from abroad and importing machinery for producing for export.

When we estimate the total tax exemptions for business investment, we arrive at a figure of roughly NT$1.5 billion for the period 1961–80. Of this amount, about 38.1 percent represented business tax exemptions, and 37 percent represented income tax exemptions. The total tax relief for exports, those refunds of taxes and duties paid for imported raw materials, came to NT$249.6 billion or 39 percent of total tax receipts from 1955 to 1980. Of export refunds, customs duties made up 61.7 percent and commodity taxes another 27.5 percent. All this represented a great loss of revenue for the government, but it is more than likely that the incentive given to businesses to undertake more investment and expand sales generated more tax revenue than was lost from state coffers.

And what of foreign investment? The government had drafted laws for foreign nations to invest in Taiwan as early as July 14, 1954, and these were amended on December 14, 1959.[39] These laws encouraged foreign investment to locate in Taiwan and made it possible for the investor to apply each year to remit foreign exchange to his home country. Article 12, for example, stipulated that the investor could apply for any amount up to 15 percent of the total sum invested. Such application could only be made two years after government approval of the original investment plan. But even that 15 percent share could be raised if the government approved, and such approval largely depended upon the available foreign exchange reserves.

Did foreign investment in the Republic of China grow rapidly during the transformation period? The answer is yes—according to table 2.6, in the years 1965–70 alone the total amount of capital inflow exceeded that for the 1952–64 period fivefold. In fact, foreign investment rapidly climbed during the 1970s, with overseas Chinese capital accounting for roughly one-third of the total amount.

Government policies to channel resources into modern factories, especially for export, also periodically took place. For example, in 1957 the government encouraged leading manufacturers to pool their funds and, with some American capital, built a new plant in Miaoli to produce synthetic textiles.[40] With capital of around US$1 million, the Artifical Fiber Corporation became the first producer of synthetic fibers in Taiwan. Other firms followed, and this industry eventually became a leading export earner.

The government then set up an export-processing zone in Kaoshiung in 1966 and two more at Nantze and Taichung in 1969.[41]

Table 2.6   Overseas Chinese and Foreign Investment (US$1,000)

Period	Overseas Chinese		Other Foreign		Total
	Value	Percent	Value	Percent	
1952–64	36,150	38.8	56,956	61.2	93,106
1965–70	126,866	27.2	339,258	72.8	466,124
1971–75	247,315	29.2	598,702	70.8	846,017
1976–81	593,819	34.7	1,115,094	65.3	1,708,913
Total	1,004,150	32.2	2,110,010	67.8	3,114,160

Source: Investment Commission, Ministry of Economic Affairs, *Statistics on Overseas Chinese and Foreign Investment, Technical Cooperation, Outward Investment, Outward Technical Cooperation*, The Republic of China, December 31, 1984, p. 5.

Occupying only 180 hectares of land, all three offered their joint-venture, foreign, and Chinese firms exemptions from import tariffs, commodity taxes, a five-year corporate tax holiday, and low-cost loans to build factories without deed taxes. Although 110 factories had closed their doors between 1967 and 1970, new applicants totaling 262 still produced for export. They attracted US$280 million worth of investment by 1979, but only 12 percent of that came from Chinese firms. These zones ultimately produced electronic components, machinery, precision optics, plastics, leather, clothing, and leisure goods. Of the nearly 80,000 people they came to employ, 60,000 were women housed in modern multistory dormitories near the factories.

Another government scheme, launched in July 1979, was designed to create a 210-hectare park only forty-five miles southwest of Taipei, in Hsinchu, for Chinese and foreign high-technology firms. Located near several major universities and institutes, the park is supposed to operate as a bonded, duty-free area with a computerized inventory control system rather than a physical wall at the boundary.[42] The park immediately took applications from firms to make minicomputers, integrated circuits, and laser optics. In this way the park, like the export-processing zones just described, began to channel new resources and technology into new product lines that are now revolutionizing all sectors of Taiwan manufacturing.

Finally, there were policies for promoting economic equilibrium. These policies can be divided into two groups by reason of the kind of economic equilibrium to be achieved. The first group of policies related to plans and spending to bring the economy's infrastrucure in line with the expanding market economy supporting the private sector. A variety of public goods and services usually are supplied to any economy by public organizations: energy, transportation, communications, education, etc. In the early 1970s government economic planners already had observed that the private sector's rapid growth and demands were outstripping the supply of public goods and services. Unless the infrastructure was improved, critical bottlenecks could very well impede the activities of private enterprise and choke off the development underway.

In 1974 the government initiated the Ten Major Development Projects for completion by 1979.[43] The government viewed these projects as necessary because private investment during the 1963–72 period had outpaced public investment for infrastructural development. These projects involved building a north-south freeway, electrifying the railway system, constructing a new international airport, establishing a nuclear power plant, constructing an integrated steel mill, opening a giant shipyard, and building a naphtha-cracking plant for the state-run Chinese Petroleum Company, as well as expanding the productive capacity of existing petrochemical firms. Immediately upon completing these projects in 1979, the government announced that twelve more such projects, costing around US$7 billion, would be completed by the end of the 1980s.[44]

The second group of policies designed to achieve economic equilibrium were monetary and fiscal policies that the government used from time to time to stabilize economic activity in order to prevent severe inflation or recession. These policies followed the conventional monetary and fiscal tools used by Western economies but with some differences. Some examples can elucidate these practices.

As the Republic of China became more dependent upon foreign trade in the 1960s, it became increasingly more difficult for the single, fixed exchange rate to accommodate the rapid changes in value of other foreign currencies, a situation that became more acute after the mid-1970s. Taiwan traders encountered very unpredictable costs whenever the value of foreign currencies shifted wildly. Therefore, in February 1978 the government introduced a managed-floating exchange rate. The Central Bank now buys and sells key currencies like the U.S. dollar to allow the exchange rate for the NT$ to shift within a narrow band of exchange-rate values. Such pegging helped minimize unexpected costs for Taiwan traders.

Another difficulty the government faced as the island economy became more trade-dependent was the volatility of the money supply. When export surpluses mounted and exporters earned huge profits, depositing these in Taiwan banks, demand deposits abruptly rose and the money supply jumped. The opposite effect took place if traders suddenly reduced their demand deposits. The government has designed some procedures to prevent such large shifts in the money supply that might adversely spark inflation or recession. It has raised the reserve requirements for savings deposits, issued new treasury bills to be purchased by banks, sold foreign exchange to banks, suspended short-term capital inflows, and allocated foreign exchange to traders for importing consumer goods and intermediate products for industry. All of these steps were made cautiously and with prudence. Therefore, the government continually intervenes in money markets in order to stabilize the value of different forms of money.

Ever since the great post–World War II inflation, Taiwan's government has been determined to use instruments at its disposal to influence interest rates. In order to reduce the real rate of interest and promote capital investment, the government has taken vigorous steps to curtail expenditures and induce higher savings. Therefore, government-controlled banks have invariably offered very high interest rates for bank deposits to attract funds into bank time deposits. This tactic proved very successful in the early 1950s, and it has been used frequently ever since. When the oil crisis struck Taiwan in 1973 and sent inflationary shockwaves throughout the island, the government quickly responded by raising the interest rate on one-year savings deposits from 8.75 to 15 percent between July 1973 and January 1974. This sudden hike within only six months brought a tremendous cashflow into banks and helped to curb inflationary spending.

As for fiscal tools, the government has used these as incentives to direct resource flows whenever it deems necessary. We have already cited the example in 1959 of the government raising indirect taxes to cool inflationary pressures. In 1960 and subsequent years tax rebates were given to manufacturer exporters to stimulate their activities. Selectively applied tariff increases and reductions also have been used to curb or promote imports depending upon the economic conditions that prevailed. But built-in stabilizers like the progressive income tax and transfer payments have not yet become important, nor will they likely be for some time to come. Income taxes make up a small share of total revenue, still only accounting for around one-third of all tax revenues in 1981.[45] Transfer payments also are very small as a share of total government spending.

The governmental agencies for coordinating the policies just described did not take form all at once. The primary institution guiding Taiwan's economic planning from the mid-1960s to the early 1970s was the Council for International Economic Cooperation and Development (CIECD), established in 1963 in the face of gradual withdrawal of U.S. aid. The CIECD was a centralized development agency that amalgamated the Council for U.S. Aid (CUSA) and three planning groups (industrial, agricultural, and communications). It was originally charged with the formulation, integration, and coordination of economic development plans and negotiations for external financial and technical assistance.

This institution was reorganized into the Economic Planning Council (EPC) in 1973, and its functions somewhat decentralized. With the outbreak of the oil crises in the 1970s, however, the changing economic climate demanded more potent and effective tactics than the EPC could provide, and a unique forum for economic policymaking evolved in Taiwan: the Financial and Economic Committee (FEC).

It was convened in January 1974 by the then governor of the Central Bank of China, Kuo-Hwa Yu. The FEC was a remarkably informal and flexible policymaking group. The members included the minister of economic affairs, the minister of finance, the chief comptroller, the secretary general of the Executive Yuan (Cabinet), and the governor of the Central Bank who served as convener. Each week from 1974 through 1977 this committee met over breakfast to discuss policies coordinating the interests of the financial, economic, monetary, agricultural, and industrial sectors of the country. No minutes of these meetings were kept nor were any memos ever written, but each Friday the committee would make policy recommendations directly to the premier. While the FEC was in charge of policy, the EPC continued in its planning role. The two functions were merged in 1977 by the creation of the Economic Planning and Development Council, a super-ministry level organization headed by Yu. The other members of the former FEC continued as members of the Economic Planning and Development Council.

This short review of government policies shows that the state has intervened to influence the private sector in many ways. But such policies are designed to nurture private enterprise and not impede its activities. Government officials and planners are convinced that the marketplace cannot provide adequate signals all the time for actors to respond in the best interests of society. Because the government also has the responsibility for national defense and for improving the welfare of the people, its economic policies often appear to be interventionist in the market and ill-suited to serve the interests of business. Many instances have also arisen whereby the government has been asked to provide subsidies for firms that have gone bankrupt, but the government has generally refused to bail out firms except in the case of large-scale public enterprises. Therefore, when difficult economic times struck, many business failures occurred. Furthermore, many critics of government have long held that the economy should be more open, like the free *entrepot* economies of Singapore and Hong Kong. But the government has resisted such moves, because national security concerns dictate that some surveillance and checks must still be exercised upon private parties that want to enter and leave Taiwan. Here too the government has tried to strike a balance between the demands of those running the defense establishment and the businessmen eager for more freedom to trade in the international market.

The Private Sector. Taiwan enterprises are predominantly small and medium-sized, operated by a single proprietor or family. Some large companies like Formosa Plastics exist, but the simple fact is that we do not find great conglomerates like Hyundai or Samsung as in South Korea. For example, as of mid-1983 the Hyundai and Samsung corporations had annual sales of US$8.0 and $5.9 billion, respectively; assets of US$6.0 and $4.6 billion, respectively; and employed 137,000 and 97,384, respectively. But Formosa Plastics, the Republic of China's largest privately owned corporation, lagged far behind with annual sales of US$1.6 billion, assets of US$1.7 billion, and a workforce of 31,211.[46]

The government does own and operate large firms to produce steel and build ships, but these are special cases. The small-scale enterprises in Taiwan are characteristic of Chinese society, and the same features exist in Singapore and Hong Kong and had long operated on the mainland before the period of Communist rule. This structural feature might very well explain why markets are so open and competitive on Taiwan. For indeed that is the case. Numerous enterprises emerge and fail every day. As one would also expect, we tend to find cutthroat pricing practices everywhere. Firms are price takers rather than price makers. They try to keep their unit costs low while expanding sales either at home or abroad. For these reasons, then, few private firms can spend very much for research and development, and consequently the Republic of China has a very low rate of R&D expenditure. Technical creativity under these circumstances is rare. Firms obtain their new technology by imitating their competitors, especially the foreign multinationals that have located on the island. Technical diffusion becomes very rapid because entrepreneurs imitate their domestic rivals, or they learn the newest state of the art from foreign firms.

As an example of imitating rivals, in 1957 the government wanted to promote plastics, and so officials persuaded Y.C. Wang, a successful businessman in his own right, to set up a factory. After several years of lackluster success, Wang finally reduced unit costs and began producing for export. Then three other businessmen without any experience in plastics quickly followed suit and built similar factories; others also entered the industry. In 1957 only 100 small firms had fabricated products from plastics supplied by Wang, but in 1970 more than 1,300 small firms purchased from the few major plastics suppliers.

Before 1960 the electronics industry did not exist, but by 1978 over 1,000 Chinese firms produced nearly 10 percent of the value of manufacturing and exporting as well. By 1983 the export value of electronic products exceeded that of textiles, giving it first place in Taiwan's manufactured exports. Again, small and medium-sized firms predominated, with half of them earning less than US$9.4 million each year. They only spent 0.4 percent of their sales on R&D compared with 8 percent in Japan and 5–8 percent in the United States.[47]

Still another case of rapid industrial growth is that of man-made fibers. The first such firm, the Artificial Fiber Corporation, began operating in 1957 with a daily capacity of four tons of rayon filament fiber. Many other firms followed suit, in nylons, polyester, and acrylic fibers in the 1960s.[48] Their growth was tremendous. In 1957 only 738 tons of such fibers were produced on the island. By 1968 a variety of such fibers was being produced to the amount of 32,580 tons, and about three-quarters of it exported. Such industries as canned pineapples, mushrooms, and other processed foods; shoes; leather; plywood; etc., sprouted up in this same period. Again, firms in these industries were small, labor-intensive, and oriented toward export.

Foreign enterprise was another important source of new technology. Between 1961 and 1970 the net long-term capital flow into Taiwan had more than doubled, and between 1970 and 1980 it rose another eightfold to make up 9 percent of total investment during that decade.[49] While part of that funding went to the new export-processing zones, all foreign investment accounted for around 4 percent of the value added in manufacturing, around 20 percent of exports, and 10 percent of manufacturing employment. In the 1950s overseas Chinese capital came to Taiwan, followed by Japanese and U.S. capital in the 1960s, with more of the same in the 1970s but augmented by European capital as well. From these foreign enterprises Chinese businesses obtained much valuable technology.

Foreign technology has entered the country through other avenues as well. In 1982 Taiwan exported US$1.8 billion worth of computer components, about 9 percent of exports for that year. One of these, personal computer boxes (PCB's), is now produced by a flourishing grassroots industry.[50] Several managers and technicians who had once worked for Ampex Taiwan, a subsidiary of U.S. Ampex, left to set up their own PCB factories. This new industry spread rapidly. PCB firms now turn out other components as well, at costs 30 percent lower than their counterparts in the United States. These same components have been widely used in the computers that have been under-selling their competitors abroad.

Borrowing from multinationals was still another means. The Singer Sewing Machine Company set up a factory in 1963 with capital of US$800,000. The government approved this investment because it hoped Singer's investment would replace sewing machine imports, save foreign exchange, and stimulate local industrial growth. That it did. By 1967 Singer's exports used all locally made parts except needles for its straight stitch model.[51] In the 1960s Singer's exports grew at 12 percent per annum, and by 1976 it exported 86 percent of its total output, with about four-fifths of that locally made. In addition, the company trained workers, held seminars, and provided standard blueprints to its parts producers. Singer did all this because it wanted to ensure that native firms adhered to its rigid specifications and that it cultivated goodwill with the authorities. Foreign firms like Singer used more foreign technology than their native competitors, but very soon much of that new technology had filtered down to other Chinese firms.

Just as small firms dominated the manufacturing sector, so too did small establishments proliferate in services. Between 1965 and 1973 the annual growth rate of labor leaving agriculture and never returning averaged 4–5 percent.[52] In this eight-year period the migration from the rural sector was the most rapid in Taiwan's entire economic history. Perhaps nearly half of the population of the Pescadores in the 1950s migrated to Kaohsiung city and environs in the transformation period. Although many of these new arrivals to the cities indeed found work in manufacturing, the services sector probably provided the greatest amount of employment.

Any visitor to Taiwan's large cities can only be amazed at the intense competition in services and the vast number of small shops, street vendors, and taxis. Competition among these units is fierce at all times; some prosper and others fail. Few ever become really large and incorporate, although some modern department stores now flourish in every major city. In 1982 the services sector employed 40 percent of the workforce and produced nearly half of the net domestic product. The economist Shirley Kuo found that the growth rate of value added in services was nearly as high as that of manufacturing between 1957 and 1981.[53]

Not surprisingly, small enterprises employ most of the workforce in services and generate most of the wage income. In the mid-1970s the firms in the commercial sub-sector of services having fewer than nine workers employed 70 percent of the workers and produced two-thirds of the wage income for that sub-sector.[54] Services are strongly linked to the other sectors, for their sales and revenue greatly fluctuate in response to economic conditions in industry and agriculture.

Although more land is now cultivated than in 1952 and the number of farm families in 1982 (803,819) exceeds that of 1952 (679,750), agriculture's share of exports (18.9 percent) and of the net domestic product (9.2 percent) was at a far lower level than it had been in either 1952 or 1965. Family farms now obtained only one-third of their income from farming compared to over two-thirds in the early 1950s. About nine out of ten farm households now work on a part-time basis whereas in the 1950s the number was around five out of ten farms.

In 1982 the total amount of paddy and upland land farmed was equivalent to that of 1965. In other words, although land cultivation continued to grow during the transformation phase, the high point had been reached in 1977, and thereafter land cultivation steadily declined.[55] Multiple cropping greatly increased along with crop yields. While farm output matched consumer demand and some produce was processed and even exported, the demand for food slowly declined. Rice consumption was only 96 kilograms per capita per year in 1982 and is expected to decline by 1.8 kilograms each year over the next decade.[56] By the mid-1970s the government began introducing subsidies to farmers. In the early 1980s the government was paying rice farmers (in kind) the cash equivalent of US$370 to $506 per hectare not to grow rice; this subsidy was costing the government millions of dollars each year.[57]

Government programs to support agriculture were varied and heavily funded. The Joint Commission for Rural Reconstruction (JCRR) began its work in 1950, and between 1950 and 1965 spent NT$4 billion on some 6,200 projects to provide farmers with new technology, information, and infrastructure.[58] This innovative administrative organ competed with the government's Department of Agriculture and Forestry, and sometimes their services overlapped. But the flexibility provided to the JCRR gave it more leverage to act with farmers in different regions and to lend more speedy assistance when needed. Government policies to encourage family farming continued through the transformation years. Some policies, however, definitely imposed a heavy burden on farmers while they assisted certain income groups living in the cities and working for the government, namely the civil service and the military.

One notable policy was the rice-fertilizer barter system, initiated in 1950, and finally phased out only during the early 1970s. In the early 1950s the government imported fertilizer from Japan and supplied it to farmers' associations, which in turn sold it to farmers in exchange for rice.[59] In those years farmers welcomed the scheme because fertilizer applications generated a high marginal output increase that yielded lucrative benefits at the fertilizer-rice barter ratio set by the government. But two new conditions wiped out these benefits. First, Taiwan developed its own fertilizer industry, and prices fell even lower than imported fertilizer. Second, the incremental output increase from fertilizer slowed down. As a result, farmers began to incur financial loss under the terms of the old fertilizer-rice exchange. Moreover, this system provided a powerful incentive for farmers to apply fertilizers only to rice rather than other high-value crops, so that the system distorted resource allocation on farms. Yet the arrangement had provided a stable supply of rice for the government to distribute to its employees. By the 1970s, the system had outlived its usefulness, and critics charged that its allocative inefficiencies were becoming excessive. Thus, the policy was finally abandoned.

The early land reform, government funding and technical support to farmers, and expanding domestic and international demand for farm output provided sufficient incentives and new technology for family farms to increase output at a growth rate of 4.2 percent per annum in 1953–1962, 4 percent in 1963–1972, and 2 percent in 1973–1982. This performance proved sufficient to supply enough food and raw materials to the urban sector at prices that people could afford without generating shortages and price inflation. On the other hand, the rapid growth of the urban sector and new export opportunities after 1965 kept demand for farm output strong so that farm prices did not begin to fluctuate violently and decline. Taiwan seems to differ from other countries during their economic transformation when their agricultural sector typically suffers protracted and severely declining terms of trade.

Having briefly reviewed the response of family farms, service establishments, and manufacturing firms to government policies both before and during the period of export-led growth, we offer these insights. First, government policies to restructure prices and financial incentives; channel resources to more competitive, high value-added activities; and restore balance in the economy through infrastructure development seem to have paid off. In the early 1950s the stability and revival of the economy was critical, and government controls achieved their ends. But continued reliance upon these controls rapidly distorted the structure of incentives and stifled entrepreneurial activities. The economy clearly was developing problems by 1956–57: more unemployment, higher inventories, and rising unused productive capacity.

Second, government reform of the exchange-rate control system and the liberalizing of trade tilted entrepreneurial activities to export and sparked a massive rural-urban migration. Economic units of all kinds vigorously responded to the new price incentives. A remarkably smooth transition to greater manufacturing and service activities took place. Family farms became more capital-intensive and diverted more resources from food grains to special crops, livestock, and aquatic products. Economic fluctuation remained minimal except for price shocks incurred from skyrocketing petroleum prices in 1973 and 1979.

Third, government policies aimed at promoting exports, stabilizing the domestic economy, and expanding the infrastructure helped to sustain the export-led growth until the world recession of 1981–82. Even then the Republic of China would emerge from that recession in 1983 and achieve the highest economic growth rate of any country in the world in 1984. The highly competitive factor and product markets worked to rapidly reallocate resources and goods and services.

The Period in Historical Perspective

The economic dualism that marked Taiwan in 1950 still persisted in 1960 but disappeared by 1981. Taiwan's population growth continued to exceed 3 percent per year in 1952–1965, and while it gradually declined during the transformation phase, it was 1.9 percent in 1981, still a very rapid growth rate for a developing country. As a country only 36,000 square kilometers in area, the population density in 1982 had become 508 persons per square kilometer, one of the highest in the world.[60] The Republic of China's experience does indicate that even under rapid population growth and with a large labor surplus, pursuing the correct economic policies can produce a rapid economic transformation. But were not the conditions in Taiwan very special for the Republic of China and its people to have achieved the successful growth they did? What about the Japanese colonial heritage and the abundant U.S. economic aid between 1950 and 1965? What of the favorable expanding international market of the 1960s and 1970s that Taiwan was so fortunate to enter?

To be sure, these conditions were helpful, but they are not sufficient to explain the remarkable economic transformation between 1965 and 1981. If certain government policies had not been initiated when they were, even those favorable conditions would not have sufficed for Taiwan to have achieved the transformation that it did. Why not? Let me offer the following argument.

Just as the Marshall Plan directed crucial economic aid to the Western European countries and helped restore the economies, so did American aid play an important role in Taiwan. American economic aid in the early 1950s financed the import of vital consumer and capital goods that could not have been produced domestically without diverting more resources from defense. Yet during these same years the Nationalist government continued to spend a very high proportion of the budget and allocate a large share, perhaps close to 10 percent, of gross domestic product for national defense. It has been pointed out that Taiwan could have grown just as fast and have consolidated her economic infrastructure for further growth as well as it did if the country had had less aid but a smaller defense budget. Though this might be true, government leaders opted for a strong defense, and they refused to cut military spending during the transformation phase, so that Taiwan's economy continued to bear a very heavy military expenditure burden even after American economic aid ended in 1965.

In 1982 the per capita military spending in the United States came to US$1,028 with a nominal per capita income for that year of US$13,242—7.7 percent of per capita income. For that same year Taiwan's per capita spending for defense came to around $US240 with a per capita income of US$2,500, or 9.6 percent of per capita income. In other words, the average citizen bears a very heavy military burden, as appears to have been the case ever since 1950. But in spite of such a burden, Taiwan's economy experienced a rapid and smooth transformation. How was that possible even after the ending of U.S. aid in 1965?

There is every reason to believe that the government could have oriented the economy toward the international market as early as 1955 if the will to do so had existed. But that was not the case. Powerful economic interests both inside and outside the government opposed any such move. The economic doctrines justifying the import-substitution strategy and tight control over the private sector still had their strong supporters in government. Is there any reason, then, to believe that Taiwan could have postponed the 1958–59 reforms until later, 1960 or beyond? The answer is yes. When we observe the policy experiences of the Philippines and the Latin American states, we note that their leaders adhered to the import-substitution strategy and the full complement of restrictive controls which that approach required until the late 1970s. Therefore, the 1958–59 reforms need not have been introduced at all or certainly much later than was the case. In other words, if persuasive arguments for them had not been made and powerful persons had not supported them, they would not have prevailed. Certainly the development pattern that unfolded after the early 1960s could not have taken place without them.

But simply launching those reforms might not have been enough. We have described how a series of follow-up policies were introduced that helped private enterprise to allocate resources through markets and carry out the transformation. If those policies had been in error, the 1958–59 reforms might not even have borne fruit. Instead, crippling inflation might have resumed; new economic controls and regulations might have been imposed to stifle private enterprise. But proper government policies did nurture private enterprise, and the timing of those policies also was crucial.

But what of markets and their role? Special attention has been focused upon the important role that markets played in allowing private enterprises to adhere to their comparative advantage and use abundant resources efficiently while gradually switching to the use of more scarce resources like capital goods. Paradoxically, the small and medium-sized firms that so readily accommodated these markets never made high R&D expenditures, nor did they generate new technology of their own. But technical diffusion did occur. Entrepreneurs borrowed from foreign enterprises and the international market. By a gradual learning-by-doing process, these entrepreneurs raised the productivity of their firms.

Our focus so far has been on the economic activities, both public and private, that helped to initiate and shape the distinctive character of Taiwan's economic transformation between 1965 and 1981. We have seen that that experience was a unique case. The ingredients that made it possible are not likely to be easily transferred to other developing countries to help them initiate their transformations. But one lesson that might be transferable and adopted by developing countries does seem important: If state policies can nurture the private sector by encouraging it to perform better, and if these policies can promote the redeployment of resources to higher value-added economic activities that comply with the comparative advantages those countries possess, then developing countries should be able to initiate their transformation phase as well. The more specialization and trade that can be encouraged under conditions of stability and peace, the greater the prospect for economic advancement and the improvement of society's welfare.

In terms of confirming or rejecting economic development theory, what does the Taiwan case tell us? Space does not permit a review of all relevant economic development theory, but by listing the essential features of Taiwan's transformation we can offer a few observations.

First, in the pre-transformation phase very little surplus labor was reallocated to other sectors because small and medium-sized firms in manufacturing and services were not growing rapidly. During the transformation phase the growth of small and medium-sized firms became more rapid because of expanding market demand, a significant change in relative prices, and new profit opportunities. Their rapid growth provided a vigorous demand for labor. Surplus labor was reallocated among all sectors.

Second, during the transformation phase the terms of trade became moderately unfavorable to agriculture, but they did not worsen over time. Real wages rose more rapidly but never out-stripped productivity. Increases in per capita income occurred because of rising productivity.

Third, capital shallowing and capital deepening occurred at the same time during the early transformation phase but capital deepening began to dominate by the 1970s and continued thereafter. This trend occurred in all sectors.

From these remarks, we can observe that the Taiwan case reveals some characteristics associated with both the classical two-sector and neoclassical models, but it does not adhere faithfully to either. The Taiwan case does show that the creation of appropriate price and income incentive structure is critical for the reallocation of resources. Further, if markets are highly competitive and can allocate resources fairly efficiently, technical diffusion, productivity gain, and employment increases can take place in all sectors. The key, of course, is that these developments take place in all three sectors and that policies are not slanted to favor a single sector over others. Finally, carefully timed and implemented economic policies that modulate the private sector to allocate resources to higher net value-added activities will be more successful than policies designed to protect select industries in the marketplace.

3

SUNG YEUNG KWACK

The Economic Development of the Republic of Korea, 1965–1981

The Republic of Korea is a developing country that has achieved remarkable economic growth over the last two decades. Since 1965, Korea has been transformed from an underdeveloped, agricultural country to a leading Newly Industrializing Country (NIC). Between 1965 and 1981, Korea's Gross National Product (GNP) multiplied twenty times from $3 billion to $63 billion; per capita GNP increased sixteen times from $105 to $1,628; and per capita consumption rose twelve times from $88 to $1,054 (table 3.1). In fact, if one excludes the OPEC countries and the centrally planned economies, the growth rate of real GNP in Korea ranked fifth in the world during the 1960s and first thereafter until 1978. At the same time, predominance in the country's industrial structure shifted from agriculture to manufacturing.

Appreciating this phenomenal growth requires an understanding of Korea's circumstances. Colonized by Japan in 1910, its status as a colony ended when the Japanese Empire surrendered to the Allies in 1945. Korea was then divided—the Soviet Union occupied the North, the United States occupied the South. Following three years of American military occupation, South Korea held its first national election in 1948 and, with Rhee Seung Man as the first duly elected president, became the Republic of Korea (from this point on, the designations Korea, South Korea, and Republic of Korea are used interchangeably). The Korean War, which began in June 1950 and ended in July 1953, further solidified the division of the Korean Peninsula into North and South.

Table 3.1   Current Level and Growth of GNP and Consumption

Year	GNP current mil. US$	Growth rate (%) Nominal	Growth rate (%) Real	Per capita GNP current US$	Per capita[a] consumption current US$
1965	3,026	12.5	5.8	105	88
1966	3,822	28.7	12.7	125	98
1967	4,736	23.5	6.6	142	111
1968	5,976	29.0	11.3	169	126
1969	7,478	30.4	13.8	210	149
1970	8,641	24.1	7.6	242	175
1971	9,462	22.5	9.4	277	205
1972	10,254	22.2	5.8	304	223
1973	13,152	29.9	14.9	383	258
1974	18,060	40.0	8.0	519	360
1975	20,233	32.5	7.1	565	401
1976	27,423	35.3	15.1	752	494
1977	35,168	27.6	10.3	944	596
1978	47,351	33.6	11.6	1,279	795
1979	60,066	26.9	6.4	1,598	995
1980	56,506	18.1	–6.2	1,479	963
1981[b]	63,370	25.7	7.1	1,628	1,054

a. Private consumption only.
b. Preliminary.
Sources: Korean Economic Planning Board, *Major Statistics of the Korean Economy*, various issues; Bank of Korea, *Monthly Bulletin*, 36:1 (January 1982), p. 133; and *Monthly Economic Statistics*, various issues.

The government of President Rhee Seung Man was toppled following large demonstrations in April 1960. An interim government introduced constitutional reforms and installed Chang Myun as president in August of that year. Chang's government, although short-lived, was democratic both in principle and in action. A military coup led by General Park Chung Hee in May 1961 turned it out of power, however. General Park officially assumed the presidency in October 1963. Under the Park regime, which spanned nearly two decades, the economy developed rapidly, despite the limited democracy that prevailed. President Park was assassinated in October 1979. General Chun Doo Whan emerged as the new leader in Korean politics, and became Korea's president in September 1980.

Korea occupies the southern half of the Korean Peninsula, which adjoins the People's Republic of China and the Soviet Union and faces

Japan across the Sea of Japan. The total land area of Korea is approximately 99,000 square kilometers (or 39,000 square miles)—a quarter of the size of Japan. Moreover, roughly 60 percent of the land is uncultivated, forested mountain slopes, leaving only 30 percent for actual cultivation and 10 percent residual for building. Two-thirds of the cultivated area is used for cereals, 50 percent of this for rice alone. Little pasture land exists in Korea since the mountainous slopes not used for cultivation are also not appropriate for grazing. Hence, Korea depends heavily on imported grain for animal feed. Given the country's small size, Korea's agricultural development policy understandably has emphasized land-saving strategies. In particular, irrigated paddies have increased substantially over the last twenty years. Irrigated land accounted for 548,000 hectares in 1965 and 833,000 hectares in 1980—a 2.8 percent annual increase on the average. Despite its largely mountainous terrain, Korea lacks mineral resources. Of special significance is the fact that Korea must import all of its oil.

In contrast to its limited land area, Korea has a large population relative to other nations. In 1965, the country's population numbered approximately 29 million, and increased to an estimated 38 million by 1980. With the exception of small city-states such as Monaco and Vatican City, Korea has the highest population density in the world. From 1964 to 1980, its population per square kilometer increased from 291 to 385 persons. However, Korea's population growth rate fell to a 1.6 percent average from 1975 through 1980, down from a 2.4 percent average between 1965 and 1970.

The total labor force of Korea has increased more rapidly than the population as a whole. The labor force grew from 8.9 million persons in 1965 to 14.4 million in 1980. Its average annual growth rate was 2.9 percent during the second half of the 1960s, 3.9 percent during the first half of the 1970s, and 4.5 percent through 1980. Two main factors accelerated this growth rate: first, demographic changes raised the proportion of the working-age population in the total population, and second, the female worker participation rate increased.

The Korean labor force is better educated than its counterparts in other developing countries. Compulsory primary education was implemented in Korea as early as 1949, and by the early 1960s the rate of primary school enrollment reached almost 100 percent. Enrollment in secondary school (middle and high school) rose at a rapid rate during the 1960s and 1970s. By 1980, middle school enrollment had reached 94 percent and high school enrollment, 85 percent. College and university education also boomed, particularly after 1975. The enrollment rate jumped from 9 percent in 1975 to 16 percent in 1980, reflecting the growing aspirations invoked by social modernization and industry's pressing need for educated workers. In 1980, Korea had eighty-five colleges and universities, eleven junior teachers' colleges, and 128 junior vocational colleges.

When Korea launched its first Five-Year Economic Development Plan in 1962, the country already possessed some basic infrastructure, most of which was constructed during the Japanese Colonial Period (1909–1945). This included railways and paved roads connecting urban areas, several modern harbors, and the electrification of a number of cities. The existing facilities were, however, insufficient for industrialization. Since the decade of the 1960s, expansion of Korea's infrastructure has paralleled its rapid industrialization, thanks to the generous influx of investment. Over the past twenty years, the largest proportions of this investment (about 23 percent of the total) went to the transport, storage, and communication industries.

Korea's Economic System

The Korean economy is a market economy in principle, relying primarily on the private sector. During the last two decades, for instance, private firms undertook about 70 percent of total investments. Because of limited resources, however, the government has viewed coordination between the public and private sector as an essential ingredient in a successful planning structure. Government policymakers carefully considered and often accepted the opinions and suggestions of business people. In turn, the private sector over the years has responded positively to government policies, mainly because of the incentive system the government implemented to induce business support. Moreover, the government has used informal devices and persuasion to bring recalcitrant companies in line. This combination of economic incentives and government decree has been effective in implementing policy. In fact, business and government have worked so well together in Korea that some Western observers have referred to the alliance as the "Korean Company."

The major institution guiding Korea's economic planning is the Economic Planning Board (EPB), established in 1961. The EPB designs the Five-Year Plans, monitors their implementation, plans budgets, su-

pervises expenditures, examines capital import projects, and accommo-
dates the often conflicting needs among economic ministries. The Minister of the Economic Planning Board (who is concurrently the
country's Deputy Prime Minister) is responsible for all economic policies. Of equal importance to planning, of course, is implementation.
Since the EPB has the dual responsibility of drawing up the
government's budget and designing the Five-Year Plans, it can ensure
program implementation through the budget it proposes. This integration of plan design and budget formulation under the auspices of one
group has proven very successful in enabling Korea to meet its economic objectives. To support the work of the EPB, the Korea Development Institute (KDI) was founded in 1971. Specifically, KDI provides
technical assistance in drawing up detailed plans to meet overall guidelines established by the EPB.

Beginning with the Park government, executive ministries including the Ministry of Construction, the Ministry of Finance, the Ministry
of Commerce and Industry, and the Ministry of Transport, carried out
directly the plans and budgets designed by the EPB. Conflicts among
these ministries were resolved at the Economic Ministers' Meeting, in
which all economic ministers and the Minister of Foreign Affairs participated. The Deputy Prime Minister chaired the meeting. President Park,
however, was known to decide major questions and disputes—unlike
his predecessors, Rhee Seung Man and Chang Myun, Park involved
himself directly in determining and implementing economic policies.
To assist him in these endeavors, he established a strong secretariat,
which served as an "inner" cabinet in advising the president and occasionally wielding more influence than did the official executive cabinet.
On the other hand, the Korean legislature, mass media, and the academic community did not play a very important role in determining
national economic policy. The Park regime was, in short, noted for
strong centralization and domination by the executive branch.

The Park system of government did possess the advantages of speed
and flexibility. The Presidential Emergency Decree, the centerpiece of
Korea's energy policy, was, for example, issued only three months after the
first oil crisis of October 1973. At the same time, Korea's centralized system
at times produced bad decisions. The most notable of these, in light of the
world economic conditions of the 1980s, was the over-investment in heavy
industries during the late 1970s, a decision that will be described later in
more detail. The government under President Chun Doo Whan has made
no significant changes in the planning structure evolved during the Park

regime. It appears that President Chun is not involved in actual policymaking to the extent his predecessor was.

Between 1945 and 1970, Korea received foreign aid or grants total-ing $4.4 billion, of which 86 percent, or $3.8 billion, came directly from the United States, with the remaining portion from the United Nations. Initially, U.S. assistance to Korea took the form of relief for the war-torn country during the U.S. military occupation (GARIOA aid). Assistance from the Economic Cooperation Administration (ECA), which empha-sized economic reconstruction, replaced GARIOA when the Republic of Korea was formed in 1948. During the Korean War (1950–1953), U.N. relief to the civilian population (CRIK and UNKRA) eclipsed ECA aid, providing food, clothing, and medicine.

With the end of the Korean War, U.S. aid increased rapidly in two areas. One was through Public Law 480, which provided Korea with American surplus agricultural products, mainly grains and raw cotton. The second was assistance from the Agency for International Develop-ment (AID), which supported economic reconstruction. The total of these two forms of aid reached a peak of $370 million in 1957. Thereaf-ter, the amount decreased continuously as American foreign assistance policy shifted from grants to loans. During the 1970s U.S. aid to Korea was minimal. Before the mid-1960s, foreign aid was important to Korea in terms of both civilian relief and economic reconstruction. AID assis-tance, in particular, contributed greatly toward the construction of Korea's consumer goods industries and electricity-generating plants. From 1953 to 1954, foreign aid comprised more than 68 percent of total imports and about 60 percent of total investment during this period.

Until the mid-1960s Korea was still a poor country with a low qual-ity of life. Yearly per capita consumption was a mere $88 as late as 1965. As the Korean economy expanded, so too the quality of life improved, as changes in the composition of consumption expenditure indicate. From 1965 through 1981, the most important change was the drop in the food portion (Engel Index) from 59.5 percent to 40.4 percent. In contrast, over the same period, the portion of furniture and household equip-ment rose from 1.4 percent to 6.2 percent; that of personal care and health expenses from 3.4 percent to 7.4 percent; and that of transporta-tion and communications from 4.4 percent to 8.6 percent. At the same time, per capita consumption rose from $88 to $1,054, a twelvefold in-crease in nominal terms or 4.6 times in real terms.

Korean life expectancy increased slightly from sixty to sixty-three years for males and sixty-four to sixty-nine years for females between

1965 and 1980. These new life expectancy levels are higher than those in most other developing countries, although lower than those in most other developed countries, where male/female life expectancies are beyond seventy years. The running-water supply per capita increased from 106 liters to 256 liters per day. Korea's water supply, however, continues to be inadequate for the needs of its population. In 1980, about half of all households did not have a piped water supply. In urban areas, most households do have piped water, but it is not cheap enough for everyday use, such as for bathing.

Despite overall improvements in the quality of life, Korea's rural areas continue to lag behind the urban centers. Some rural homes are not presently electrified or even supplied with piped water. Ironically, televisions have become a familiar sight in these areas, while refrigerators are scarce. Many rural towns are still not connected with the national highway system, and they are experiencing shortages in medical and educational services. Since the early 1970s, the Korean government has tried to meet these shortcomings by emphasizing rural development, and thus far its policies have shown some promising results.

Economic Growth

Between 1965 and 1981, Korea achieved an 8.6 percent annual rate of real GNP growth.[1] The growth of the economy is best viewed as taking place in three distinct phases: the period prior to the first oil shock in October 1973, the years between the first oil shock and the second shock in 1979, and from 1979 on. During the first of these phases, the Korean economy sustained a rapid growth rate, despite a recession in the early 1970s. On average, the rate of growth in real GNP registered 9.8 percent between 1965 and 1973. The engines sustaining the growth during these years were the expansion of exports and investments.

During this period exports grew at an average annual rate of 45 percent, from $175 million to $3,271 million. The expansion was due primarily to three factors. The first was a favorable international economic environment, which saw total world imports expand from $176 billion in 1965 to $536 billion by 1973. This boom in imports reflected the fact that the industrialized countries had not yet erected import barriers against exports from developing countries and were, on the contrary, quite active importers of cheaper goods from Newly Industrializing Countries such as Korea. A second significant factor was the

Korean government's policy of promoting exports, which was set in motion in 1965. Initially, the government introduced a number of fiscal and financial incentives, such as high interest rates. In addition, the government activated an export-targeting system. Finally, it established the Korea Trade Promotion Corporation (KOTRA) in 1962 to encourage overseas marketing. A third factor was Korea's abundant and highly productive labor force. This gave Korea a strong comparative advantage in producing labor-intensive commodities and provided the impetus for the notable expansion of exports.

Moving into the second phase of growth, Korea was able to successfully overcome the negative effects of the shock generated by the oil-price hike in 1973. The rates of increase in both real GNP and exports continued at a rapid pace. From 1976 to 1978, Korea recorded the highest growth rates among all oil importing countries. The ability to sustain this high growth during these years can be credited to the continuous expansion of exports and investments. The development of an export market in the Middle East for the Korean construction industry was an especially significant factor.

From 1979 to 1981, however, Korea managed a growth rate of only 2.4 percent and faced serious stagnation and inflation problems. Along with unfavorable world economic conditions, resulting in part from the second oil shock, domestic demand was sharply reduced by tight stabilization policies and by the political disruption caused by the 1979 assassination of President Park. Shrinkage in domestic demand produced stagnation in manufacturing and construction. In addition, the grain harvest of 1980 fell 22 percent, in real terms, due to unfavorable weather conditions. And rising international interest payments and debts abroad sharply increased external interest payments. All these events culminated in a real growth rate of minus 6.2 percent in 1980—the first negative rate since Korea launched its development policy in 1962. In 1981, the real growth rate did recover to 7.1 percent as agricultural harvests as well as domestic demand increased.

According to a study by the Bank of Korea, between 1971 and 1981 the Korean economy (excluding agriculture, forestry, and fisheries) grew, on the average, 10.4 percent each year.[2] Of this, 8.4 percent stemmed from increases in factor inputs and 2 percent from increases in the productivity of these factors. Increases in labor input contributed 35.6 percent of total growth, while that of capital, 45.2 percent. Hence, the contribution of increases in capital was more significant than that of labor. The results are in sharp contrast to the U.S. experience, where the

Table 3.2   Average Annual Real Growth Rate by Sector (percent)

	1965–69	1970–74	1975–79	1980	1981[b]	1965–81
Total gross national product	10.0	9.1	10.1	–6.1	7.1	8.6
Agriculture, forestry & fishing	3.1	3.4	4.0	–22.0	23.0	2.8
Mining & manufacturing	19.3	18.6	15.5	–1.1	6.8	15.9
Mining	4.1	8.0	5.6	–1.0	6.8	5.5
Manufacturing	21.6	19.4	15.9	–1.1	6.8	16.9
Social overhead capital & other services	12.9	9.7	9.3	–3.4	2.0	9.2
Construction	27.9	6.0	15.3	–0.8	–5.6	13.6
Electricity, gas & water	24.7	17.1	17.3	0.7	9.0	18.1
Transportation, communications & storage	24.7	15.2	15.9	3.4	8.3	16.9
Other services[a]	10.2	9.2	6.8	–6.1	1.5	7.4

a. Insurance; Financing; Ownership of dwelling; Public administration; Wholesale and retail; Community, social, and personal services; and Rest of the world.
b. Preliminary.
Sources: Korean Economic Planning Board, *Major Statistics of the Korean Economy*, various issues; Bank of Korea, *Monthly Bulletin*, 36:1 (January 1982).

contribution of labor input has been much larger than that of capital. Increases in productivity are usually associated with advances in technology and the quality of factor inputs. The high rate of school enrollment, leading to a high-quality labor force in Korea, may have resulted in Korea's technical advancements. In any case, the contribution to economic growth of a rise in productivity has been greater in Korea than in the United States.

The manufacturing sector led the growth of the economy between 1965 and 1981, registering a 16.9 percent annual real growth rate (table 3.2). The average annual growth rates of the manufacturing industry for the second half of the 1960s, the first half of the 1970s, and the second half of the 1970s were 21.6 percent, 19.4 percent, and 15.9 percent, respectively. The social overhead capital and other services sector was the second fastest growing industry during this period. From 1965 to 1981, the average growth rate of construction, in real terms, was 13.6 percent; that of electricity, gas, and water was 18.1 percent; and that of transportation, communications, and storage was 16.9 percent. Over the same period, primary industries and other services showed a lower average growth rate than that of total GNP. Primary industries grew only 2.8 percent in average real terms, while other services increased 7.4 percent on the average.

This difference in growth rates among sectors produced structural changes within the Korean economy. In 1965, the proportion of primary industries to GNP production was 37.6 percent; that of manufacturing, 17.9 percent; that of social overhead capital, 8.7 percent; and that of other services (including the rest of the world), 33.8 percent. In 1981, however, the ranking between primary industries and mining/manufacturing was reversed. The proportion of primary industries decreased to 18 percent—half of that registered in 1965. In contrast, the share of manufacturing nearly doubled to 29.5 percent. Social overhead capital also nearly doubled to 16.5 percent. The share of mining, however, decreased slightly from 2 percent to 1.4 percent, while the share of other services (including the rest of the world) increased from 33.8 percent to 34.6 percent.

One interesting occurrence during 1975 was the drop into the negative numbers of the proportion representing the rest of the world. Since 1975, its share at absolute levels has grown at an increasing rate. This reflects the fact that Korea's net payment of interest on foreign loans and assets abroad has been exceeding overseas earnings of its labor.

Development of Manufacturing. The development of the Korean manufacturing industry over the last two decades occurred in two stages. During the first, covering the period through 1968, Korea's light industries (such as textile, apparel, plywood, and footwear) expanded rapidly in line with the growth of foreign import demand. Armed with a strong advantage in unskilled labor, these industries had conquered the world market by the end of the 1960s. Among the light industries producing consumer goods, those in textile and apparel were the only traditional industries in the manufacturing sector already developed prior to the big push of the 1960s. Other light industries were essentially new, established after 1962. Nevertheless, at the beginning of the 1960s Korea's industrial sector was more highly developed than that of most other underdeveloped countries.

The second stage in the growth of the manufacturing sector was led by the development of heavy and chemical industries, which include those producing chemicals, petroleum, coal, rubber, plastics, nonmetallic mineral products and basic metals, fabricated metal products, and machinery and equipment. By the end of the 1970s, heavy and chemical industries were growing faster than light industries. Between 1965 and 1980, the proportion of heavy and chemical industries to overall production of manufacturing industries increased from 34.2 percent to 53.2 percent; and to exports, from 15.3 percent to 47.6 percent.

Several important changes in the economic situation of the country led to the shift from light to heavy and chemical industries. The first was the weakening of Korea's comparative advantage based on unskilled labor, in the face of growing competition from less industrialized countries where the wage rates of unskilled labor were still lower. In addition, major traditional export industries in Korea were reaching the limits of their potential to expand. The plywood industry, for example, had achieved such a dominant position in the world market by the end of the 1960s that further expanding its share became difficult or very costly. Moreover, textiles and footwear faced rising import barriers in the developed countries. In order to expand total exports, therefore, Korea turned to new export industries that were expected to have a comparative advantage based on abundant skilled labor. Shipbuilding, electronics, and steel were such industries because they required a large skilled labor force for their assembly process. In fact, only the assembly process within these industries was developed in Korea, and it was geared for the export, not domestic, market.

A second reason behind the shift from light to heavy industries lies in the backward linkage effect of export expansion. The rapid growth of manufacturing goods created an equally rapid growth in the demand for intermediary goods. During the first half of the 1960s, Korea imported most intermediary goods. Between 1968 and 1971, however, some chemical and heavy industries (such as fiber spinning, textile fabrics, rubber products, chemicals, and iron and steel) began to produce intermediary goods as substituters for imports. Most investment in this area was made in medium-scale plants.

The third impetus to the development of heavy industry in Korea was a shift within the world manufacturing industry. Beginning in the mid-1960s, some heavy and chemical industries manufacturers moved their operations from industrialized countries to the Newly Industrializing Countries, including Korea. These industries fell into three groups: (1) heavy industries where the assembly process was so labor-intensive that industrialized countries had lost their comparative advantage (shipbuilding, for example); (2) industries whose technology developed so quickly that the industrialized countries moved to monopolize advanced technology and to export low-level technology (electronics, for instance); and (3) high pollution-producing industries (chemical production, for example). Most heavy and chemical industries that eventually developed in Korea encompassed the industries of the three groups mentioned above.

The push for heavy and chemical industries in Korea occurred in two thrusts: 1968–1976 and 1977–1979. During the first period, the government selectively chose projects for investment with emphasis on those industries that produced basic intermediary inputs for other industries, namely, iron and steel, cement, fertilizers, and petroleum. In short, these industries produced for domestic demand rather than for exports, substituted for imports, and used low-level technology.

From 1977 to 1979, on the other hand, the government pumped huge amounts of investment, totaling 2,806 billion won, into large-scale projects in heavy and chemical industries. This investment amounted to approximately four times that funneled into light industry and close to the amount planned for the entire Fourth Five-Year Plan (1977–1981). The majority of large plants built in Korea during this period met serious shortages of demand in both the domestic and world markets. Most analysts believe that the 1977–1979 push for heavy and chemical industries was too ambitious.

A report released in 1981 by the Economic Planning Board pinpointed the effects of this economic measure.[3] First, it contended that underinvestment in light manufacturing industries caused severe supply shortages in many consumer necessities, which, in turn, brought about steep inflation. Second, the productivity gap between small and large firms widened. The report went on to state, "In order to promote exports and to realize large-scale economies, big firms have been given priorities, and small and medium firms relatively disregarded in the government's allocation of loanable funds and other funds and other administrative preferences. Consequently, dozens of conglomerates, mainly relying on trading companies, have been formed through expansion and takeover of existing firms, while the level of productivity and technology in small and medium firms has become relatively stagnant."[4]

As the shortcomings of these investments became evident, the government took steps to stop them in 1979. It then attempted to resolve the problems that resulted, including the "big" recession of that year. An important objective of the industrial policies of the Fifth Five-Year Plan (1982–1986) is to eliminate existing structural problems and to prepare the economy for another era of high growth.

The degree of self-sufficiency—the ratio of domestic production to total domestic demand (i.e., domestic production plus imports minus exports)—of Korean industry, as a whole, grew from 86.7 percent in 1970 to 90.3 percent in 1975 and 91.3 percent by 1978 (table 3.3). Manufacturing recorded the largest increase between 1970 and 1975, from

Table 3.3   Change over Time in Self-Sufficiency

	1970	1975	1978
Agriculture, forestry & fishing	88.7	88.2	91.5
Mining	49.9	18.9	21.5
(Coal)	(79.5)	(57.9)	(58.9)
Manufacturing	76.2	90.1	89.4
Other industries	98.7	102.1	102.6
Total industries	86.7	90.3	91.3

Note: Self-sufficiency=Domestic production/(domestic production + imports - exports)
Source: Lee, Soo Rae, "Analysis of Korean Economic Structure by Input-Output Table 1978," Bank of Korea, *Monthly Review*, 35:4 (April 1981), p. 42.

76.2 percent to 90.1 percent. The degree of self-sufficiency in this sector, however, decreased slightly to 89.4 percent in 1978. This drop stemmed from the development of heavy and chemical industries that required large doses of imported materials and intermediary goods. With regard to the manufacturing industry, the degree of self-sufficiency in light industry rose rapidly in the 1970s and was higher than 100 percent by 1978. In contrast, self-sufficiency in the heavy and chemical industries increased at a much slower pace and was less than 100 percent in 1978.

Development of Agriculture. Korea is often cited as a country that has successfully developed its agricultural sector. Production has increased and diversified, and rural life has been modernized. All agricultural production (including that of grains, vegetables, and fruits) rose continuously except during 1980, when bad weather conditions led to a poor grain harvest. Dramatic improvements in land productivity based on technological advancements account for most of the growth of agricultural production. As a case in point, growth in grain production came about solely by means of technological improvements as the land devoted to grain cultivation declined steadily from 1965 to 1980 (by almost one-third, from 3 million hectares to 2 million hectares). The significant areas of technological modernization included diffusion of new high-yield grain species and improvement and expansion of inputs, such as fertilizers and mechanization.

As the level of income has increased, food consumption patterns have changed. This shift of demand in food has brought about a change in the composition of agricultural production. The demand for vegetables, fruits, and dairy products has increased at a rapid pace.

Production of these goods has, in turn, grown at a greater rate than that of grains to meet demand. Vegetable production rose almost fivefold between 1965 and 1980, for example, and fruit production nearly three-fold. As a result, cultivated areas have been transformed from grain production to vegetable and fruit production.

With the ongoing shift in food consumption patterns, Korea's dependency on imported grains has increased. By 1977 Korea had almost reached a level of self-sufficiency in rice, the principal staple in the national diet. However, while the import of rice has decreased, the import of wheat and corn increased dramatically. The degree of Korean self-sufficiency in total grains has dropped continuously from 91.1 percent in 1965 to 65.6 percent in 1979 and 50.7 percent in 1980. The increase in imported corn, in particular, was directly related to the growth of dairy farming, as corn is used as livestock feed. As in the development of the manufacturing sector, the government took a leading role in the growth of agriculture. Its primary objective was technological improvement. As already noted, policy measures included dispersion of new species, land development, farm mechanization, and increased use of fertilizers.

In addition to this technological push, the government also implemented a two-tiered pricing policy and a New Community Movement, both of which had a significant impact on agriculture. After the Korean War, the prices of rice and barley were suppressed to achieve price stability. Indeed, keeping the price of grain low was a major policy tool for price stability during the 1950s. At that time, the government could fairly easily suppress grain prices because of the large importation of U.S. grains under the Public Law 480. While Korea's cheap grain policy was taken as an anti-inflation measure, it also was implemented to relieve the low-income class from the specter of starvation. In spite of cheap grain, the hyperinflation that followed the Korean War continued. By contrast, the nominal income of the low-income class was very low, and high unemployment existed, especially in the urban areas. In such a situation, the Korean government considered the low-price grain policy absolutely necessary to insure that food was available to the needy.

The Park government reinforced this policy, but for a reason related to low-wage polices. As the export drive was undertaken, a low-wage level became an important tool in achieving comparative advantage. To keep wages low, the Park government felt that the price of grain should be kept low. This policy of low-wage/grain prices led to decreases in the production of rice and barley. Hence, agriculture was sacrificed for industrialization in Korea during the 1960s. After 1968, the Korean government changed its cheap-grain policy. In 1969, the government established a two-tiered grain pricing policy, purchasing grains, rice, and barley from farmers at higher prices than its selling price to consumers. This new pricing policy raised the income of farmers without increasing the market price of grains. Concomitantly, however, the policy brought about serious government deficits and increases in the money supply.

The New Community Movement was a major comprehensive effort on the part of government to improve rural life. The movement, which started in 1971, was based on the idea of self-help. Throughout the 1970s, most government expenditures for rural and agricultural development went into this movement. To increase income, the movement promoted diversification of production and accelerated the cultivation of commercial crops,vegetables, and fruits. Small-scale rural manufacturing, using local resources and materials, was also encouraged. To improve rural living conditions, investments in the infrastructure increased, with government financial support. New roads and bridges were constructed, and electricity and water supplies installed. Many traditional homes were transformed into modern dwellings with indoor plumbing and running water. The movement did, to a large extent, assist in raising rural income and improving rural living standards.

Prices, Exchange Rate, and Monetary Policy

Inflation. In table 3.4, the rates of change in price levels in Korea are presented in terms of the deflator for GNP, wholesale prices (WPI), and consumer prices (CPI). Between 1965 and 1981, inflation rates in the different measures of prices showed little difference, holding at 16 percent on average. The prices changed in the same direction, even over the short term. Moreover, the rate of increase of the GNP deflator remained very close to the rate of inflation of consumer prices. This is because the GNP deflator and consumer prices include the movement of the prices of services, whereas wholesale prices do not.

The interval between 1965 and 1981 is subdivided into four periods according to whether the prices of foreign goods, including primary goods, rose substantially and whether exchange rates were adjusted: 1965–1972, 1973–1974, 1975–1978, and 1979–1981. The 1965–1972 and 1975–1978 periods were characterized by very minimal unexpected changes in import prices and devaluations of the won. During

Table 3.4	Rate of Inflation of Korea, 1965–1981 (percent, average)		
Year	GNP Deflator	WPI[a]	CPI[b]
1965	6.2	9.9	13.6
1966	14.5	9.0	11.8
1967	15.6	6.4	11.1
1968	16.1	8.4	10.9
1969	14.8	6.4	12.5
1970	15.6	9.1	16.1
1971	12.1	8.8	13.4
1972	15.6	13.8	11.7
1973	13.2	6.9	3.2
1974	29.6	42.1	24.3
1975	24.7	26.6	25.3
1976	17.7	12.1	15.3
1977	16.3	9.0	10.1
1978	20.6	11.7	14.4
1979	19.3	18.8	18.3
1980	25.8	38.9	28.7
1981	17.5	22.5	23.3
Average (1965–81)	17.4	15.3	15.5
(1965–72)	13.8	9.0	12.7
(1973–74)	21.4	24.5	13.8
(1975–78)	19.8	14.9	16.3
(1979–81)	20.9	26.7	23.4

a. Wholesale price index.
b. Consumer price index.
Source: Bank of Korea, *Monthly Economic Statistics*, various issues.

the 1973–1974 and 1979–1981 intervals, on the other hand, the price of crude oils and primary raw materials rose very significantly on a worldwide basis and devaluations of the won occurred.

Comparing the changes in prices among the different periods reveals that when foreign prices rose significantly, wholesale prices rose at a higher rate than did consumer prices and the GNP deflator. On the other hand, when domestic conditions took precedence, consumer prices and the GNP deflator increased at higher rates. Although these results may seem surprising, the reasons behind them are fairly simple. A change in the prices of imported goods directly causes a change, in the same direction, in the prices of industrial goods. Consequently, wholesale prices respond more quickly and profoundly to a change in foreign prices than do consumer prices. The inflationary pressures internally generated from excess demand for goods and labor, however, seem to be reflected fully in the prices of services and agricultural goods. Since consumer prices and the GNP deflator give more weight to the prices of agricultural goods and services than do wholesale prices, significant changes in domestic factors, such as the weather, money supply, and wage rates, tend to exert more influence on consumer prices and the GNP deflator.

While wholesale and consumer prices exhibited similar trends over the long run, the short-term movements of the two prices did not coincide as closely. The differential behavior between them indicates a difference in commodity composition, in addition to different degrees of sensitivity to changes in labor costs, import prices, and excess demand/supply conditions. Wholesale prices, constructed at the base year 1975, are composed of prices of industrial goods, which are given the weight of 77.5 percent, and the prices of agriculture, forestry, and fishery goods, whose weight is 22.5 percent. On the other hand, consumer prices are based on 37.4 percent of the price of industrial goods; 38.5 percent of the price of primary goods; and 24.1 percent of the price of services.

Services and primary (agriculture, forestry, and fishery) goods used a higher proportion of labor input per unit of output than did industrial goods, according to a Bank of Korea study based on the input-output relationship of Korea in 1978.[5] In contrast, the production of industrial goods used more intermediate material inputs. By raising the price of services and primary goods, labor costs more significantly influence the rates of change in consumer prices than in wholesale prices. Intermediate raw material prices, however, have a greater impact on wholesale prices than on consumer prices, since they affect the prices of industrial goods.

Inflation is attributed variously to the domestic cost of production, represented by labor costs (domestic cost view); the openness of the economy vis-à-vis the world (internationalist view); excessive monetary expansion (monetarist view); and rigidities in the economic structure, represented by the responses of supply and demand to price changes (structuralist view). Inflation is measured in terms of either wholesale prices or consumer prices. The relationships of various causes of inflation to wholesale and consumer prices are not identical. Special attention therefore is given to differential effects.

First, consider labor costs. Between 1966 and 1979, nominal wage rates increased at an annual rate of 26.4 percent for manufacturing, 26.1 percent for agriculture, and 29.4 percent for services. The rise in labor productivity varied among the sectors. After taking labor productivity into account, the increase in unit labor cost registered for manufacturing industries was 13 percent annually; followed by agriculture, forestry, and fisheries at 21 percent; mining at 22 percent; and services at 31 percent. Differential increases in unit labor costs, along with the differences in the weights accorded to labor costs, result in a differential trend between wholesale and consumer prices. Specifically, a change in the wage rate and in labor productivity tends to have a stronger influence on agricultural and service products than on manufactured goods. Accordingly, a change in labor costs affects consumer prices, which include the service sector, more than it affects wholesale prices.

Next, consider foreign prices. Korean exports and imports are small when compared to global transactions. Nevertheless, exports and imports represented more than one-half of Korea's total GNP after 1972, gradually increasing to more than 100 percent by 1981. Given the small size of Korean trade vis-à-vis the world economy and its large share of foreign trade as described above, prices in Korea would be expected to be affected by prices of foreign goods, including variations in exchange rates.

Korea has imported increasingly large amounts of raw materials relative to its total nominal imports. The share of raw-material imports has been about 60 percent, while the share of raw materials and capital goods in total imports has remained at a consistent 80 to 90 percent level. Thus, increases in the price of imports necessarily raise the cost of producing goods requiring (directly or indirectly) imported inputs and increase as well the prices of import-competitive goods, thereby significantly influencing Korean prices.

In Korea, prices of imported raw materials largely determine the prices of intermediate inputs. Considering the higher weight given to intermediate inputs in manufacturing and industrial goods, import prices (including foreign prices) affect wholesale prices more than they affect consumer prices. In fact, all other things being equal, a 10 percent increase in import prices is estimated to produce a 3.6 percent rise in wholesale prices and a 1.7 percent upswing in consumer prices, based on the input-output relationship in 1978.

A money supply in excess of a given level of demand for money is also thought to be responsible for inflation. As table 3.5 reports, the annual increase in the money supply (currency plus demand deposits, M1 definition) averaged 30 percent during the 1965–1981 period. The specific annual growth rates, however, deviated widely from the average. A comparison of inflation and the growth rate of the money supply

Table 3.5   Wholesale Prices and Money Supply (percent)

Year	Wholesale prices	Money supply (M1)	Real GNP	Ratio of money supply to real GNP	Ratio of nominal GNP to money supply
1965	9.9	34.2	5.8	26.8	−13.3
1966	9.0	29.7	12.7	15.1	−5.3
1967	6.4	44.5	6.6	35.6	−21.5
1968	8.4	44.6	11.3	29.9	−16.6
1969	6.4	41.7	13.8	24.5	−14.6
1970	9.1	19.7	7.6	11.2	−1.9
1971	8.8	18.7	9.4	8.5	0.3
1972	13.8	45.1	5.8	37.1	−17.0
1973	6.9	40.6	14.9	22.4	−12.6
1974	42.1	29.5	8.0	19.9	18.5
1975	26.6	25.0	7.1	16.8	8.5
1976	12.1	30.7	15.1	13.6	−1.2
1977	9.0	40.7	10.3	27.6	−14.6
1978	11.7	24.9	11.6	11.9	−0.1
1979	18.8	20.7	6.4	13.4	4.7
1980	38.9	16.3	−6.2	39.2	12.1
1981	22.5	4.7	7.1	−2.2	25.2
Average	15.3	30.1	8.7	20.7	3.8

Note: For comparability nominal GNP used for the computation of the velocity of money is defined as real GNP times wholesale prices; the use of actual nominal GNP does not change results significantly.
Source: Bank of Korea, *Monthly Economic Statistics,* and *Monthly Bulletin,* various issues.

suggests that other factors have been inducing sizable variations in prices.[6]

The ratios of nominal GNP to money supply, which is termed the velocity of money, were calculated to determine their constancy. The velocity of money fluctuated widely between 1965 and 1981, with a minimum change of minus 17 percent in 1972 and a maximum change of 25 percent in 1981. Since velocity is affected by expectations on inflation and interest rates, the large variance of the velocity over the sixteen-year period appears to reflect varying expectations in these areas. This, in turn, indicates uncertainty regarding changes in policy and in the international environment, such as the Smithsonian exchange-rate realignments, as well as rising primary and oil prices. Because of fluctuations resulting from shifts in the demand for money, a change in the money supply caused a change in prices over the short run only to a marginal extent and in an unpredictable manner. The average velocity change between 1965 and 1981 was small—just 3.8 percent—compared to the large variations in velocity on an annual basis. This confirms that the money supply tends to be associated with prices over the long term, given a stable demand for money. A rise in the supply of money generally leads to an increase in the demand for goods and services. Thus, consumer prices are likely to be influenced more rapidly than wholesale prices.

The apparent relationship between money and prices over the long run does not necessarily mean that money growth automatically leads to inflation, because it also influences the level of output. The growth of money could be merely a result of the passive accommodations of the monetary authority to inflation and GNP, brought on by other non-money supply factors. To determine the causal relationship, table 3.6 presents the amount of money (M1) supplied annually from 1965 to 1981 by government, private, and foreign sectors. In this table, the negative numbers in the government sector represent budget surpluses, while those in the foreign sector reflect balance of payments deficits. During the time intervals of oil price shocks and exchange rate depreciations, i.e., 1974–1975 and 1979–1981, the foreign sector absorbed money from the other sectors, while the money supply from the private sector increased significantly through augmentations in loans from banks. The money supply through the foreign sector is beyond the direct control of the Bank of Korea. Changes in Korea's domestic credit indicate the direction of policy.

Monetary growth during the first and second oil crises appears to have been the result of an active policy to offset the effect of balance of payments deficits. This active policy may justify the contention that changes in the money supply can be treated as exogenous during these years. The growth of the money supply in other periods, however, is likely to have come about to accommodate the demand for money, thereby implying the endogenous character of the money supply.

Finally, consider the effect rigidities in economic structure have on inflation. The responses of the supply of goods and services to changes in demand differ from one industry to another. Similarly, changes in the amount demanded in response to shifts in the supply of goods and services vary depending upon the characteristics of the goods and services in question. These differences in demand/supply responses affect the pattern of inflation differently.

Table 3.6   Money Supply by Sector in Korea (billion won at end of year)

Year	Money supply (M1)	Government sector		Private sector		Foreign sector		Other sector
1965	65.6	14.9	(22.7)	32.4	(49.4)	18.6	(28.4)	—
1966	85.1	11.7	(13.7)	24.5	(28.8)	51.8	(60.9)	–2.9
1967	123.0	11.5	(9.3)	46.1	(37.5)	80.4	(65.4)	–15.0
1968	177.9	–2.0	(–1.1)	118.0	(66.3)	81.4	(45.8)	–19.5
1969	252.0	–22.3	(–8.8)	202.3	(80.3)	107.9	(42.8)	–36.0
1970	307.6	–52.8	(–17.2)	277.3	(90.2)	110.2	(35.8)	–27.2
1971	358.0	130.7	(36.5)	407.3	(113.8)	37.8	(10.6)	–20.4
1972	519.4	51.8	(10.0)	420.2	(80.9)	102.5	(19.7)	–19.5
1973	730.4	45.4	(6.2)	450.5	(61.7)	299.6	(41.0)	–60.3
1974	945.7	121.0	(12.8)	1,131.0	(119.6)	–116.4	(–12.3)	–189.9
1975	1,181.7	414.5	(35.1)	1,213.5	(102.7)	–169.4	(–14.3)	–275.9
1976	1,544.0	369.2	(23.9)	1,257.9	(81.5)	308.9	(20.0)	–392.0
1977	2,172.6	364.5	(16.8)	1,378.3	(63.4)	976.0	(44.9)	–546.2
1978	2,713.8	464.0	(17.1)	2,397.9	(88.4)	724.9	(26.7)	–873.0
1979	3,274.5	334.9	(10.2)	3,970.9	(121.3)	236.2	(7.2)	–1,267.5
1980	3,807.0	731.2	(19.2)	6,188.6	(162.6)	–582.4	(–15.3)	–2,530.4
1981	3,986.0	1,659.2	(41.6)	7,549.4	(189.4)	–2,264.1	(–56.8)	–2,958.5

Note: Numbers in parentheses are a percentage of M1. Other sector consists of such assets and liabilities as suspense accounts, interoffices personal and real estate, capital accounts, and others.
Source: Bank of Korea, *Monthly Economic Statistics*, various issues.

The supply of and demand for industrial goods are sensitive to changes in prices, whereas the supply of and demand for agricultural products—because they are goods of necessity—are insensitive to price changes. A high price elasticity of supply of and demand for industrial goods makes the adjustment of prices to a change in excess demand/supply come about quickly. In contrast, the price insensitivity of the supply of and demand for agricultural goods leads to wide fluctuations in prices when excessive demand or supply occurs. If the share of agriculture's output to total GNP is large, the economy's structure can be highly rigid. Such rigidity in the economy tends to cause prices to fluctuate with large variations when there is a shortage of supply resulting from unfavorable weather or an unexpected surge in demand for agricultural goods from abroad.

The share of agriculture, forestry, and fisheries to real GNP dropped from 43 percent in 1965 to about 19 percent in 1981. This substantially increased the flexibility of the country's economic structure to changes in prices. Nevertheless, Korea's growth rate of output and inflation rate have thus far behaved unsystematically, thus creating large fluctuations in the prices of agricultural goods. As stated earlier, the government has been actively involved in setting prices and interest rates. The prices of utilities administered by the government, for example, have not changed in line with market demand and supply conditions. Government intervention in the price mechanism means that the economic structure of Korea is more rigid than would otherwise have been expected. The cost-push phenomenon attributable to government intervention, as well as the rigidity of the response of the agricultural sector, introduced into the economy substantial inflation, although this is extremely difficult to quantify. Structural inflexibility and price management by the government influence consumer prices more than wholesale prices, since the latter depend largely on the prices of industrial goods.

Individual factors as well contributed to the development of inflation in Korea, each to a different degree and over time. The periods 1973–1974 and 1979–1980 were intervals during which a substantial hike in foreign raw material prices and adjustments in the exchange rate occurred. Because of dependence on prices of industrial goods, wholesale prices rose more than consumer prices during these two periods. The contribution of import prices to wholesale and consumer prices was 75 and 45 percent, respectively, of the changes in prices that occurred. While no substantive changes occurred in foreign prices during the intervals 1965–1972 and 1975–1978, there were high growth rates in the money supply, a poor harvest due to bad weather conditions, a shortage of skilled laborers, and an increase in domestic absorption, among other things. These demand/supply conditions led to high labor costs and shortages of agricultural supplies. Consequently, the resulting increases in the prices of services and of agricultural goods, as well as prices of industrial goods, were accompanied by rising consumer prices, which increased more than wholesale prices. Labor costs and demand/supply factors contributed 65 and 75 percent increases, respectively, in wholesale and consumer prices.

Looking over the entire period between 1965 and 1980, foreign prices influenced domestic prices, particularly wholesale prices, to a significant degree. This impact is to be expected, given the Korean economy's small and open character vis-à-vis the world, as previously discussed. In contrast to other countries, labor costs in Korea appear to have little effect on wholesale prices. This may be because the manufacturing industries in Korea were more capital-intensive over recent years than in other countries. It may also be attributable to Korean government intervention in the labor market. Finally, factors affecting demand/supply conditions—including money, economic output structure, and exports—accounted for approximately 40 percent of the inflation rate.

Exchange Rate Policy. Since exchange rate adjustments affect both economic growth and inflation, an attempt is made to sort out the basis for exchange rate variations. In 1964, Korea officially moved from a fixed parity to a unitary floating exchange rate system. Although the exchange rate system has been "floating," its actual operation has not been significantly different from what would be expected from a fixed-parity basis to the U.S. dollar with discontinuous devaluations and gliding parity. Table 3.7 shows the changes in the nominal exchange rate of the Korean won vis-à-vis the U.S. dollar from 1965 through 1981. The nominal rate was allowed to float for a short interval during the spring of 1965, between 1968 and June 1971, and again from early 1972 until June of that year. For the remainder of the period, the exchange rate was established with discontinuous devaluations.

Sizable devaluations of 64 percent in 1964, 12 percent in 1971 and 1972, 19 percent in 1975, 25 percent in 1980, and 12 percent in 1981 occurred. Between January 1975 and December 1979, the exchange rate stayed at the January 1975 level. In January 1980, however, the government allowed more frequent adjustments of small amounts in the exchange rate for the purpose of minimizing the undesirable shock effects of the one-time sizable adjustments.

One of the objectives of Korean economic policy has been to sustain growth in exports.[7] This also has been an aim of the country's exchange rate policy. The real exchange rate indicates the prices of foreign goods relative to Korean goods in the world market. It has a significant impact on the determination of the amount of Korean exports. Consequently, when Korean prices and foreign prices (in their respective currencies) vary, maintaining the real exchange rate requires changing the nominal exchange rate. This in turn satisfies the purchasing power parity rule. The constancy of the real exchange rate has helped to prevent Korean exports from becoming expensive relative to competing goods in the world market.

The nature of the discontinuous devaluations of 1964, 1971, and 1974, as well as the gliding parities of 1980 and 1981, are instructive. The

Table 3.7   Exchange Rate of Won to US$

Date (year, month)	Exchange rate (won/US$)	Date (year, month)	Exchange rate (won/US$)
1961.2	130.00	1980.7	612.70
1964.5	255.51	1980.8	616.30
1965.12	272.06	1980.9	625.00
1966.12	271.46	1980.10	651.60
1967.11	268.11	1980.11	658.80
1968.12	281.50	1981.1	665.70
1969.11	304.35	1981.2	670.50
1971.6	370.80	1981.3	672.80
1972.12	398.90	1981.4	678.90
1973.12	397.50	1981.5	683.80
1974.12	484.00	1981.6	685.10
1980.1	580.00	1981.7	686.90
1980.2	580.70	1981.8	685.50
1980.3	586.10	1981.10	687.20
1980.4	590.50	1981.11	689.90
1980.5	596.20	1981.12	700.50
1980.6	603.00	—	—

Source: Bank of Korea, *Monthly Economic Statistics*, various issues.

devaluations in 1964 and 1974 were more than the amount needed to maintain purchasing power parity, and so the won was devalued in real terms. The Korean government designed these devaluations to stimulate exports further. In contrast, the devaluations of 1971 and those during the 1980s were not large enough to restore the real exchange rate fully to its previous levels. These limited devaluations reflected concern regarding the impact of inflation on Korea.

Beginning in March 1973, most developed countries moved from the fixed exchange rate system to a floating exchange rate system. Korea, however, pegged its exchange rate to the U.S. dollar (as did many other developing countries). This reluctance to adopt the floating system likely stemmed from the uncertainties of exchange rate movements expected from the absence of well-developed money and credit markets in Korea. In addition, if the exchange rate variations were large, they might have had an unfavorable impact on the external transactions and inflation rate of the country.

Since the exchange rates of the currencies of Korea's major trading partners vary, the exchange rate of the Korean won, as measured against these currencies, also varies. During the period 1977–1978, the effective exchange rate of the won depreciated. In 1980, the effective rate appreciated by one percent. The Korean government introduced gliding parity after 1980 to offset partially a change in the effective exchange rate by varying the nominal exchange rate of the won with the U.S. dollar. Thereafter,the nominal exchange of the won appreciated or depreciated according to the movement of the effective and real exchange rates.

Objectives of Monetary and Fiscal Policies. Monetary and fiscal policies, applied judiciously, can have a significant macroeconomic impact on a national economy. Such policies can minimize economic fluctuations, promote economic growth, and bring the balance of payments into equilibrium. Korea's monetary and fiscal policies have stabilized short-run economic fluctuations and promoted long-term, rapid economic development. The charter that established the Bank of Korea stipulates the objectives of stabilizing the value of money in order to achieve economic growth, and developing a sound credit system in order to promote efficient use of natural resources.

The link between monetary and fiscal policies lies in the management of investment funds to achieve targeted real growth rates and inflation rates. In the process of its economic development, Korea has faced two resource gaps. The first has been a foreign resource gap—that is, an excess of imports over export earnings, which has been filled by foreign aid and/or additional foreign capital borrowings. The second gap has been on the domestic side—an excess of investment demand over saving that has been financed by deficits in the government budget. The government's budget deficits have been financed almost exclusively by new borrowings from the Bank of Korea and reductions in cash balances. These changes have affected the money supply and credit conditions by changing the net domestic sources of the monetary base.

Monetary Indicators. A monetary indicator should reflect the state and timing of general economic conditions. In other words, it should signal at the appropriate time whether the economy is in an inflationary or deflationary state, so that policymakers will recognize the necessity of taking corrective action. In addition, the monetary authority must be able to control the behavior of the indicator. In Korea, two monetary policy indicators have been used: interest rates and aggregate money supply. The money supply meets the two requirements of a monetary indicator stated above. Interest rates do not. Interest rates are set directly by the monetary authority on commercial bank deposits and loans. Agreements reached within the Bankers Association of Korea (whose membership is composed of commercial banks) determine actual interest rates. Interest rates for non-bank financial intermediaries and public bonds move closely in line with those of commercial banks. Because the officially established interest rates are usually lower than, and thus do not represent, the rates determined by the interplay of demand and supply schedules in the market place, they are not reliable monetary indicators in Korea. The following is a historical sketch of the aggregate money supply as a monetary indicator in Korea.

1965–1969. Narrow money (M1)—the currency in circulation and demand deposits of commercial banks—was the monetary indicator during the 1965–1969 period. The monetary authority based the targeted rate of monetary growth on the planned growth rate of GNP, the anticipated inflation rate, and the expected change in income velocity of money (caused by monetization of the non-monetized or barter exchange sector of the economy). The main policy tool to attain the target rate was management of bank loans to the private sector through control of the claims of the Bank of Korea on deposit money banks.

1969. To regulate the excessive reserve money supply emanating from government and the foreign sector, the reserve base of the Bank of Korea was adopted as a new monetary target. By thus targeting the reserve money base of the central bank, the monetary authority aimed at controlling the money supply. The actual money supply is affected to some extent by the behavior of commercial banks as well as the public's desire to hold money. From 1965 to 1981 the ratio of M1 to the reserve base ranged between 0.94 and 1.42, while that of M2 was 1.96 to 5.60. This variation is far from constant, implying that little control can be exerted on the money supply by targeting the monetary base.

1970–1977. Toward the end of the 1960s, large investments made in the past began to build high inflation in the economy and to make the balance of payments worse. The monetary authority recognized that all these factors retarded steady, ongoing economic growth. In order to regulate the growth of investment demand and economic growth, management of domestic credits supplied by the banking system was necessary. Accordingly, the monetary indicator was changed from the Bank of Korea's reserve base to loan credits given to the private sector by commercial banks, the supply of which was more closely related to broad money (M2) than to narrow money (M1). Hence, domestic credits or a broadly defined money supply became the monetary indicator.

1978–present. In line with the second oil price shock in 1979 and the currency devaluations, inflationary pressures have built up in the economy. Consequently, monetary policy has shifted toward achieving price stability. The monetary authority, therefore, now considers monetary aggregates (M1 and M2) to be the most useful indicators in the management of price stability.

Establishment of Target Money Growth Rate. To implement monetary and fiscal policies, the government formulates a so-called "Fiscal Stabilization Plan" on an annual and quarterly basis. The plan explicitly establishes the targeted growth rate of monetary aggregates, such as M1, M2, and domestic credits. Each year the Economic Planning Board draws up the "Overall Resources Budget," which specifies policy targets— real GNP growth, inflation rate, balance of payments, and overall resource allocation. Based on the Overall Resources Budget, the Ministry of Finance and the Bank of Korea estimate the required growth rate of monetary aggregates. The framework used for the estimation is based on the demand for money; that is, the growth rate of money supply is equal to the growth rate of money demand, which in turn is the growth rate of nominal GNP minus the growth rate of the income velocity of money. The estimate of the growth rate of income velocity (nominal GNP divided by money) takes into account the credit conditions and the degree of monetization of the economy, as structural and behavioral changes occur. The growth rate of M1 and M2, estimated in this manner, is further refined by incorporating subjective judgment on economic disturbances and other events.

Available monetary policy tools in Korea include discount rates, open market operations, and required reserve ratios. The economic environment, however, has not been suited for all these instruments. As discussed previously, interest rates charged by banks are, by and large, exogenously determined and are below the market rate. Moreover, discount rates have not been effective in achieving monetary growth targets. With lower interest rates on government bonds and a shallow securities market, the Bank of Korea has been unable to operate an open market as a means of controlling the money supply and credit conditions. Consequently, the Korean monetary authority until recently primarily used direct controls over the supply of bank credits and the legal reserve requirement to control growth rates of money. From 1965 to 1981, the reserve ratios in Korea changed frequently. This is in contrast to the more advanced economies, where the reserve ratio is not normally subject to recurring change because it may impose an abrupt effect on the free reserve of commercial banks, and consequently the money supply.

Korea's reserve ratio applies uniformly to all commercial banks, ignoring differences in liquidity among individual banks. To counteract this shortcoming, the Bank of Korea operates a monetary stabilization account by issuing monetary stabilization bonds to control the day-to-day liquidity position of commercial banks. The interest rate on the monetary stabilization bonds is relatively low compared to other securities. Hence, they are issued mainly to commercial banks and non-bank financial intermediaries, rather than to general investors. The percentage ratio of the bonds to Ml has been rising at a rapid pace, indicating the bonds' growing importance as a monetary policy instrument in Korea.

In an attempt to introduce an open-market operation system in Korea, the government began to issue treasury bills in 1977. This move aimed to finance at least part of the budget deficits by selling the bills to general investors, thus minimizing the growth of direct borrowing from the Bank of Korea for this purpose. However, this open-market operation has not been very active. This is not unexpected, since short-term money and credit markets are linked to foreign financial sectors and are not effectively developed in Korea.

Financial Markets

Mobilization of domestic savings and retention of control over the private sector have been the dual objectives of government financial policy in Korea. The effective implementation of this policy has been closely connected with the development of financial institutions and markets. Over the last two decades, financial institutions in Korea played an important role in the country's economic development by supplying funds to corporate sectors and by providing facilities to save household wealth in financial form. The ratio of money stock (M2) to GNP rose from 9.4 percent in 1965 to 35.8 percent in 1980, and that of financial assets to GNP rose from 89.3 percent to 252.4 percent. In addition, the ratio of a change in financial assets to total capital formation increased from 96 percent in 1965 to 185 percent in 1980. These statistics show that financial intermediaries succeeded in inducing savers to save their wealth in financial form. At the same time, financial institutions increasingly needed the savings flow to meet the demand for external funds by firms.

Ongoing diversification accompanied this expansion in Korea's financial sector, including the Bank of Korea, banks in general, non-bank financial institutions (such as insurance, trust, and short-term financial companies), and security markets. Total new funds expanded eighty-two times from $209 million (55.7 billion won) in 1965 to $17,079 million (10,377 billion won) in 1980. In comparison, GNP rose 24-fold. While the banks' proportion of new flows of total funds (including foreign funds) decreased from approximately 58 percent in 1965 to 48.5 percent in 1980, the share held by non-bank financial institutions increased from around 14 percent to 30.5 percent. This increase illustrates the growing importance of non-bank intermediaries in the financial market. Security markets (both stocks and bonds) also expanded as part of the diversification process, but their proportion of the total supply of funds was not stable over the time period.

The Bank of Korea, in its role as the country's central bank, determines the allocation of loans, interest rate levels, and the supply of money and credit. The decision-making organization within the bank in this area is the Financial and Monetary Management Committee, which is presided over by the Minister of Finance.

The primary goal of the Korean government has been economic growth. To meet this objective, it has placed financial markets under its strict control. Financial policies have been an important instrument in implementing Korea's export drive and push toward industrialization. To promote investment, the Bank of Korea has maintained interest rates of bank institutions at low levels. In line with this approach, the government has also suppressed the rates of non-bank financial institutions. As a result, demand for loans from the formal financial markets typically has exceeded supply.

Interest rates on loans from special purposes have been lower than those on ordinary loans. Loans for export and equipment have, in general, been made at the lowest rates. Loans were especially important incentives for export promotion over the last two decades. To reduce the excess demand for bank loans, the government has regulated credit rationing with sectoral guidelines that specify the qualifications of borrowers. This method, however, has not removed all excess demand.

Banks, therefore, have raised effective interest rates on loans by various indirect methods. They have collected interest rates in advance, for example, and have required borrowers to open installment savings accounts of large amounts.

This discretionary lending system under tight government regulation has promoted industrialization. About half of all bank loans have been allocated to manufacturing and approximately one-third to social overhead capital and other services. In contrast, primary industries have received only around one-tenth of all loans.

Only five nationwide commercial banks operated in Korea in the early 1960s. During the two decades that followed, however, ten domestic commercial banks and thirty-three foreign bank branches opened their doors. Moreover, before 1961, there were no specialized Korea banks. During the 1960s, six specialized banks (all of which are still active in Korea) began operation. Four of these went into business between 1961 and 1963.

Of the specialized banks, the earliest, the Medium Industry Bank, opened in 1961 to provide loans as working capital to small and medium-sized firms in the manufacturing industry. Also in that year, the National Agricultural Cooperatives Federation and its member cooperatives added a credit department to supply financial support to farmers. In 1962, the Central Federation of Fisheries Cooperatives and its member organizations created a similar department. The Citizens National Bank, founded in 1963, specialized in banking services for households and small-sized firms—necessary at the time since the services of ordinary commercial banks were not yet available to small customers.

In 1967, two additional specialized banks opened that had a particularly important impact on the Korean economy. The first, the Korea Housing Bank, supplied long-term loans to build new housing for the low- and middle-income classes and financially supported the Korea Housing Corporation, which built apartment complexes for these citizens. The Korea Foreign Exchange Bank, on the other hand, filled the gap in foreign exchange services previously handled by a department of the Bank of Korea. Specialized banks do provide deposit service, but, with the exception of the Korea Foreign Exchange Bank, their loans are restricted to their specialized purposes. The Exchange Bank is no longer considered a specialized bank, although it provides some unique foreign exchange services. Today, other commercial and specialized banks are active in the foreign exchange.

Loans from the government and the Bank of Korea are a major source of funds for Korea's specialized banks. These loans are under the direct supervision of the Ministry of Finance. In contrast, the Bank of Korea continues to control directly commercial banks. The Bank of Korea's control over the country's banking system weakened substantially when specialized banks joined the system. As in the case of many developing countries, the most important role of Korean banks is to mobilize domestic savings for investment funds. Prior to 1966, however, banks in Korea were virtually inactive in this area because of government policies that discouraged their use for voluntary savings.

Perhaps the most significant government action preventing the growth of bank savings was its "cheap money policy": the Bank of Korea (which regulates all bank interest rates) imposed nominal interest rates on deposits lower than 15 percent during the first half of the 1960s. Given the concurrent high inflation rate (in the range of 10 to 35 percent), real interest rates were, in most cases, negative. Hence, no incentive existed for saving in banks. This situation continued until the reforms of September 1965, which doubled nominal interest rates on deposits and led to positive real deposit rates.

The reform measures of 1965 were, in fact, more effective than the Korean government expected.[8] Time and savings deposits increased 50 percent within the first three months and doubled every year thereafter over the following four years. The ratio of time and saving deposits at banks to GNP increased from 3.8 percent in 1965 to 6.8 percent in 1966, and to roughly 21 percent during the 1970–1979 period, reaching 26 percent by 1981. The rapid rise in bank savings over this interval was apparently a result of a shift of savings from other institutions and of an increase in savings. As savings deposits grew, so did bank loans. But when non-bank financial institutions started to expand after 1969, the banks' share of outstanding loans to total existing loans began to decrease, from 48 percent in 1970 to 38 percent in 1981.

Non-bank financial institutions include the Korea Development Bank (KDB), the Korea Export-Import Bank, saving institutions, trust companies, insurance companies, and short-term finance companies (STFC). The development of the non-bank sector was a major financial trend in the 1970s. The total outstanding loans of non-bank institutions increased 46-fold from 202 billion won in 1970 to 9,331 billion won in 1981, while that of banks rose 23-fold from 722 billion won to 16,481 billion won. This rapid growth was, for the most part, the result of the establishment of new non-bank institutions (particularly STFCs) to generate funds from informal (underground) money markets. They have provided higher interest rates on deposits than banks and, thus, have been impressive in their success in mobilizing savings deposits. The proportion of non-bank institutions in total savings and time deposits increased from 12.5 percent in 1970 to 22.3 percent in 1981.

The government's effort to develop new financial institutions began with the Third Emergency Measure of August 1972. The Third Emergency Measure went beyond the measures of 1965 by directly freezing all informal market loans, and requiring that these loans be reported to the government and converted into five-year loans after a three-year grace period. Likewise, the measure required that shareholders' loans to their own firms be converted into equities in the firms. There is no evidence that capital flights abroad developed around that time, probably because of tight restrictions on foreign capital transactions, despite the possibility to the contrary.

Concomitantly, the government established new financial institutions to replace Korea's existing informal market. Investment and finance companies, as well as merchant banking corporations, were short-term finance companies (STFCs) developed by the Korean government. The Korea Investment and Finance Corporation, established in 1972, was the first investment and finance company set up by the government. By the end of 1981, the number had increased to twelve. These companies provide the same services as did the broker in the informal money market—they mobilize temporary surplus funds and re-lend them to businesses on a short-term basis. The function of the merchant banking corporations (founded in 1977 and numbering six by 1981) is basically the same as that of the investment and finance companies. However, they also re-lend foreign funds borrowed from world capital markets and at times provide long-term investment capital.

The government created mutual savings companies to substitute for the informal consumer loan market, called the *kae*, and based on the traditional mutual savings method of money collected from and used by members. In fact, mutual savings companies are essentially formal *kae* dealers under government supervision. The Korean consumer loan market continues to be limited in scope. This is because of strict government controls on interest rates and loan allocations. The fact that the informal market is still operating in this area implies that the formal market cannot yet provide sufficient credit and consumer loans to the private sector.

Even after the financial reforms of 1965, government regulation of interest rates of formal institutions produced a huge excess demand for loans from these institutions, while at the same time an idle money balance existed. The combination of excess demand for loans and an idle balance created an informal market whose lending terms were flexible and beyond government control. As described earlier, the Third Emergency Measure of 1972 aimed to formalize the activities of the informal market (or, more simply, the black/underground market).

Two types of markets have existed within the informal money market. One of these, the short-term money (business or call money) market, has provided working capital for businesses. Temporary surplus money held by firms and individuals is lent to money brokers, who then make loans to the business community. Although the informal financial market is often described as unorganized, the opposite has been true of the short-term financial market in Korea, at least insofar as business working capital is concerned. Most borrowing and lending have been carried out very efficiently on a call basis, because money brokers keep up-to-date information about their clients and terms of lending.

The actual size of this informal market has never been accurately established. According to the Bank of Korea, the household claims on the informal market amounted to 102 billion won at the end of 1972 and increased to 186 billion won by the end of 1981. This estimate for 1972 is smaller than that suggested by Cole and Park, who state that the outstanding balance was equal to almost 40 percent of total bank loans in 1964 and 1965, and estimate claims at 350 billion won as of July 1972.[9] The Cole and Park estimates were used in connection with the Emergency Measures of August 3, 1972.

Koo, Hong, and Shin of the Korean Economic Institute recently produced a comprehensive study of the informal market in Korea.[10] The following statistics are based on this study. As table 3.8 summarizes, Koo, Hong, and Shin estimated the size of the informal market to be 1,100 billion won at the end of 1981, or approximately three times the figure estimated for 1972. The size of the underground market relative to total lendings of deposit money banks, money supply, and total debts of the corporate sector apparently declined substantially between 1972 and 1981. This decline seems to substantiate the view that funds in the informal market have shifted to formal financial institutions.

All funds in the informal financial market have encompassed short-term working capital. Maturities usually are no longer than three months. In general, interest rates that money brokers pay to money suppliers are 3 to 5 percent per month. In turn, the brokers charge borrowers interest rates between 5 and 7 percent per month, depending on

Table 3.8   Estimates of Informal Market Size
               (billion won, end of year)

	1972	1981	Percent change 1972–82
Market size			
Bank of Korea	102.1	185.8	1.812
IMF[a]		1091.0	
KEI[b]	350.0	1100.0	3.14
KER's estimate relative to total, lendings of deposit			
money banks	0.29	0.07	
Money supply (M1)	0.67	0.27	
Household assets[c]	0.19	0.07	
Corporate debts[c]			
Total	0.15	0.04	
Financial institutions	0.39	0.10	

a. IMF estimate of 1977 (749.36) times (1 + growth rates from 1977 to 1981, reported by the Bank of Korea).
b. KEI (Korea Economic Institute) estimate is (lending ratio, 0.29) times money supply (M2) –shift to non-bank institutions (3392).
c. Based on assets at the end of the year.
Sources: Koo, S.M., S.Y. Hong, and J.M. Shin, *A Study in Informal Financial Market in Korea* (Seoul: Korea Economic Institute, 1982).

the risk premium. While their levels differed, the interest rate in the informal market has moved very close to time-deposit rates in financial institutions, particularly since 1974. This implies that the formal and informal markets have been integrated to a significant extent over recent years. The existence of the informal market per se, however, suggests that it provides services of financial intermediation that are not otherwise supplied by the formal market. Such services likely include more speedy transactions between lenders and borrowers, and under more realistic terms. In this sense, the informal market is complementary to the formal market.

Besides providing working capital for businesses, the informal market has a second type of operation: consumer loans to households. During the 1960s and into the early 1970s, households in Korea did not have access to banking services. Instead, consumer loans were, by and large, supplied by private money lenders and the *kae*. In contrast to the informal short-term money market, this consumer loan market was not well organized and also much smaller. A report of the Citizen's National Bank confirms this.[11] A substantial portion of household savings has been held by the informal market, amounting to 64 percent of the savings in 1981. On the other hand, households borrowed funds from the informal market at a rate of close to 80 percent of their debts. These funds have been used mainly to purchase residences, supply working capital for unincorporated firms, and repay existing debts.

Security Markets

To mobilize domestic savings, the government attempted to develop security markets. The first important policy step in this direction was the enactment of the Capital Market Promotion Law in 1968, which promoted the sale of government-owned securities to the public by specifying conditions for the sale. The law was instrumental in expanding the number of market transactions and in encouraging the sale of stocks to the employees of issuing firms. Further, the law created the Korea Investment Corporation to underwrite the sales of securities and carry out such functions as stabilizing security prices through market operations and providing financing to security companies. The government also provided tax incentives for companies to open up to public ownership. In fact, the Public Ownership Inducement Law of 1972 established the legal basis for the government to compel large enterprises to open up their ownership.

In 1974, the government announced two additional sets of measures. The first included the Regulations on Business Financing and Concentration of Business Ownership, as well as the Agreements for Financing Control of Subsidiary Companies. Under these measures, all large companies heavily dependent on bank loans had to go public or risk having new bank loans cut off. The primary objective of the second law, the Comprehensive Capital Market Development Plan, was to establish investment trusts for newly issued stocks and bonds. The Korea Investment Trust Company was founded for this purpose by the joint investment of security brokerage firms and other financial institutions. Furthermore, the government introduced an installment security savings plan, administered by brokerage firms, to promote investments by small investors. Ten percent of all newly issued stocks were by requirement allocated to the members of the plan. Other policy measures to promote security markets followed these initial government efforts, resulting in ongoing market growth. The total number of companies listed on the securities market increased from 24 to 343 between 1967 and 1981. At the same time, the amount of stock transactions rose 100-fold, from 25 billion to 2,534 billion won, while bond transactions increased from 0.04 billion to 1,410 billion won.

From 1976 to 1978, the private sector in Korea held an excess of idle funds, most of which derived from labor export earnings in Middle East construction. As these speculative funds were invested, the stock market became overheated. Many construction company stocks, for example, whose face value had been 500 won were traded at more than 5,000 won. The speculation ended in 1979 with a rapid drop in stock prices. The recession of that year only exacerbated the situation. Stock transactions decreased from 1,741 billion won in 1978 to 1,134 billion won in 1980. Many stockholders suffered large financial losses and money shifted from the stock to bond market. This chain reaction points up the continued instability of Korean security markets.

Investment, Savings, and Rates of Return

Savings and investment are necessary ingredients for economic growth. The rapid expansion of Korea's economy over the last two decades would not have been possible without the enormous investments the country undertook during that period. In fact, since 1968, Korea invested more than one-quarter of its total GNP. This enormous investment was financed through aggressive mobilization of domestic savings and inducement of foreign capital. The average ratio of nominal gross capital formation (that is, gross domestic capital formation and the increase in inventory stock) to nominal GNP was approximately 10 percent between 1953 and 1960. This ratio surged upward beginning in 1961, but remained under the 15 percent level through 1965. It reached the threshold point for higher investment in 1966, leaping to 21.6 percent. Thereafter, the ratio never dipped below 25 percent, except in 1972 (table 3.9).

Most of these investments were undertaken by the private sector. Since 1963, the Korean government has carried out less than 18 percent of the total. To promote investment by the private sector, especially in manufacturing industries, the Korean government has provided various incentives. It has offered many specialized, long-term loans with favorable interest rates for such investments through deposit banks as well as through the Korea Development Bank (KDB, the Korea Reconstruction Bank's replacement). With its volume of loans expanded by

Table 3.9   Ratio of Nominal Investment to Nominal GNP (percent)

Year	Total	Fixed capital formation	Increase in stocks
1965	15.0	14.8	0.2
1966	21.6	20.2	1.4
1967	21.9	21.4	0.5
1968	25.9	25.0	0.9
1969	28.8	25.8	3.0
1970	26.6	24.4	2.4
1971	25.2	22.5	2.7
1972	21.7	20.6	1.1
1973	25.6	24.0	1.6
1974	31.0	25.5	5.5
1975	29.4	26.0	3.4
1976	25.6	23.8	1.7
1977	27.3	26.0	1.3
1978	31.2	30.7	0.5
1979	35.4	32.5	2.9
1980	31.5	32.7	−1.2
1981[a]	27.2	28.3	−1.1

a. Preliminary.
Source: Bank of Korea, *Economic Statistics Yearbook*, various issues and 1982, pp. 280–81.

the government, the KDB was designed to supply long-term credit for investment. In fact, it has provided more long-term credit than have all deposit banks. The KDB has also administered the National Investment Fund, the largest source of specialized, long-term funds for fixed capital formation. Specialized loans such as these have carried interest rates lower than those for short-term working capital, but higher rates than those for export financing. In 1972, for example, the interest rate on export loans was 6 percent; on specialized funds, 10 percent; and for discounts on bills, 15.5 percent. Although most of the deposit bank loans for equipment purchases and construction have come from these specialized funds, the proportion of these loans in total loans of commercial banks has been near 20 percent.

The Korean government, by restricting imports, has also given favorable treatment to the use of capital goods. In cases where capital goods were not produced domestically, but were to be invested in industries chosen by the government, loans in foreign currency have been allowed and tariffs waived for their import. The government likewise has made available investment incentives (to certain industries) affecting corporate income tax. These incentives have included three options offered to new investors: (1) total exemption from corporate taxation for three years and a 50 percent reduction in tax for two additional years; (2) a corporate tax reduction of up to 8 percent of the total value of the investment; or (3) the doubling of normal depreciation allowances. The taxation on undistributed profits invested in new technology was also reduced to 8 percent. The government offered investment incentives discriminately, concentrating on the export and import substitution industries. In the 1970s, however, heavy and chemical industries (involving chemicals, basic metals, machinery, and equipment) had priority.

In the initial stages of its economic growth, Korea depended heavily on foreign capital. The proportion of foreign capital to total capital formation was approximately 40 percent during the latter half of the 1960s (table 3.10). Thereafter, until 1977, this proportion declined (in line with the ongoing development of the Korean economy) to an estimated 30 percent in the early 1970s and to 2.2 percent by 1977. Beginning in 1979, however, Korea once again became a substantial borrower of foreign capital. The proportion of foreign capital in total capital formation, therefore, increased to 21.6 percent in that year, 32.4 percent in 1980, and 30.4 percent by 1981.

Two factors brought about this sudden increase in foreign loans. The first was the rise of interest payments on foreign debts, including remittance of profit to investors of foreign capital. The amounts involved grew rapidly from $75 million in 1970 to $3,689 million in 1981. The second factor was the sharp rise in the prices of petroleum imports in 1980. Although the volume of petroleum imports decreased slightly that year, the value of imports almost doubled between 1979 and 1980, from $3.4 billion to $6.2 billion. In 1981, the value again rose to $6.9 billion, despite the fact that volume fell. The ratio of petroleum imports to total exports of goods and services increased from 17.4 percent to 27.4 percent in 1980 alone. It remained at the 25 percent level throughout 1981.

From 1965 to 1980, 85 percent of foreign capital represented net borrowings. In the 1950s and 1960s, net transfers (especially aid from the U.S.) composed most of the foreign capital and was characterized by a declining trend. Net borrowings began to increase rapidly from the mid-1960s and surpassed net transfers beginning in 1968. Net borrowings supplied less than 8 percent of total funds for investment by the early 1970s and less than 4 percent after 1975 (table 3.10). Of net transfers, private transactions have predominated, with official transfers

Table 3.10   Domestic Savings and Foreign Capital (percent)

Year	Total[a,b]	Domestic saving			Subtotal	Foreign capital		Statistical discrepancy
		Subtotal	Private	Government		Net transfer (Aid)	Net borrowing[c]	
1965	100.0	49.6	38.1	11.5	42.2	44.2 (29.0)	-2.0	
1966	100.0	54.6	41.6	13.0	39.0	26.5 (12.5)	12.5	
1967	100.0	54.0	35.6	18.4	40.2	21.7 (9.3)	18.5	
1968	100.0	51.0	27.5	23.5	43.1	14.6 (6.8)	28.5	
1969	100.0	58.8	37.9	20.9	36.9	11.4 (5.0)	25.5	
1970	100.0	60.1	34.6	25.6	35.3	7.9 (3.6)	27.4	
1971	100.0	56.9	33.3	23.6	44.0	7.4 (2.1)	36.6	
1972	100.0	71.7	53.1	18.6	26.7	8.3 (0.0)	18.4	
1973	100.0	84.3	66.9	17.4	15.4	5.9 (0.0)	9.5	
1974	100.0	61.3	51.7	9.6	43.2	4.2 (0.0)	39.0	
1975	100.0	63.2	49.7	13.6	35.5	3.8 (0.0)	31.7	1.2
1976	100.0	90.6	66.4	24.2	9.5	5.0 (0.0)	4.5	-0.1
1977	100.0	92.1	71.6	20.6	2.2	2.3 (0.0)	-0.1	5.7
1978	100.0	84.7	63.9	20.6	10.6	3.2 (0.0)	7.3	4.8
1979	100.0	75.1	54.6	20.4	21.6	2.1 (0.0)	19.5	3.3
1980	100.0	63.2	43.6	19.6	32.4	2.5 (0.0)	29.8	4.4
1981[d]	100.0	73.4	47.1	26.3	30.4	3.0 (0.0)	27.4	-3.8

a. Same as that of Table 9 and Table 12.
b. Based on current price.
c. Direct investment included.
d. Preliminary.
Sources: Bank of Korea, *Economic Statistics Yearbook, 1982*, p. 245 and pp. 320–21. Bank of Korea, *National Income in Korea, 1975, 1976*, pp. 180–81.

representing only one-tenth of the total since 1977. Most foreign investments in Korea between 1962 and 1981 were in the form of loans and amounted to $35 billion at the end of 1981. Direct investments comprised just 5.5 percent of the total, and short-term debts were around $12 billion.

As the flow of foreign capital to Korea declined, domestic savings rose at a rapid pace. The portion of domestic saving in total savings represented less than 50 percent until the mid-1960s. Beginning in 1965, the proportion increased steadily until 1977 (from 49.6 percent to 92.1 percent) with the exceptions of 1971 and 1974 (table 3.10). Thereafter, it decreased to 63.2 percent in 1980, with a small upturn in 1981 to 73.4 percent.

The increase in domestic savings through 1977 was, for the most part, due to the rise in savings of the private sector. Although the proportion of private sector saving typically has been erratic, it did increase from 38.1 percent in 1965 to 71.6 percent in 1977. The proportion of government savings, on the other hand, remained relatively stable—in the neighborhood of 20 percent—over the same period. Government savings has been largely composed of net saving, with only 1 to 2 percent represented by provisions for depreciation (table 3.11). This reflects the fact that the share of savings in total government expenditures and the ratio of total government expenditures to GNP have remained relatively stable. The former has been, by and large, between 30 and 40 percent, while the latter has hovered around the 20 percent level.

In the formation of private savings, corporations played a more significant role than households, at least up to 1975: they supplied 35 percent of total saving in the second half of the 1960s, 33 percent in the first half of the 1970s, and approximately 40 percent between 1975 and 1977. Beginning in 1978, the proportion of corporate savings declined slightly, but still kept close to the 30 percent level, as table 3.11 shows. The major form of corporate savings has been provisions for depreciation, while net savings has been of secondary importance. Throughout the years between 1965 and 1978, provisions for depreciation were the largest source of investment funds in Korea—contributing from 25 to 30 percent of total savings. In contrast, the share of household savings in total savings was 1.2 percent, on average, during the second half of the 1960s. During the 1970s, however, household savings grew rapidly. It jumped from 14.9 percent during the first five years of the decade to an estimated 26 percent by 1976, with increases continuing through 1978. In 1977 and 1978, household savings recorded the highest proportion in

Table 3.11   Composition of Capital Finance (percent)

	1965–69[a]	1970–74[a]	1975	1976	1977	1978	1979	1980
Total	100.0	100.0	100.0	100.0	100.0	100.0	100.0	100.0
Government	17.5	19.0	14.18	26.3	21.1	20.9	20.7	19.8
Provisions for depreciation	2.2	1.7	1.7	1.9	1.7	1.2	1.3	1.3
Savings	15.3	17.3	13.1	24.4	19.4	19.7	19.4	18.5
Private	36.2	47.9	52.3	69.3	73.3	66.9	56.5	45.8
Corporations	35.0	33.0	38.2	42.9	39.9	31.7	27.3	26.1
Provisions for depreciation	24.9	26.5	25.7	29.1	28.1	21.8	19.8	25.8
Savings	10.1	6.5	12.5	13.8	11.8	9.9	7.5	0.3
Household savings	1.2	14.9	14.1	26.4	33.4	35.2	29.2	19.7
Foreign capital	40.3	32.9	—	—	—	—	—	—
Net transfer[b]	23.7	6.7	—	—	—	—	—	—
Net borrowing	16.6	26.2	31.7	4.5	–0.1	7.3	19.5	29.8
Statistical discrepancy	6.1	0.2	1.2	–0.1	5.7	4.8	3.3	4.4

a. Average.
b. From 1975, included in government or private sectors; this discontinuity does not mislead the trend because this item was less than 5 percent after 1975.
Sources: Bank of Korea, *Economic Statistics Yearbook*, various issues.

total savings (table 3.11). This dramatic increase in household savings was also reflected in the rapid rise of the average savings propensity of households, from 0.2 percent in 1965 to 15 percent in 1978.

The government has controlled directly all interest rates on savings and loans by banks. Thus, the interest rate on savings has depended on government policy, rather than directly on demand and supply of the marketplace. Government policy on bank interest rates has undergone three distinct phases. Prior to September 1965, the government kept interest rates on savings and loans in the formal financial markets at low levels. Because of the concurrent high inflation rate, this "cheap money" policy produced negative real interest rates for a number of subsequent years. In the early 1960s, the *nominal* interest rate on bank time deposits was 15 percent per annum and that on installment savings, 10 percent. At the same time, consumer prices for all urban areas rose 19.7 percent in 1963, 29.5 percent in 1964, and 13.6 percent in 1965.

As a result, the *real* interest rate on time deposits actually registered negative 4.7 percent in 1963, negative 14.5 percent in 1964, and 1.4 percent in 1965. Similarly, the *real* interest rates on installment savings for the same years were negative 9.7 percent, negative 19.5 percent, and negative 4.5 percent, respectively.

During the second phase of government interest policy (from September 1965 through the end of 1971), the nominal interest rates on savings were set high enough to encourage savings in banks. The reforms instituted in September 1965 raised nominal interest rates on time deposits and installment savings (the only two significant forms of saving deposits in banks) to 30 percent per annum. Although the government began to lower the rates beginning in 1963, they remained above 20 percent through 1971. Over the same period, the inflation rate was also relatively moderate—no higher than 14 percent annually, except in 1970 when it inched up to an estimated 16 percent. Consequently, the real interest rates remained positive.

The third phase covered the period after 1972, during which the government's "cheap money" policy was revived and the nominal interest rates kept, once again, at low levels. In fact, nominal interest rates dropped from 21.3 percent to 17.4 percent in January 1972 alone, and plummeted to 12.6 percent only seven months later. Thereafter, the rates continued to be low with intermittent increases and dips. Real interest rates on time deposits were even lower—less than 3 percent, except in 1974, 1977, and 1978, when they registered above 5 percent. The rates on installment savings were restrained to levels similar to those on time deposits.

One significant change in policy was made during this third phase regarding the structure of interest rates on time deposits based on maturities. Previously, interest rates for short-term maturity dates were substantially lower than for long-term maturities. In January of 1974, the government reduced the differentials in interest rates among different maturities. This action on the term structure was implemented to encourage and mobilize both short-term and long-term savings.

Interest rates on savings of non-bank institutions have had large spreads, depending on such factors as maturities, attachments of recourse, and the special purposes of each institution. The objective of investment and finance companies, initially established in 1973, was to bring together short-term idle money. Trust companies, on the other hand, concentrated on mobilizing long-term, large-scale assets, while mutual savings companies set their goals on amassing long-term, small savings from the low- and middle-income classes. It is, therefore, not a simple matter to compare the interest rates of these institutions among themselves or with those of banks. In general, however, the interest rates on savings of similar maturities of non-bank institutions have been slightly higher than those of banks.

Unlike interest rates on savings held in financial institutions, the average yields of stocks and bonds in Korea have relied on the interplay of market demand and supply. Consistent data on the average dividend yield of stocks, however, are available only after 1967 and on that of bonds, after 1976. As already noted, Korean security markets have suffered several steep rises and falls. Because of this instability, stocks have not been a good substitute for bank or non-bank financial institutions in terms of long-term investments. The average dividend yield on stocks is one component of the yield on stock, which also includes capital gains arising from price appreciations. Thus, dividend yields are likely to be lower than the interest rates offered by bank and non-bank institutions on savings. The Korean experience bears this out, particularly during the latter half of the 1960s, when the formal financial institutions offered very attractive interest rates and the average yield on stocks was just one-half of the rates on bank savings with one-year maturity (table 3.12). In contrast, bonds have been excellent substitutes for long-term investments, at least according to available data. The average yield on bonds, without exception, has been much higher than bank interest rates. After 1978, in particular, the rates on corporate bonds were more than 8 percent higher.

Interest rates on savings and yields of securities have not been enough to stimulate savings. To fill this gap, the government has provided tax incentives. In 1962, the first tax incentives for household savings were introduced, allowing income tax exemptions for interest on savings in formal financial institutions. Initially, all interest earnings from bank savings were thus tax-exempt. Beginning in 1965, interest earnings from installment and mutual savings were also given tax-exempt status. After 1972, however, interest earnings from most short-term savings were excluded from tax exemption, with the exception of dividend income. The government took additional steps to use the tax system to induce savings: it allowed the deduction of some part of savings from the income tax base. Another income tax law, announced in 1974, provided such deductions for special savings and insurance established for the low and middle classes. A third government tax incentive lowered tax rates on interest and dividend earnings to 5 percent.

Table 3.12   Average Yields on Stocks and Bonds (annual rate, percent)

Year	Stock	Corporate bond
1966	N.A.	—
1967	11.6	—
1968	13.7	—
1969	12.6	—
1970	17.0	N.A.
1971	18.4	N.A.
1972	13.8	22.9
1973	7.3	21.8
1974	13.2	21.0
1975	12.0	20.1
1976	12.7	20.4
1977	14.2	20.1
1978	12.9	21.1
1979	17.8	26.7
1980	20.9	30.1
1981	16.3	24.4

Note: Yield on stocks is dividend yield.
Source: Bank of Korea, *Economic Statistics Yearbook*, various issues.

Along with these tax incentives, the government gave higher interest rates to household savings than to ordinary time deposits. In addition, household checking deposits have been allowed to earn interest, while business checking accounts have not. The interest rates offered on time deposits of mutual savings companies have always been the highest of all savings accounts among financial institutions. As a further incentive, holders of bank savings have priority in obtaining consumer loans at the banks where they hold their accounts. Because interest rates on bank loans have been much lower than those in the informal money markets, this incentive has been particularly attractive to savers. Holders of special savings accounts also have some priority in obtaining newly issued stocks and recently constructed apartments.

Foreign Economic Relations

Balance of Payments. The balance of payments records an individual country's external transactions of goods, services, and financial capital. More specifically, transactions of tangible commodities are recorded in the trade account, and those of intangible services (such as transportation, travel, and investment income) are included in the invisible trade account. Both are combined to form the current account. The capital account of the balance of payments incorporates changes in claims and liabilities on financial capital, such as government and corporate bonds, and on equity capital among nations.

Table 3.13 presents the overall picture of Korea's balance of payments since 1965. Imports of commodities have been consistently greater than commodity exports, resulting in ongoing deficits in the trade account. The size of the deficits, in fact, increased steadily from $240 million in 1965 to $1,040 million in 1971. Thereafter, they briefly tapered off during 1972 and 1973, but worsened considerably following the 1974 oil crisis, when they increased to more than $1,900 million in 1974 and $1,600 million in 1975. After some improvement in 1976 and 1977, deficits are again on the increase, reaching $3 to $4 billion a year from 1979 to 1981.

As table 3.13 shows, the invisible trade account registered net surpluses each year prior to the first oil crisis in 1974. However, it has since reversed itself into a net deficit position ranging between $71 and $1,500 million, except in 1977 and 1978. The relatively large deficits in the invisible trade account during 1980 and 1981 were caused by an excess of investment income payments over receipts. This reflects the fact that foreign investors' claims on Korea were far greater than Korea's investment position abroad—an imbalance that a surplus of goods, services, and income from the construction export boom to the Middle East has not fully offset. The current account balance (which includes net transfers) was in deficit throughout the period presented in table 3.13 and experienced fluctuations in line with those of the trade account balance. This similarity of movement stems from the fact that invisible trade and net transfers were small relative to the trade account balance. Korea's domestic saving has not met the need for a high level of investment. The government has actively encouraged the import of foreign capital to fill the saving-investment gap and to close the foreign exchange gap resulting from ongoing current account deficits.

The nature of foreign capital flows into Korea, initiated primarily by the government, contrasts sharply with that of industrialized countries where such flows are motivated by private agents who seek maximum returns on investment portfolios. In Korea, foreign loans (which represent most of the long-term capital inflow) for the most part have been secured directly by the government or its agencies. The amounts

Table 3.13　Balance of Payments of Korea, 1965–1981 (million US$)

Year	Current balance Total (A)	Trade balance Total	Trade balance Exports	Trade balance Imports	Invisible trade (net)	Net transfers	Long-term capital (B)	Basic balance (A+B)	Short-term capital (C)	Errors & omissions (D)	Overall balance (A+B+C+D)
1965	9.1	−240.8	175.1	415.9	46.1	203.3	37.3	46.4	−23.1	−7.1	16.2
1966	−103.4	−429.6	250.3	679.9	106.5	219.6	211.8	108.4	6.4	4.4	119.2
1967	−191.9	−574.2	334.7	908.9	157.1	225.2	201.2	9.3	85.9	23.0	118.2
1968	−440.3	−835.8	486.2	1,322.0	169.3	226.1	433.8	−6.5	13.2	−20.2	−13.5
1969	−548.6	−991.7	658.3	1,322.0	197.3	245.8	576.2	27.6	56.5	−7.6	76.5
1970	−622.5	−922.0	882.2	1,804.2	119.3	180.2	448.8	−173.7	122.4	−5.2	−56.5
1971	−847.5	−1,040.6	1,132.2	2,178.2	27.8	170.6	527.8	−319.7	134.6	13.1	−172.0
1972	−371.2	−574.5	1,675.9	2,250.4	32.9	169.8	505.1	133.9	−16.3	30.1	147.7
1973	−308.8	−566.0	3,271.3	3,837.3	67.1	190.1	666.3	357.5	84.0	18.8	460.3
1974	−2,022.7	−1,936.8	4,515.1	6,451.9	−308.3	222.2	946.4	−1,376.3	−45.4	27.9	−1,093.0
1975	−1,886.9	−1,671.4	5,003.0	6,674.4	−442.2	326.7	1,178.3	−708.6	679.5	−121.5	−130.6
1976	−313.6	−590.5	7,814.6	8,405.1	−71.8	348.7	1,371.2	1,057.6	356.5	−240.5	1,173.6
1977	12.3	−476.6	10,046.5	10,523.1	266.0	222.0	1,312.7	1,325.0	21.4	−31.7	1,314.7
1978	−1,085.2	−1,780.8	12,710.6	14,491.4	224.0	471.6	2,166.3	1,081.1	−1,171.0	−312.0	−401.9
1979	−4,151.1	−4,395.5	14,704.5	19,100.0	−194.6	439.0	2,662.9	−1,488.2	843.6	−328.7	−471.3
1980	−5,320.7	−4,384.1	17,214.0	21,598.1	−1,385.9	449.3	1,856.5	−3,464.2	1,944.5	−369.9	−1,889.6
1981	−4,436.2	−3,418.5	20,880.6	24,299.1	−1,518.4	500.7	2,841.9	−1,594.3	−82.3	−620.4	−2,297.0

Note: Exports and Imports are on FOB basis. The distinction between long-term and short-term is based on the original maturity of one year.
Source: Bank of Korea, *Monthly Economic Statistics*, various issues.

of these loans are largely determined by the Korean government, based on economic growth targets, export and import targets, and the desired level of international reserves. Moreover, even loans from banking institutions or private enterprises usually require the approval of the government, particularly as to volume and terms of conditions (e.g., interest rates and repayment period). In contrast to this government-induced financial flow, direct foreign investment has been relatively insignificant in Korea, hovering around the $100 million mark each year since 1965.

As table 3.13 indicates, the value of long-term capital inflow has, on average, roughly corresponded to the amount of current account deficits. For three years beginning in 1976, however, the long-term capital balance was even greater than the current account deficit, possibly due to the replenishing of foreign exchange reserves that had dwindled to low levels after the oil crisis in 1974. As a result, the basic balance (i.e., the sum of current and long-term capital accounts) recorded surpluses from 1976 through 1978. Most of the net short-term capital flows during this period were trade credits provided by foreign exporters to domestic importers. Short-term trade credits also financed, to a limited degree, Korea's current account deficits. Errors and omissions of the balance of payments are unidentified transactions and include speculative, short-term capital inflows.

A balance of payments deficit is financed by decreasing reserve assets and increasing liabilities of the banking system. Changes in the reserve assets, in turn, affect the money supply via the net foreign asset position of Korea's central bank, the Bank of Korea. Under Korea's present managed floating system, the monetary authority has, on occasion, intervened in order to maintain the desired exchange rate vis-à-vis foreign currencies.

Trends and Characteristics of Export. Although Korea's exports have expanded at a rapid rate, its share in nominal world trade remains small. The value of world exports grew at an average annual rate of 17.2 percent from 1968 to 1980, while Korean exports increased by an average annual rate of 37.5 percent. In line with these percentage differentials in growth rates, the share of Korean commodities in global transactions jumped from 0.21 percent in 1968 to approximately 1.00 percent by 1980; the proportion, however, is still an insignificantly small part of world trade. The volume of Korean exports has also undergone dramatic increases, particularly when compared to the country's real output. Korea's real volume of exports increased 26 percent, on an average annual basis between 1965 and 1981, while real GNP grew a mere 8.7 percent. At the same time, the share of exports in GNP rose from 5.7 percent in 1965 to 48.7 percent in 1981.

Most of Korea's exports are manufactured goods that are highly sensitive to a change in foreign income (income elasticity of export volume is around 3.5). Thus, the rapid growth of exports was due mainly to favorable international economic factors, such as rising income in the U.S. and Japan. However, export growth also can be attributed to government policy initiatives designed to pinpoint industries and commodity items best suited for international competition and to promote such exports through a variety of incentives, including tax credits and favorable interest rates. In addition, the competitive price levels of Korean exports have helped bring about the country's rapid export growth, since the elasticity of exports demanded with regard to relative price is in the neighborhood of 1.2. The competitiveness of Korea's exports in the world market has resulted from the country's high labor productivity. Over the period 1965 through 1981, Korea's real GNP grew at a rate of 8.7 percent per year, on average, a rate slightly higher than the growth rate of Japan (7.2 percent), and much higher than that of the United States (3.1 percent). Korea experienced a notably higher growth rate in labor productivity (13 percent) than either Japan (9.1 percent) or the United States (2.3 percent).

Structural Changes in the Export Industry. The structure of Korea's export industry has changed over the past two decades. Korean exports first shifted from primary products to light industry products, and then toward heavy/chemical industry products. In 1962, primary products made up 72.6 percent of all exports, followed by light industry products at 20.3 percent and heavy/chemical industry products at 7.1 percent. After only five years, light industry products represented 63.9 percent of total exports, while primary products dropped to 27.5 percent and heavy/chemical industry rose slightly to 8.6 percent. The share of light industry remained stable at an estimated 70 percent until 1974, when it fell to 50 percent. This abrupt decline was matched by an increase in the share of heavy/chemical industry products from 21 percent in 1972 to 42 percent in 1980.

As of 1980, the dominant export commodities continued to be traditional items, such as textiles and clothing, which are unskilled, labor-intensive industries. These two products alone represented about 30 percent of all exports. Advancing quickly, however, are new products, including electrical machinery, iron and steel, and ships, which are skilled labor-intensive products. Moreover, high technology and capital-intensive products are beginning to take on significance among the country's exports.

The changes in export structure reflect the implementation of Korea's development strategy, which began in 1962. During the initial stages of industrialization, the government promoted the export of goods whose production or assembly depended heavily upon unskilled labor at low wage levels, and therefore held a comparative advantage in world trade. As the economy accumulated more capital and technological skills, however, Korea's comparative advantage shifted to skilled labor-intensive and/or capital-intensive products. Figure 3.1 illustrates how different export structures characterize the different stages of economic development in Korea and Japan. As the graph shows, Japanese exports are largely oriented toward products which are technology-intensive, resource-consuming, and mass-produced (such as machinery, transport equipment, and iron and steel). In contrast, Korean exports consist, by and large, of simple labor-intensive products, such as textiles, wood products, and metal products.

Another significant phenomenon is that the share of Korean exports to various countries has changed since 1965. Table 3.14 represents the percentage components of Korea's total exports in trade with industrialized countries, oil-exporting developing countries, and non-oil-exporting developing countries between 1965 and 1980. In addition, industrialized countries are also subdivided into the United States, Japan, and other countries. One obvious pattern table 3.14 shows is the steady decline of the market share of industrialized countries. At the same time, oil-exporting, developing countries have increased their share considerably. Non-oil-exporting developing countries have experienced only slight share increases over the same period. Among the industrialized countries, the share of Korean exports to the United States and Japan decreased, while exports to other industrialized nations, particularly Europe, have taken an increasing share.

This trend came about primarily because of Korea's determined efforts to diversify its markets, thereby reducing the variability of exports by decreasing its dependence on the United States and Japan, and to expand its export volume on a worldwide basis over the long term. The alternative—a continued concentration of exports on a few markets—would have likely invoked resistance on the part of domestic

Figure 3.1   Comparison of Manufactured Goods Export Structure for Korea
             and Japan

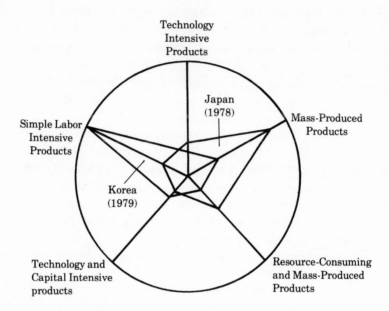

Notes:
1) technology intensive products: precision instruments, motors, aircraft, ships, railway
vehicles, metal-working machinery, printing and book binding machines, heavy electric
machinery.
2) mass-produced products: telecommunication equipment, domestic electric equipment,
other electric equipment, motor cars, agricultural machinery, industrial machinery.
3) resource-consuming and mass-produced products: petrochemical products, cost products, iron and steel products, paper manufactures, non-ferrous manufactures.
4) technology and capital intensive products: cement, rubber manufactures, leather
manufactures, textile manufactures, office machinery, musical instruments, cycle bodies,
fabricated metal products, watches and clocks.
5) simple labor intensive products: wood manufactures, textiles, pottery, toys, miscellaneous manufactured articles.
Source: Paeng, Dong Joon, "Korea's Trade Structure in the 1970's," *Quarterly Economic
Review* (December 1980), Bank of Korea.

Table 3.14   Direction of Exports (percent)

Year	Industrialized countries				Developing countries	
					Oil exporting	Non-oil-exporting
	U.S.	Japan	Other	Total	countries	countries
1965	35.2	25.1	14.3	74.6	0.7	24.7
1966	38.4	26.2	17.0	81.6	0.8	17.6
1967	42.9	26.5	13.5	82.9	0.7	16.4
1968	51.7	21.9	11.8	85.4	0.6	14.0
1969	50.7	21.4	10.6	82.7	0.8	15.5
1970	46.7	28.0	12.1	86.8	1.1	12.1
1971	49.8	24.5	11.3	85.6	3.1	11.4
1972	46.9	25.2	13.9	86.0	2.7	11.6
1973	31.7	38.5	14.7	84.9	2.0	9.5
1974	33.5	30.9	18.2	82.6	3.8	11.7
1975	30.2	25.4	21.0	76.6	6.6	15.1
1976	32.4	23.4	22.7	78.5	9.3	11.0
1977	31.1	21.46	21.5	74.0	12.4	12.5
1978	32.0	20.6	21.9	74.5	10.9	13.5
1979	29.2	22.3	21.9	73.4	11.1	14.3
1980	26.4	17.4	20.4	64.2	12.8	18.3

Source: International Monetary Fund, *Direction of Trade*, various issues.

producers in the importing countries as the market share of Korean commodities increased. Moreover, the income and demand conditions in the few importing countries would have constrained the expansion of Korean exports.

Structure and Characteristics of Imports. Like the export sector, Korean imports have also experienced notable changes. Between 1965 and 1981, real imports increased at an average annual rate of approximately 20 percent. The higher growth rate of real imports as compared to real GNP (which increased at an average annual rate of 8.7 percent over the same period) raised the share of imports in GNP from 13 percent in 1965 to 54 percent in 1981. Raw materials and grains have made up a substantial portion of imports. Consequently, real imports not only depend on real productive activity in Korea, but also on government policy with regard to imports, including the exchange rate and availability of foreign exchange. Thus, the growth rate of real imports has been loosely related to the growth rate of GNP and somewhat affected by changes in prices. The income elasticity of import volume is likely to be about 1.3, whereas the elasticity

with respect to a change in relative price is probably around 0.8, according to the estimates of Kwack and Mered.[12]

The share of goods and raw materials for domestic use in total
imports during the 1970s was about 20 percent. The share of goods and
raw materials for exports and domestic use, together, is estimated to
have been approximately 40 to 60 percent of total imports during this
period. This high percentage of raw material imports in Korea can be
partly explained by the country's poor endowment of natural resources. After 1973, however, the share of imported raw materials in
total imports grew less rapidly or even decreased. This downturn may
reflect significant reductions in world raw-material prices and a reduction in the raw materials required per unit of production. Capital goods
were second to raw materials in percentage of import share, representing almost 38 percent between 1965 and 1980. The import of capital
goods was needed for investments in new plans and equipment.

The share of non-competitive goods (that is, products that are not
produced in Korea) in total imports was 30 to 38 percent during the
1970s. A sharp increase in their share from 31.6 percent in 1972 to 38
percent in 1976 was due primarily to higher crude oil and grain prices
in the world market. Since 1977, however, the share of these noncom-
peting items has declined steadily toward a trend level of 30 percent.

Since 1965, Korea's import-market structure has changed in a pattern similar to that of the export market. The share in Korea's imports of
industrialized countries decreased from 85.4 percent in 1965 to 61.5 percent in 1980. The most notable drop occurred in the U.S. market share,
from 39.3 percent to 21.9 percent. The share of oil-exporting developing
countries increased from 0.1 percent to 26.3 percent over the same period. The share of non-oil-exporting, developing countries, on the other
hand, declined between 1965 and 1980.

The sharp increase in the share of oil-exporting developing countries was mainly due to price increases in crude oil from OPEC nations,
which provide Korea with all of its crude petroleum needs. The relative
stability of the shares of industrialized nations, excluding the U.S. and
Japan, and of non-oil-exporting, developing countries is a result of
Korea's desire to diversify its exports over countries in the world and
secure the sources of raw materials in developing countries. Korea's
imports from non-oil-exporting, developing countries have led to
Korea's exports to those countries.

Korea has imposed various restrictions on imports in order to protect its domestic industries and improve its balance of payments situa-

tion. The most widely used import restrictions are quantitative controls, such as quotas and tariffs. The Korean government periodically has made efforts to liberalize trade restrictions. The pace of such liberalization, however, has not been even, and at times it has faced resistance from vested interests in the business community or from deterioration of the balance of payments. Until 1967, Korea operated under a so-called "Positive List" System, which classified all imports into prohibited, restricted, or automatic approval items. Quotas were imposed on restricted goods, and their importation was related to the performance of domestic exports.

Between the last half of 1964 and the first half of 1965, the number of items eligible for importation increased substantially, from 500 to 1,500. Thereafter, the total continued to rise rapidly, particularly those in the automatic-approval category. In contrast, the number of prohibited commodities declined markedly between the second half of 1965 and the first half of 1967. In 1967, a "Negative List" approach to import control replaced the "Positive List" system. Under the new system, all commodities not listed as prohibited or restricted were classified as automatic approvals. This change indicates Korea's movement toward lower trade restrictions.

The tariff system in Korea can be characterized as having high rates and a complex structure. For this reason, a revision toward simple unitary rates increasingly has found support. Thus far, however, reforms in this direction have not taken place. As an additional reform objective, tariffs on products at each level of fabrication using the same basic materials would be equalized and the degree of escalation of tariffs from lower to higher levels of fabrication reduced. Even under a reform bill, tariff rates in Korea would continue to be high.

To shed some light on tariff rates, the ratios of custom duties and other charges on trade to total value of imports are computed. These ratios, called "effective tariff rates," depend not only on the individual tariff rates, but also on the proportion of non-taxable imports. The effective rate remained at the 7 percent level in 1981, representing a decrease from the 8 to 10 percent levels between 1976 and 1979. The higher rates during this three-year interval were due to increases in other charges, such as defense taxes. The average tariff rate of small European countries in 1977, by comparison, was 5 percent. Hence, Korea's tariff rates have been higher than those of other industrialized nations.

Capital Borrowings and Service on the Foreign Debt. As table 3.15 shows, private direct investment represented a relatively small portion

Table 3.15   Foreign Direct Investment and Loans in Korea, 1962–1981
               (million US$)

Years	Total	Long-term	Short-term	Direct investment	Total
		Loans		Direct	
1962–1966	347.2	330.0	17.2	17	364.2
1967–1971	3,376.7	2,528.1	848.6	96	3,472.7
1972	829.8	805.5	24.3	61	890.8
1973	1,074.3	999.6	74.7	158	1,232.3
1974	1,986.4	1,517.6	468.8	163	2,149.4
1975	2,845.2	1,733.5	1,111.7	69	2,914.2
1976	2,610.8	1,948.4	662.4	106	2,716.8
1977	2,627.4	2,259.3	368.1	104	2,731.4
1978	3,189.4	3,409.5	−220.1	100	3,289.4
1979	7,015.6	4,585.3	2,430.3	126	7,141.6
1980	8,471.5	4,389.5	4,082.0	96	8,567.5
1981	7,295.5	6,085.1	1,210.4	105	7,400.5
Total	41,669.8	30,591.4	11,078.4	1,201	42,870.8

Source: Korea Economic Planning Board, *Major Statistics of Korean Economy*, various issues.

of external capital inflow, amounting to $1.2 billion between 1962 and 1981. Japan, the United States, and the Netherlands provided the largest proportion of foreign investment. During the period 1962–1978, Japan supplied 57.9 percent of total foreign investment, followed by the United States at 19.2 percent and the Netherlands at 7.2 percent.

Before 1967, Korea's borrowings were negligible (table 3.15). During the Second Economic Development Plan (1967–1971), however, Korea began to borrow heavily from abroad. The amount of new foreign loans increased dramatically in 1972, the first year of the Third Economic Development Plan. It jumped again in 1975 in line with Korea's trade balance deterioration following the oil crisis and worldwide recession. Since 1978, the financial capital inflows in the form of long-term and short-term loans have increased continuously (from $3.2 billion in 1978 to $7.3 billion in 1981), resulting from an ongoing deterioration of the trade balance and expanding investment at home. We estimate that, at the end of 1981, the amount of gross long-term debts brought into Korea after amortization of principal debt was roughly $21 billion. In addition, the amount of short-term debts, including borrowings from Euro-dollar markets, was in the neighborhood of $12 billion. Thus, we estimate that Korea's gross financial debt was $33 billion at year-end 1981.

As foreign debts have increased, debt service (repayments of principal and interest on outstanding debts) also has risen from $3.4 million in 1972 to about $5.0 billion in 1981. This trend has raised concern over whether the debt service is manageable. We use two types of debt service indicators to address this issue: the ratio of debt service payments to exports of goods and service, and the ratio of debt service payments to GNP value in terms of U.S. dollars. While the former measures a country's ability to make payments on schedule, the latter represents its capacity for producing outputs with which to service its debts. The debt service ratio to exports, called the debt service ratio, changed from 5 percent in 1967 to 18 percent in 1981. During this period, the ratio fluctuated considerably and hit 18 percent in 1981, mainly due to a substantial rise in U.S. interest rates, oil import bills, and decreases in exports. The ratio to GNP has risen monotonically, indicating that the debt service tends to become a burden over time.

These two indicators suggest that Korea's debt conditions have already moved in an unfavorable direction. High and rising debt service payments have not affected adversely Korea's borrowing costs to any great degree, however. The continuous rise in debts, and particularly in short-term debts relative to total debts, may force Korea to implement policy measures that are undesirable in the long run. Hence, Korea may benefit by initiating corrective measures to raise the saving rates and to promote export expansion.

Distribution of Income

Korea is often cited as a developing country that accomplished rapid economic growth without dramatically skewing income distribution. The data behind this claim, however, are far from complete.[13] No national income survey has ever been published. Furthermore, all statistics on household income distribution have come from raw surveys in which the size of the sample was extremely small and excluded important subgroups (such as the upper and lower classes). Functional income distribution (namely, the distribution between labor income and property income derived from published national income account data) is considered reliable. Although the available data are not completely dependable, they may indicate trends in income distribution.

The modernization of the Korean economy has been reflected in the change in distribution of national income (GNP plus government subsidies less indirect taxes and capital consumption allowance). Up to the mid-1960s, income from unincorporated enterprises (the unmodernized sector where labor income is intertwined with property income) composed more than 50 percent of national income. In 1965, the income of this unmodernized sector represented 51.9 percent of total national income. Thereafter, the proportion decreased to 40.8 percent in 1970 and 26.9 percent by 1980. The decrease in this share is related to the decline of small-size farming, which has represented over one-half of the unincorporated enterprises. The proportion of agriculture in national income declined from 32.7 percent in 1965 to 14.6 in 1980.

While the proportion of income from unincorporated enterprises decreased, that of incorporated enterprises (where labor income can be separated from property income) increased dramatically. Between 1965 and 1980, the share of compensation of employees in national income rose from 31.8 percent to 49.4 percent. The share of property income also increased from 10.6 percent to 17.6 percent. These changes in the distribution of functional income did not occur continuously over the fifteen-year period. During the first half of the 1970s, for example, income distribution became static. The share of labor income and that of property income decreased slightly, while that of unincorporated enterprises remained at the same level.

Notable structural changes in the Korean economy came about after 1975, and, in line with this, significant shifts in functional income distribution took place. Within five years, the share of compensation of employees increased from 38.4 percent to 49.4 percent, and that of property income from 12.7 percent to 17.6 percent. At the same time, the share of unincorporated enterprise income dropped sharply from 40.8 percent to 26.9 percent. Of particular note is the fact that the ratio between compensation of employees and income from property remained roughly 3-to-1 throughout the growth period; that is, 31.8 percent to 10.6 percent in 1965, 39.5 percent to 13.9 percent in 1970, 38.4 percent to 12.7 percent in 1975, and 49.4 percent to 17.6 percent in 1980. This 3-to-1 ratio, in fact, is the same as that of most developed countries.

The income distribution of households by size in lieu of source is called "size income distribution" or "personal income distribution." This particular income distribution is relevant to a discussion of equity in income distribution. Its statistical analysis, however, is suspect due to the unreliability of its data. No comprehensive, original data, covering all income groups, are currently available. Moreover, all existing statistics on household income were calculated indirectly from raw data that,

Table 3.16	Probable Share of Total Income by Income Group (percent)				
Decile	1965	1970	1976	1978	Mean income 1976 (000 won)
First (poorest)	1.32	2.70	1.84		248
Second	4.43	4.56	3.86		520
Third	6.47	5.81	4.93		665
Fourth	7.12	6.48	6.22		838
Fifth	7.21	7.63	7.07		953
Sixth	8.32	8.71	8.34		1,124
Seventh	11.32	10.24	9.91		1,336
Eighth	12.00	12.17	12.49		1,684
Ninth	16.03	16.21	17.84		2,404
Tenth (richest)	25.78	25.41	27.50		3,707
				Avg=	1,348
Below 40%	19.3	19.6	16.9	15.5	
Above 20%	41.8	41.6	45.3	46.7	
Gini coefficient	0.3439	0.3322	0.3808	0.4000	

Source: Choo, Hakchung and Daemo Kim, *Probable Size Distribution of Income in Korea: Over Time and By Sectors* (Seoul: Korea Development Institute, 1978); and Economic Planning Board, *Economic White Papers, 1981*, p. 351.

as we mentioned previously, had serious sampling problems. These statistics, therefore, give probable size distribution.

Table 3.16 presents the probable size distribution of income in Korea. The table indicates that the size distribution improved slightly during the second half of the 1960s, but worsened in the first half of the 1970s. In other words, income inequality in 1976 was greater than in 1965. The Gini Coefficient, an index of the inequality in size income distribution, decreased from 0.3429 in 1965 to 0.3322 in 1970, but increased to 0.3808 in 1976. The share in total income of the poorest 20 percent of the population rose from 5.75 percent in 1965 to 7.26 percent in 1970, but decreased to 5.70 percent in 1976. The share of the wealthiest 20 percent showed the opposite movement, decreasing slightly from 41.81 percent in 1965 to 41.62 percent in 1970 and increasing considerably to 45.34 percent in 1976. These trends are quite interesting, if not surprising, because they contradict the popular belief that during economic development, movement toward income equality always follows on the heels of an initial deterioration in income distribution.

Separating overall income distribution into its components—urban and rural households—presents a more concrete picture of trends in this area. The size distribution of income for urban households in Korea changed in line with that of overall households; that is, an improvement in the latter half of the 1960s was followed by a downturn in the first half of the 1970s. The Gini Coefficient in 1976, however, was slightly lower than that in 1965, suggesting that income inequality in 1976 was not worse than in 1965. In contrast, inequality was slightly more pronounced in 1976 than in 1965 in the case of overall size distribution of income. The income distribution of rural households may explain this difference.

For rural households, the size distribution experienced ongoing deterioration even in the latter half of the 1960s. The Gini Coefficient for rural household income increased continuously from 0.2852 in 1965 to 0.2945 in 1970 and 0.3273 in 1976. Hence, the equity of rural income distribution was definitely worse in 1976 than in 1965. There is little concrete data to explain this trend. One possible reason may be the commercialization of the agricultural sector, along with the diversification of agricultural products. The commercial production of fruits, vegetables, and dairy products has increased more rapidly than that of grain. This trend, in turn, seems to have made the wealthier farmers more prosperous because fruits, vegetables, and dairy products have produced more profits than ordinary grains, and because the more well-to-do have tended to be concentrated in the cultivation of fruits, vegetables, and dairy products, since more capital is required in this production area.

Income inequality in rural Korean households has been relatively low compared to other developing countries, which have had to cope with land tenure systems. In Korea, arable land has been fairly evenly distributed among small farmers due to land reform measures carried out in the late 1940s and early 1950s, which redistributed about 80 percent of all land farmed under tenancy conditions as well as virtually all land owned by absentee landlords. Furthermore, these laws prohibited individuals from owning more than three hectares of land. Prior to these reforms, approximately one-half of Korean tillers were classified as tenants; afterwards, most of these owned their own farmlands.

During the second half of the 1960s, the overall size distribution of income improved due to increasing income equality among urban households. During the first half of the 1970s, on the other hand, the size income distribution appears to have deteriorated in both rural and urban sectors. The gap between rural and urban income in Korea widened in the 1960s, but narrowed in the 1970s, due to a shift in govern-

Table 3.17   Comparison of Rural and Urban Income (income in 1,000 won, ratio in percent)

	1965	1970	1976	1980
Rural household income (1)	112	256	1,156	2,693
Urban household income (2)	112.6	381	1,152	3,205
Rural income per capita (3)	17.8	43.2	208.7	536
Urban income per capita (4)	20.3	71.4	228.1	683
Parity ratio (1)/(2)	99.6	67.2	100.3	84
Parity ratio (3)/(4)	87.7	60.5	91.5	78

Source: Working materials from the World Bank and Korea Development Institute: Ministry of Agriculture, *Yearbook of Agriculture and Forestry Statistics,* 1981; and Economic Planning Board, *Major Statistics of Korean Economy,* various issues.

ment policy regarding grain prices. This policy change in the late 1960s dramatically increased the controlled prices of grain, thereby improving the terms of trade in agriculture, and closing the gap between rural and urban households.

The parity ratio of rural household income to urban household income decreased from 99.6 percent in 1965 to 67.2 percent in 1970, rising thereafter to 100.3 percent by 1975 (table 3.17). The parity ratios of per capita income between rural and urban areas showed a similar movement, although they were slightly lower than the ratios of household income. This difference stems from the fact that rural families tend to have more members than urban families.

The income distribution of households is affected by a variety of factors, including wage differentials based on different levels of education, different types of work, and employees' gender. Hence, it is of interest to summarize wage differentials along these lines. The ratio of wage earnings of higher education graduates to those of graduates from primary schools decreased from 314.8 percent in 1967 to 291.4 percent in 1970, increasing to 384.5 percent by 1976. In contrast, the ratio of secondary school graduates' wages to primary school graduates' wages increased slightly from 124.6 percent in 1967 to 125.2 percent in 1970, decreasing to 119.3 percent in 1976, while the wage earnings' ratio of high school graduates to primary school graduates remained stable (around the 178 percent level) throughout the same period. These changes in wage differentials reflect the fact that Korea faced a shortage of skilled labor in the 1970s. The wage differential between highly educated workers and other laborers decreased between 1967 and 1970 and then increased between 1970 and 1976. This movement is not surprising;

the same trend occurred in the size distribution of income for urban households.

Another wage differential has existed between blue-collar and white-collar workers. The wage gap between these two groups fell during the second half of the 1960s, but increased again during the first half of the 1970s. The average earnings of white-collar workers were 182.5 percent of that of all workers in 1966. This percentage decreased to 146.9 percent in 1970, increasing once again to 175.9 percent by 1976. In contrast, the percentage of blue-collar workers' earnings to average earnings followed the opposite path, increasing during the latter half of the 1960s from 88.7 to 88.9 percent, and decreasing to 86.5 percent by 1977. The wage gap between blue-collar workers, therefore, enlarged in the late 1960s and narrowed in the early 1970s. The change in this differential, as in the differential between the wages of highly educated workers and other laborers, corresponded to the change in the size income distribution of urban households.

Changes in income inequality among urban households can be explained in terms of these changes in the wage differentials between education and occupation groups. The wage differential between the sexes also influences income distribution. The wage earnings of male laborers are much higher than those of female laborers, education and age being equal. Although the data are not available, the wage differential between male and female labor services seems likely to narrow over time. Regardless of sex, wage earnings of high school graduates are in the neighborhood of 130 percent of those obtained by primary school graduates. Moreover, the ratio of wage earnings of highly educated laborers to those of primary school graduates is approximately 2.4. One interesting observation is that average earnings of female workers who are 30 years old or above are similar to earnings of male laborers. This is because female workers who are unskilled and not in managerial positions tend to gradually withdraw from the labor force as they become older to take care of domestic and household-related services and financial matters, and because of the limited job opportunities for female laborers.

Concluding Remarks

Between 1965 and 1981, Korea underwent remarkable development and transformation. Real GNP increased by approximately 10 percent per year and the major industry shifted from agriculture to manufacturing. This notable success, however, produced economic problems in the early 1980s associated with an unbalanced rigid economic structure and continuous balance of payments deficits.

Policymakers as well as the public in Korea have recognized the need to correct the existing economic problems, and have searched to determine the main reasons why these problems evolved. Policymakers have vigorously sought measures to remedy the problems, under the emerging new order of the world economy. One noteworthy outcome of this effort has been the recognition of the importance of openness in the economic and political areas of the country. This recognition is likely to lead to developing a base from which both the public and the government are willing to work together for better economic conditions in the future. Such willingness, together with flexibility in the policy-implementation mechanism, will produce the foundation for sustaining economic expansion in the 1980s, although growth rates are expected to be lower, and inflation and uncertainties greater.

This prediction emerges from our belief in what we see as the inherent characteristics of the Korean people. They are outward-looking, dynamic, and hardworking, and place priority on respect and self-improvement. Spurred on by this significant pool of human resources, we expect that Korea will move rapidly from a newly industrializing country to a developed country.

4

TIBOR SCITOVSKY

Economic Development in Taiwan and South Korea, 1965–1981

To help the developing countries develop and the poor to escape poverty was perhaps the noblest and most ambitious aspiration of the postwar world—first voiced by President Truman in his Point Four Program of 1949. His fine words mobilized a lot of resources and effort; unfortunately, the outcome of all the development aid, development advice, and development policies was mixed and often disappointing. All too often the industrialization of traditional agricultural societies merely transformed rural under-employment into open, urban unemployment, which is more painful and objectionable in social and human terms. Many of the poorest countries grew more slowly than the advanced countries, falling further and further behind; even the fast-developing countries grew in a lopsided way, increasing instead of diminishing the inequality between rich and poor. Indeed, increased inequality of income distribution, both between and within countries, seemed to be an almost inevitable accompaniment of economic development—certainly in its early stages.

But development experiences were vastly different, ranging from retrogression in one Asian and nine African countries, whose populations grew faster than their national income, to almost 7 percent annual

This chapter appeared in slightly different form in *Food Research Institute Studies*, Vol. XIX, No. 3, 1985, pp. 215–64. Reprinted with permission.

Table 4.1   Average Annual Growth Rates in Real Terms,
                 1965–1981 (percent)

	Korea	Taiwan
Population	1.9	2.3
Employment	3.4	3.7
Gross national product	8.7	9.4
Gross domestic product	8.6	9.4
Manufacturing output	20.6	15.5
Exports (quantum index)	26.0	18.9
GNP per capita = GDP per capita	6.7	6.9
Labor productivity[a]	5.2	5.4
Real wages in manufacturing	7.9	7.3
Consumers' expenditures per capita	5.5	5.2

a. GNP per employed person.

growth in per capita gross domestic product (GDP) over two decades
(1960–80) in five Asian countries and city-states.[1] Two of those five,
South Korea and Taiwan, not only grew very fast but did so without
experiencing the customary great and increasing inequalities and the
emergence of mass unemployment.[2] Indeed, by the double criterion of
growth and equity, they have been the most successful of all the developing countries.

Per capita GNP in real terms grew marginally faster in Taiwan than
in Korea, at an average annual rate of 6.9 percent compared to Korea's
6.7 percent between 1965 and 1981 (table 4.1). Taiwan also had slightly
less unemployment, an even more egalitarian income distribution, and
a much higher standard of living. Taiwan's GDP per capita was
US$2,570 by 1981, whereas Korea's was US$1,697. In effect, Taiwan was
six years ahead of Korea: Korea's per capita income in 1981 was about
the same as Taiwan's in 1975.

But international comparisons, based on monetary estimates made
in national currencies and then converted into a common currency at
current exchange rates, are subject to notoriously wide margins of error.
Indeed, two similar estimates, based on different data in slightly different ways, have yielded an eight- and a ten-year gap.[3] Moreover, one
must also bear in mind that Korea produces its lower GDP with greater
effort. In 1980, the average length of the working week in Korea's manufacturing industries was in excess of fifty-nine hours, 16 percent
longer than Taiwan's fifty-one-hour week. Correcting for that factor
makes Taiwan's per capita GDP appear almost twice as high as Korea's.

Table 4.2   Social Indicators

	Korea	Taiwan
Life expectancy at birth (years)	65	72
Infant mortality per 1,000 live births	37	25
Daily calorie intake per capita	2,785	2,805
Daily protein intake per capita (grams)	69.6	78
Residential floor space per capita (m^2)	9.5	15.7
Households with running water (percent)	54.6	66.8
Households with television sets (percent)	78.6	100.4
Households with passenger cars and motorcycles (percent)	5.8	108.4
Electric power consumption per capita (KWH)	914.8	2,131.2

On the other hand, Koreans spend a much higher proportion of their lower GDP on private consumption: two-thirds as compared to Taiwan's one-half. Accordingly, the difference between the two countries' levels of living is not as great as the discrepancy between their per capita GDP would suggest.

Social indicators are sometimes more useful for assessing differences in levels of living than estimates in money terms. Those available for both countries are listed in table 4.2; they suggest that Taiwan enjoys a considerably higher level of living than Korea. The only visible social indicator is the number of motorized vehicles (passenger cars and motorcycles) per household. It suggests that in Taiwan just about every household owns such a vehicle, while in Korea only one in twenty households does; the difference is striking in the contrast between Taiwan's busy country roads and small-town streets and Korea's much quieter countryside.

None of the other social indicators is apparent; indeed, the tourist is likely not only to fail to notice Taiwan's greater prosperity but actually to get the impression that the difference between the two countries goes the other way around. Seoul, certainly, looks more affluent than Taipei, judging by the appearance of its main thoroughfares, the impressiveness of its commercial and office buildings, and the elegance of its stores and shopping areas. The explanation of the conflict between what the tourist sees and what the statistics show derives from the unequal distribution of income and of the things that income buys. All the social indicators of table 4.2 are averages and indicate average tendencies; whereas the tourist is shown only the best, and his eye instinctively looks for the best. In an egalitarian society the best is not much better

Table 4.3   Gini Index of Inequality of Income Distribution

	1965	1970	1976
Korea	0.344	0.332	0.381
Taiwan	0.322[a]	0.293	0.289
Japan	0.380	0.420[b]	
United States		0.362[c]	
Brazil	0.520[d]	0.630	

a. 1966
b. 1971
c. 1972
d. 1960
Source: The comparisons are based on Gini indexes of inequality: obtained for Taiwan from Kuo, Ranis, and Fei, *The Taiwan Success Story* (Boulder, Colo.: Westview Press, 1981); for Korea from Park, *Human Resources and Social Development in Korea* (Seoul: Korea Development Institute, 1980), p. 289; and calculated for other countries from data in World Bank, *World Development Report 1982*, pp. 158–59.

than the average, but the two differ greatly in a society with great inequalities.

Income distribution in both Taiwan and Korea is much more equal than in any other developing or newly industrializing country for which relevant statistics are available, but it is more egalitarian in Taiwan than in Korea. Inequalities in Korea are much the same as in the advanced industrial countries: somewhat less than in France and Italy, greater than in the United Kingdom and the Scandinavian countries, and just about the same as in the United States and Canada. Taiwan, on the other hand, is the most egalitarian of all capitalist countries, a finding that corresponds to the very small average size and limited dispersion of the size of Taiwan's business firms, and also explains the absence of an elite wealthy and numerous enough to support the elegant shops and finance the imposing office buildings that give Seoul its appearance of affluence (table 4.3).

One more important difference between the two economies has been the much lower rate of inflation in Taiwan than in Korea. Between 1965 and 1981, the consumer price index rose three and one-half times in Taiwan, ten times in Korea, corresponding to average annual price inflation rates of 8 and 15 percent, respectively. Compared to other countries, Taiwan did about as well—or as badly—as Japan or the United States; Korea had more inflation than any of the industrial countries, but less than the major Latin American economies.

Table 4.4   School Enrollment Rates

	Primary school	Secondary school	College and university
Korea	111	76	12.4
Taiwan	99.7	80.3	10.3
Advanced industrial countries	102	88	37
Italy	102	73	27
Switzerland	86	55	17

Note: School enrollment rate is defined as students enrolled as a percentage of the population in the appropriate age group.

Similarities in Tradition and Background

Detailed analysis and comparison of the two countries' economic conditions and performance suggest that the similarities are due largely to similarities in their history and traditions. Korea's lag behind Taiwan is more than explained by the later date at which its growth policies began: the other differences are well accounted for by the two countries' divergent economic policies. Unexplained and puzzling is the close similarity in growth rates despite the very different ways in which the two countries went about promoting growth.

To begin with the similarities, both countries—indeed, all five of the high performers—share a common Chinese tradition and Confucian philosophy. That explains, first of all, the great reverence and importance attached to learning in both countries and the very high educational and skill levels of their populations. They started from a very low level at the end of the war, especially in Korea where the literacy rate was 13.4 percent in 1945 (as against Taiwan's 21.3 percent by 1940), and where there was no large influx of a highly educated middle-class population such as benefited Taiwan in the late 1940s. Since then, illiteracy has been almost completely eradicated in both countries, and today Taiwan provides nine years and Korea six years of free and compulsory schooling. School enrollment rates at the primary and secondary levels are almost equally high in the two countries and only slightly lower than the average in the advanced industrial countries (table 4.4). That is especially impressive in Korea, where modernization started later, compulsory education ends sooner, and public expenditure on education is lower (averaging 3.5 percent of the GDP as against Taiwan's 4.5 percent), but where consumers make up for those disadvantages by paying for the greater part of their children's education out of their own pockets, bringing the total private and public expenditure on education to an astonishingly high 9 percent of the GNP.

A second condition of those countries' great economic success that can be traced back to their common tradition is the ability and willingness to work hard. Chinese tradition has many strands, but it seems to include a work ethic not unlike the Protestant and Jewish work ethics. The drive and ambition of Korean and Chinese businessmen, as well as their ability to work hard and long hours, are commented on by nearly every outside observer of the two economies, and so are the "untiring concentration and pertinacity" of their workers.[4] One is tempted to add the two countries' very long working week as a further manifestation of the work ethic, but in view of the very limited bargaining strength of their unions, it is hard to tell to what extent those long working hours are voluntary and to what extent they are imposed.

A third factor that probably also contributed to the two countries' economic success is the Chinese tradition in labor relations, which comprises both greater wage flexibility and greater employment stability than in Europe and America, and which was fully maintained and perhaps even strengthened under Japanese rule. Both countries adhere to the Chinese custom of paying bonuses to workers at major festivals and the end of the year; even if these constitute a much smaller proportion of the annual wage than they do in Japan, they nevertheless are likely to contribute to the two countries' high personal savings rate and to impart a measure of downward flexibility to wages. Again, relations between employer and employee are more permanent in the two countries than they are in the West, with employers under both moral and governmental pressure to take care of their workers even when business is slow.

Korea and Taiwan are also similar in that both were under Japanese rule, Korea for thirty-five years and Taiwan for fifty years, and that fact has facilitated their subsequent growth in at least two ways. First, the Japanese introduced the new, high-yielding strains of rice, established agricultural research institutes, and generally did much to develop the two countries' farm productivity and food production; moreover, they built roads, railways, harbors, and whatever beginnings of industry the two countries had, thus providing an excellent start and base for subsequent development. A second and very important consequence of Japanese rule had to do with the confiscation of Japanese property when their rule came to an end. The Japanese acquired a sizable part of the land (21 percent of all arable land in Taiwan) and built most of the modern manufacturing plants in both countries, and since they owned all the large enterprises and most of the largest landed estates, the confiscation of their property by the liberating armies and its handing over to the new governments drastically reduced the inequality of private wealth holdings in both countries. In Korea, moreover, the Korean War destroyed much physical property, and since most of the loss was borne by the wealthy, that too helped to reduce inequalities of wealth.

Even more important in equalizing the distribution of wealth were the thorough land reforms in both countries, which not only distributed among small tenant farmers the large estates formerly held by the Japanese, but also forced the large indigenous landowners to sell all their land over three hectares (except in Korea's upland areas) at prices very much below market values. Korea's and Taiwan's land reforms were identical in almost every detail.[5]

The stability of employment is another contributing factor in the equal distribution of income. Yet another important reason was the rise of farm families' earnings to the level of urban wage-earner families' incomes. In Taiwan, that came about largely through the operation of automatic market forces, aided by favorable circumstances. Impelled by high and rising labor costs in cities, an increasing proportion of new factories and offices was established in rural areas and offered additional employment opportunities to farmers and their families. The poorest farmers especially availed themselves of the opportunity: by 1975, 66 percent of their total earnings came from jobs off the farm. Nor was the corresponding percentage for all farm families much lower: 53.7 percent in 1975, rising to 72.7 percent in 1979. That is why, in contrast to most developing countries where mass migration into the cities depletes rural areas, Taiwan's rural population remained fairly stable, with members of farm families commuting or taking part-time jobs in nearby cities during off-peak seasons. The favorable circumstances that aided the process were a small, decentralized country, good roads, a mild climate, and a motorcycle in every family. Korea went out of its way to encourage a similar development but, perhaps for want of similarly favorable circumstances, had very limited success. It managed nevertheless to equalize rural and urban incomes through the costly expedient of a farm-price support program combined with subsidized low food prices for consumers.

Thanks to all those equalizing factors and influences, the degree of income inequality by the mid-1960s had fallen to just about the same level in the two countries. Since then, inequalities have declined yet further in Taiwan but increased in Korea, which explains why Taiwan is today the more egalitarian country. An explanation for these diverging trends is offered below in the discussion of economic policies.

Two additional similarities between the countries are the exceptionally generous economic aid both have received and the exceptionally heavy burdens of military expenditures they are saddled with: the first is an addition to economic resources, the second a drain on them. Both countries have also received substantial military aid from the United States in the form of military equipment, but since much of it seems to call for a larger defense establishment, military aid probably encourages domestic defense spending more than reduces it. Defense spending in Taiwan hovers around 10 percent of GNP; in Korea, thanks to an American military presence, it is 5 to 6 percent. But even that is much higher than the 3.8 percent average of industrial countries and the 3 percent average of newly industrializing countries.[6] The annual aid Taiwan received until 1966 averaged 5.1 percent of GNP, just enough to finance the above-normal part of its defense spending.[7]

Such a simple-minded calculation, of course, ignores that Taiwan would probably have spent as much on defense even if it had received no economic aid, and that aid may well have been crucial in the early 1950s for controlling inflation and securing the survival of the government of the Republic of China on Taiwan. But beyond assuring those initial conditions, aid cannot really be said to have accelerated growth.

Korea's situation is somewhat different. The aid it received exceeded defense expenditures, averaging 8.3 percent of GNP before 1965 and continuing, at a somewhat lower level, until 1972.[8] The economy, however, was much more devastated by war than Taiwan's, and the aid to rebuild the war-torn country was more comparable to that received by Japan and Western Europe. Unlike Taiwan, where in the early years (1951–53) part of the aid was focused on rebuilding agriculture, in Korea "the Rhee government was committed to increasing private and government consumption through the maximization of aid and imports, rather than to the future growth of output."[9] Later on, of course, aid financed a good part (an average of 10.2 percent from 1965 to 1981) of total investment and so contributed to growth. The section on sources of investable funds also deals with the contribution of foreign loans, which was sizable in Korea but zero in Taiwan during the 1965 to 1981 period.

One more similarity between the two countries worth mentioning here was their very limited imports of entrepreneurial skill and technical know-how in the form of direct foreign investments. In Taiwan, they constituted a mere 6.5 percent of fixed investment in manufacturing industries between 1967 and 1975; in Korea, they were equally insignificant until 1972, when they rose to about 20 percent, coming mainly from Japan and going mainly into textiles, electronics, and hotel business.[10] The reasons for their limited need of direct foreign investment are obvious. Perhaps as part of their excellent educational systems and traditions of hard work and untiring application, both countries are well provided with native entrepreneurial skills, drive, and ambition. Moreover, they had no need for imported technical knowledge as long as they had previous experience. That, probably, is why in Korea the increase in foreign direct investment coincided with the decision to shift to more capital-intensive industries. Even at that stage, however, direct foreign investment in Korea was low compared to other developing countries, perhaps owing to the Koreans' preference for going it alone. They learned shipbuilding by employing Norwegians from closed-down Norwegian shipyards and gained their expertise in construction by contracting to do construction work abroad.

These similarities in the two countries' backgrounds help to explain not only their similar economic performances but also the exceptional nature of their success when compared to the record of other developing countries. To explain differences between the two countries themselves, one must look at their differing policies. The effectiveness of those policies and the divergencies between them are discussed in detail below. To introduce the discussion, however, it is useful to look at the general spirit and underlying philosophies that pervaded economic policymaking in the two countries.

The Philosophy behind Taiwan's Economic Policies

Taiwanese officials will occasionally say that their economic policy is to let market forces take their course. That, however, is a highly oversimplified and exaggerated statement. Taiwan has long had and still has plenty of economic controls, which are well used to implement the government's growth policies as set out in a succession of Four-Year Plans; one could hardly call the country's economy a hands-off, laissez-faire economy. Yet the Taiwanese also know how to press market forces into the service of their economic policies.

In the early 1960s, the Nineteen-Point Economic Financial Reform of the Third Four-Year Plan greatly encouraged investment by private enterprise. In Taiwan today, government does not have the strong ascendancy over private business it still has in Korea, and economic controls tend to be moderate and often make use of the market in a selective and quite sophisticated way. The Taiwanese, like the Koreans, have encouraged exports by creating an essentially free-trade, free-market regime for exports and export production; moreover, unlike the Koreans, they have shown great respect for the strength of market forces, manifest by the careful moderation of their policies when they aim at modifying or deflecting those forces and in the gradual, stepwise fashion in which they change economic controls and policies. Finally, while Korea's development weakened the pull of market forces, Taiwan's strengthened it.

For a market economy to function properly, it must be competitive. Competition depends on the presence of many small firms and the absence of overwhelmingly large ones. In Taiwan, those conditions of competition and the proper functioning of markets are better fulfilled than in most other private enterprise economies, thanks partly to deliberate policies, and partly to fortuitous circumstances.

To begin with, heavy industries like steel, shipbuilding, and petrochemicals, whose great economies of scale render them natural monopolies in a small country, are publicly owned in Taiwan, probably more for lack of sufficient private resources and interest than for reasons of policy. Privately owned manufacturing firms were usually small in size and few in number in primitive economies, whose forced economic development in the mid-twentieth century typically took the form of growth in the size rather than in the number of firms, owing partly to economies of scale and partly to its being so much harder for government to facilitate the establishment of new firms than the growth of already established ones.

Astonishingly enough, Taiwan managed to take the opposite route to development. Between 1966 and 1976, the number of manufacturing firms in Taiwan increased by 150 percent, while the average size of the individual enterprise, as measured by the number of employees, increased by only 29 percent. In Korea, where development took the more common route, the relation between those two changes goes the other way around. The number of manufacturing firms increased by a mere

10 percent, while the number of employees per enterprise increased by 176 percent.

The result of Taiwan's route of development was the much smaller size of private manufacturing enterprises and the more competitive spirit that goes with it. Not counting the very small firms with less than five employees, which are not registered in the Korean census, the average Taiwanese firm in 1976 was only half as big as the Korean, with 34.6 employees compared to 68.8 in Korea. Moreover, the very small firms, ignored by the Korean census, constituted 43 percent of all manufacturing firms in Taiwan, bringing the average size of all Taiwanese firms down to 27 employees. The disparity in firm size between the two countries seems even greater when one looks at their largest firms. In 1981, the $10 billion gross receipts of Hyundai, Korea's largest conglomerate, were three times as big as the $3.5 billion gross receipts of Taiwan's ten largest private firms combined.

What explains this? There are at least four reasons for the faster increase in the number of Taiwanese firms. One is the immigration of overseas Chinese, who brought with them 30 percent of the total inflow of foreign capital and used it mostly for establishing independent enterprises of their own. A second is Taiwan's much higher personal savings rate, which generally makes it easier to secure the capital for establishing independent businesses. A third factor is probably the much smaller size of the average firm, which makes it easier and cheaper for newcomers to enter the market.

A fourth and possibly most important factor is Taiwan's policy of helping people with entrepreneurial inclinations and know-how but insufficient capital to establish themselves as independent businessmen. For the market to function well, labor, capital, and entrepreneurship must be somehow brought together. One usually thinks of the entrepreneur as the initiating and moving spirit, but real-life capital markets do not lend money to penniless entrepreneurs, and the capitalist owner of a small firm—as most firms are in Taiwan—can seldom afford to hire entrepreneurial talent. To remedy that situation, Taiwan has established forty-nine industrial parks and districts, some of them specialized (like the Youth Industrial Parks and the Science-Based Industrial Park), which provide infrastructure facilities, enable new investors to rent rather than buy land and buildings, and provide generous loans. In such areas, the technical skills of scientifically trained people are accepted as an important part (up to 50 percent) of their personal investment.

Those were the factors facilitating the establishment of new enterprise. Equally important for keeping alive the competitive spirit was the very slow growth of the average enterprise. Yet there is no evidence of official policy deliberately aimed at limiting either the size or the rate of growth of private firms. Indeed, Taiwan has many large private industrial groups, which, though much smaller in size than those in Korea, are sufficiently large and important to have contributed 30 percent of the country's total GDP in the 1980s. The explanation of the relatively slow growth of the size of firms, therefore, lies not in the presence of policies limiting but in the absence of policies encouraging their growth.

This brings us to the subject of monetary policy. The crucial difference between the two countries lay in their very different monetary policies. Taiwan's novel monetary policy was all-important for bringing about conditions favorable to the market economy's functioning as it should, although its effect on the size and growth of firms was an unintended side effect.

The rate of interest, or more correctly the structure of interest rates, is the one price or set of prices whose determination cannot be left entirely to the free play of market forces. Different countries pursue different monetary and interest-rate policies, yet there is a theoretically definable, though practically very hard-to-ascertain equilibrium or natural rate of interest that equates the demand for investable funds at full employment to the supply of full-employment savings; Taiwanese monetary policy may be said to have consistently tried to ascertain what the equilibrium interest rate was and to keep actual interest rates close to that equilibrium level. The beginnings of that monetary policy go back to the early 1950s, more than a decade before the period under review, but since the same policy is still being adhered to today, and since it has profoundly affected and continues to affect many aspects of Taiwan's economy, a short account of it seems to be in order.

At a time when the universally approved and practiced policy in developing countries was to keep interest rates low to encourage capital accumulation and growth, Taiwan broke new ground and raised the interest rates paid to savers and charged to borrowers to levels almost unheard of at that time. Originally, the policy was devised, outlined, and advocated as a means of curbing China's hyperinflation during the war and civil war, by a Chinese economist, Professor S.C. Tsiang, in two Chinese-language articles published in 1947 in the *Shanghai Economic Review*. Adoption of his policy had much to do with bringing that inflation to a halt.

A high interest-rate policy is, of course, a standard remedy for inflation, but totally unexpected was another effect that also followed Taiwan's adoption of the policy: the acceleration of capital accumulation and growth. Savings deposits accumulated very fast following the substantial raising of the interest paid on deposits, presumably because savers found the high interest rate so attractive that they stopped putting their savings into unproductive but price-increasing hoards of goods and real estate. They may also have increased their saving as a proportion of income. At the same time, however, that high deposit rates raised both the savings rate and the proportion of savings channeled into bank deposits, lending rates apparently were not high enough to reduce business' demand for investable funds to below the rate at which funds became available. In other words, the high deposit and loan rates instituted in Taiwan came close to but did not exceed the equilibrium rate of interest as defined earlier, which explains why raising interest rates raised the level of investment or capital accumulation.

In addition, the raising of interest rates is also likely to have rendered investment a more efficient and more effective engine of growth. For interest rates held below their natural level create excess demand for investable funds and so force the banks to ration credit. Credit rationing, however, usually favors large firms, the banks' established customers, or those whom government wants to favor, and these are not always the ones who earn the highest rate of return on their investments. Accordingly, credit rationing by bank or government policy is likely to crowd out some high-return investments that would not be crowded out if the interest rate were the main factor limiting the demand for credit. In other words, rationing credit by interest rates instead of by bank managers and government officials is almost certain to raise the average return on the total volume of investment, thereby further accelerating growth.[11]

Those advantages of a carefully managed interest-rate policy in both containing inflation and promoting investment and growth have become well known in the literature of development economics, and the policy has been advocated for and imitated by other countries as well. Indeed,the originator of the policy and Taiwan's pioneering role in developing its application have been all but forgotten, which is regrettable because Taiwan's prolonged and consistent adherence to it has also had further advantages much less known but no less important. One is that high interest rates render profitable and encourage the use of labor-intensive methods of production. In developing countries where labor is plentiful but all else is scarce, that is an important advantage: it increases the employment of labor by creating more job opportunities for any given level of investment, and it raises labor's share in the national product. Taiwan is unique among developing countries in that its unemployment rate has been consistently and often much below 2 percent throughout the entire period under review. That excellent record must be credited, in large part, to its high interest-rate policy. Note that so-called Marxian (or structural) unemployment is minimized. In other developing countries such unemployment is due to manufacturing plants and equipment of such nature and quantity that employment for all those who seek it cannot be provided, however high the effective demand for output. That is the reason why stimulating demand has never been an effective employment policy in the developing world.

The high demand for labor due to Taiwan's encouragement and use of labor-intensive methods of production also raised wages and thus labor's share in the national product. Indeed, labor's share in Taiwan's national product has steadily risen, and property's share fallen over the past one and one-half decades, and since wage income is both lower on average and more evenly distributed than property income, that gradual shift in incomes away from capital and in favor of labor has been the main factor in explaining the diminution over time of income inequalities in Taiwan.[12]

Having dealt with the two reasons why the choice of labor-intensive methods of production was an advantage, we can now discuss another advantage of Taiwan's high interest-rate policy that also has to do with income distribution. Every market transaction gives rise to a gain, and the way that gain is divided between the transacting parties depends on the price at which they effect the transaction. The rate of interest is the price the borrower pays the lender for the loan, and it determines the division between them of the total gain from the loan. The higher the rate of interest, the greater the lender's and the smaller the borrower's share, so that high interest rates favor the lender and limit the borrower's gain.

The person in the street tends instinctively to consider such a state of affairs reprehensible, because the word "lender" conjures up a rich capitalist and the word "borrower" a poor wretch attempting to stave off starvation. That imagery has its origin in medieval Europe and may still make sense in primitive agricultural communities, but the situation is very different when it comes to bank lending and borrowing in today's newly industrializing economies. There, the typical lender is a small saver, the typical borrower is the corporation, often the large corporation, so that high interest rates favor the low-income saver and limit the profits of business enterprise. In other words, high interest rates transfer a large part of business profits to small savers in the form of interest on their savings, which supplements their wage and salary income. Accordingly, this is yet another factor that contributes to Taiwan's egalitarian income distribution.

One advantage of having high interest rates on savings deposits has already been dealt with: it encourages small savers to increase both their saving rate and the proportion of their savings that they put into bank deposits and so make available for productive use. Another advantage is that it limits profits, which restrains the rate at which the size of the individual enterprise grows. As already shown, the individual firm's size in Taiwan has grown very slowly and stayed small, which has helped to maintain competition.

Yet another advantage of small firms is that they render the always painful adaptation of the economy to changing circumstances a little more bearable. Right now, the world economy is going through a major convulsion that calls for the scaling down of some established industries and the creation and expansion of new ones. Examples abound in the United States, Britain, West Germany, and elsewhere of the great and successful resistance large firms can put up to the necessary cutting down of their operations, thereby prolonging the agony but not obviating the necessity of change. High bankruptcy rates in Taiwan suggest that there, too, painful changes in the pattern and scale of manufacture are called for, but the small size of the average firms facilitates the adjustment process. The subject will be discussed further at the end of this paper.

A final potential advantage of limited profits, mentioned here only for completeness' sake, is their tendency to keep entrepreneurs on their toes and so maintain their efficiency and initiative. Too high and secure profits, whether assured by monopoly advantage or government protection, can destroy entrepreneurial drive. In America, Europe, and Latin America, inefficiency, failure to innovate, and poor economic performance in general have often been traced to that factor. Ironically, in Korea there is no evidence that the large profits and fast accumulation of great fortunes that Korea's economic policies made possible had any unfavorable effects on the drive, stamina, and efficiency of Korea's businesses. Perhaps this is due to the Chinese cultural background.

The Philosophy behind Korea's Economic Policies

The main difference between Korea's and Taiwan's economic policies lies neither in their aims nor in their achievements, but in the much more forceful and aggressive spirit with which Korea's policymakers pursued their aims. In a private enterprise economy, of course, profit and self-interest are the main motivations of economic behavior, and government's main policy tool is the set of incentives and disincentives with which it tries selectively to change the thrust of the profit motive. This is true in both Korea and Taiwan, but there is a great difference in the number and nature of inducements used and in the forcefulness with which they are applied.

Nearly every industrializing country publishes periodically an economic plan that sets forth the government's intentions for its own expenditure on infrastructure and other government projects, together with projections of the private sector's future development. Those projections can vary from rough guesses to carefully worked-out sectoral patterns of compatible and feasible growth that the government hopes for, or expects to occur, or encourages, either by merely announcing it or by the use of incentives and disincentives. Accordingly, one cannot tell just by the publication of an economic plan and its wording the extent of government's influence and control over economic affairs.

There is, however, much evidence to show that during the period considered, which largely coincides with the Park regime, government influence over economic affairs was much greater and more detailed in Korea than in Taiwan.[13] The machinery of economic planning was larger, more elaborate, more centrally and prominently placed in the Korean government's administrative hierarchy, and well-provided with channels of communication for consultation with business. The Prime Minister chaired the Central Economic Committee, and the chairman of the Economic Planning Board held the rank of Deputy Prime Minister. A Product Evaluation Board engaged in market research and provided rate-of-return and profitability estimates for the Economic Planning Board, which also acquired an impressively large and competent research arm with the founding of the Korea Development Institute. Close contact between government officials, researchers, and private business was maintained in monthly Export Promotion Meetings and specialized Working Groups. None of this seems to have had a counterpart in Taiwan.

Korean policymakers also, until recently, have made extensive and forceful use of a wide range of incentives, both of a general and a particular nature, designed to assure private industry's close compliance with their plans. The main incentive is differential access to credit and concessionary cost of credit. Both countries have for many years granted credit at lower cost to approved industries, but the criteria that qualify a borrower for low-cost credit tend to be more generally defined in Taiwan than in Korea, and the cost concession is typically twice or even three times greater in Korea than it is in Taiwan. Moreover, in view of Korea's generally lower average interest rates and inflationary climate, the real interest cost of such concessionary loans in Korea has often been zero or even negative. Most of Korea's concessionary loans are given by specialized banks and non-bank financial institutions, many of which are under the direct control of the Minister of Finance (rather than the Bank of Korea). Furthermore, in Korea, borrowing abroad by private firms also hinges on express authorization by government.

On the disincentive side, firms that fail to do what government wants them to do often find that their loan applications are ignored or their outstanding loans fail to be renewed. Those are extremely effective instruments in a country in which business relies heavily on bank credit. From 1972 through 1981, the sum of the current and fixed liabilities of Korean manufacturing enterprises expressed as a percentage of their net worth was 364 percent—more than twice as high as in Taiwan and four times as high as in the United States. Moreover, almost two-thirds of that debt was short-term (current liabilities), which makes the profitability—even the survival—of manufacturing firms depend greatly on interest rates, the banks' willingness to prolong expiring short-term loans, and consequently on the goodwill of government, which owns and controls the banks.

The same is true of the differences between the two countries' use of tax incentives. A five-year tax holiday for approved investments, remission of duties on imported inputs into export production, and exemption of exports from indirect taxes are standard in both countries, but Korea also provides an assortment of inducements for export and for investment in specified industries in the form of lower rates of profits tax and very generous depreciation allowances and wastage allowances. On the disincentive side, the tax returns of Korean firms that do not toe the line drawn by government are said to be subject to especially careful scrutiny.

In short, the Korean authorities have a very strong control over decision making by private business, because "it does not take a Korean firm long to learn that it will 'get along' best by 'going along.'"[14]

Control is greatly facilitated by frequent personal contact between government officials and businessmen, which is made easy because production is concentrated in relatively few firms. Such concentration, in turn, is one of the results of Korea's substantial credit and tax concessions, because they have enabled the firms that went along with the government's economic plans and made the investments called for in those plans to make very large profits, whose accumulation and reinvestment over the years explains their very fast growth.

Mention has already been made of the much larger size of the average firm in Korea than in Taiwan; Korea, a relatively small country of thirty-eight million people, has conglomerates that are huge by any standard. The twenty largest Korean conglomerates are responsible for producing half the value added in manufacturing, and the four largest (Hyundai, Sam Sung, Daewoo, and Lucky) each had an annual gross turnover between US$5 and $10 billion in 1981. Even the smallest of them had a larger turnover than the gross sales of Taiwan's ten largest companies combined. As remarkable as the size of those companies is the speed with which they have grown from very small beginnings. For example, the oldest and largest company, Hyundai, started in 1950 as a small construction and auto-repair shop; today it employs 150,000 workers, lists forty-three overseas offices on five continents, and has gross sales of US$10 billion.

The fast growth of those companies, thanks to the government's generous credit and tax incentives, must have played an important part in increasing the inequality of incomes during the 1970s, and it may have other untoward consequences as well. The diminished resilience of an economy when individual firms grow to excessive size has already been alluded to. Another potential danger of the excessively large size of business firms is that they may wield excessive influence over government policy. Observers generally agree, however, that the Korean government definitely has the upper hand, at least as far as determining the direction in which the economy is going. Problems that may be created in the future by large size and insufficient competition in the private sector are discussed in the last section of this chapter.

Agriculture

Taiwan and Korea are the world's second and third most densely populated countries (after Bangladesh), and both of them have poor soil, of which only a quarter is arable in Taiwan and slightly less (22 percent) in Korea. Intense cultivation, however, goes a long way in both countries to compensate for the scarcity and poverty of arable land. Furthermore, in Taiwan, the subtropical climate renders double cropping, and in the south even triple cropping, possible, thereby considerably increasing the utilization of land, labor, farm machinery, and intrastructural facilities. Indeed, the increased practice of multiple cropping has been an important element of agricultural development, and Taiwan's multiple-cropping index had risen to almost 190 percent by 1964.[15] In Korea's less favorable climate, double cropping is possible only by alternating rice with barley (an unpopular food), and the multiple-cropping index has not risen above 140 percent.

During the colonial period the Japanese instituted agricultural experiment research stations, a network of extension offices, the provision of inputs (seed and fertilizer) in kind, lending of equipment, organization of cooperative societies both for marketing and for the distribution of credit and fertilizer, and the building of an infrastructure of roads, railroads, and harbors. The Japanese seem to have concentrated especially on Taiwan, where the climate was more favorable, colonial rule lasted longer (fifty years), and the rulers and subjects got along somewhat better than in Korea.

World War II in Taiwan and, more severely, the Korean War in Korea destroyed much of the infrastructure, lowering farm output by 36 percent in Taiwan and 60 percent in Korea. Taiwan's agriculture had just about recovered by the time the Korean War ended, while Korea's was in shambles. From that time on, the average annual growth rate of the two countries' farm output was almost the same: 5 percent until 1965 and 3 percent after in Korea; 5.1 percent up to 1965 and 2.8 percent after in Taiwan. Accordingly, the two countries were equally successful in rebuilding and expanding their farm output, but Korea had to offset a much greater war devastation and a later start.

That is why Korea had almost managed to eliminate its large agricultural import surplus by the end of our period (1981). Taiwan, on the other hand, achieved a sizable export surplus on farm products already before 1965, which then declined and changed into a deficit by 1973, due to a shift in production from rice to livestock, vegetables, and fruit. The shift was prompted by the rising dietary standards of an increasingly affluent population and also by the hidden but substantial tax on rice, although that was replaced by a subsidy by the mid-1970s. As a result of that shift, and as a result also of the expanding export market for delicacies like mushrooms and asparagus, rice and other staples make up less than 40 percent of Taiwan's farm output today, while livestock alone constitutes 36 percent. This caused a greatly increased demand for imported animal feed, which explains Taiwan's trade deficit on farm products. (Taiwan still has an export surplus in human food, but imports of fodder and lumber turn the scales and account for its import surplus in agriculture.) In Korea, on the other hand, livestock is a mere 6 percent of farm output and food grains still constitute 80 percent of the national diet.

In short, Taiwan's growing trade deficit in farm products signifies not decline but progress—though the increasingly affluent public's demand for more sophistication, variety, and high quality in its diet is outrunning agriculture's ability to meet that demand, given the limited quantity of land and the competing demands on the agricultural labor force.

For despite the higher value of its farm output, Taiwan employs a much smaller proportion of its labor force on the farm than does Korea. Farm families constitute much the same proportion of the population in Taiwan (29.8 percent) as in Korea (28.4 percent), but the percentage of the labor force employed on farms is only 19.5 percent in Taiwan compared to 34 percent in Korea. The explanation is that many members of Taiwan's farm families commute on a full-time, part-time, or seasonal basis to nonfarm jobs in manufacturing, teaching, and administration, so that almost three-quarters (72.7 percent) of the average farm family's income comes from nonfarm employment; whereas in Korea, the nonfarm income of farm families is only about 20 percent of their total income.

That situation has come about spontaneously. High urban wages increasingly have persuaded new manufacturing business to locate in rural areas, and short distances, good roads (72 percent are paved), good public transportation, and the possession of motorcycles have induced members of farm families to commute to those new jobs rather than to move. An important consequence has been the raising of farm households' incomes to the level of urban incomes. This is an important part of the explanation of Taiwan's favorable income distribution, and it is something that many countries have striven for but few achieved.

Korea tried to bring about a similar situation by offering tax advantages to firms locating in rural areas, but found it easier to persuade industry to move to the countryside than to persuade members of farm households to take employment in those industries. Some workers—including urban workers—have moved to the vicinity of rural factories, but disappointingly few commute to those factories. The reasons for the policy's failure are not fully known, but they probably have to do with transportation problems in a country more highly centralized than Taiwan, with much poorer roads (only 32 percent paved); inadequate bus transportation; a climate that prevents commuting by motorcycle or bicycle during much of the year; and frequent curfews after dark, a major impediment to rural commuting in a country with a work week almost sixty hours long and a cultural tradition of socializing with fellow workers after work.[16] Nevertheless, Korea too brought farm-family incomes to the level of urban wages but in a much more costly way: by paying farmers a high price for rice and barley, which is then resold to consumers at a much lower price. The cost of that subsidy, paid out of general government revenues, is estimated at about 1.4 percent of the GNP.[17]

While Taiwan enjoys the advantages of a more favorable climate and an earlier start from a higher base, which enables it to produce proportionately more farm output with the aid of a smaller percentage of her labor force, Korean agriculture accomplished more during this period. Korean farm output increased slightly faster (7 percent) than Taiwan's, but labor productivity in farming increased about twice as fast. Part of that shows up in the employment statistics, which indicate that farm employment increased somewhat in Taiwan and declined slightly in Korea, but the more detailed studies of the two countries' agriculture show that, at least during the 1965–75 period, the number of days worked in farming fell at an average annual rate of 3 percent in Korea and at not quite two-thirds of one percent in Taiwan. The average annual rise in labor productivity during that period is estimated at 2.78 percent in Taiwan and at 5.65 percent in Korea. What accounts for the difference?

In Korea, the great rise in the productivity of farm labor is usually attributed to the great increase in the application of chemical fertilizers, by over 125 percent between 1965 and 1975. In Taiwan, fertilizer use increased 60 percent over the same period. Similarly, Korea's stock of fixed capital in farming increased by 183 percent during that period, compared to an estimated 77 percent in Taiwan. Finally, the rise in the value of Taiwan's farm output was partly due to Taiwan's shifting production from standard crops to much higher-priced (and higher value-added) livestock, vegetables, fruits, and mushrooms—all of which are more labor-intensive than rice or other standard crops.[18]

Export Promotion

Fast economic growth in both countries began with the 1960s, and is called "export-led growth" because its driving force seemed to be the exceptionally fast expansion of the export of manufactures, explained in turn by the adoption of export-promotion policies. However, since those policies consisted of little more than the removal or offsetting of man-made obstacles to international trade, one cannot understand why they were so successful without knowing something about the policies and the situation they replaced.

The classic and almost universally adopted development policy of the immediate postwar years was import substitution: encouragement through import restrictions and tax concessions of the domestic manufacture of goods previously imported. The main aim of that policy was increased self-sufficiency and diminished dependence on the vagaries of world trade, but it was hoped that productivity and total output would also grow in the process. Increased self-sufficiency seemed eminently desirable in the light of the experience of the depressed 1930s when the prices of the poor countries' primary-product exports fell drastically in relation to the prices of their manufactured imports, and perhaps even more desirable during World War II, when the manufactured exports of the advanced countries were simply unavailable.

Self-sufficiency, however, is a very costly and hard-to-achieve luxury because the products a country imports are almost always ones that are comparatively difficult for that country to manufacture. To overcome the disadvantage has proved so costly and difficult that, apart from the limited success of the simplest forms of (so-called primary) import substitution, the policy was a disappointment everywhere. Self-sufficiency made little headway: little growth accompanied each country's efforts to produce what they had a disadvantage in producing. As a final blow, what little gain in self-sufficiency was achieved seemed hardly worth having during those years of uninterrupted prosperity, continued trade liberalization, and ever-expanding world trade.

The force of that argument was brought home strikingly by the experience of such city-states as Singapore and Hong Kong. They were far too small even to try for self-sufficiency and had no choice but to focus on producing what they were good at producing and to exchange that for what they wanted to consume. They then found that the road they had followed for want of any other could not have been better. The contrast between their phenomenally fast growth and the import-substituting countries' much slower growth is a measure of the economic gains to be had by exploiting one's comparative advantage and of the cost incurred by trying to overcome one's comparative disadvantage—at least in a period when world trade conditions are favorable to the expansion of exports by new countries and new firms.

Among the large countries having a choice between alternative policies, Taiwan and Korea were the first to recognize the gains from encouraging the production for export of products they advantageously could manufacture. Beginning in the early 1960s, both countries engaged in export promotion, which consisted partly in dismantling or offsetting previous protectionist policies discriminating against exports and partly in actively encouraging measures in favor of exports. Dismantling and offsetting included remitting duties on imported inputs for export production and, in Korea, on imported inputs into domestically produced intermediate goods used in export production; establishing export-processing zones and bonded factories whose main purpose was to cut red tape; and abolishing multiple exchange rates in favor of a single rate that ended the overvaluation of domestic currency, which had been the hallmark of import-substitution regimes.

The second set of measures included cheap bank loans for exporters (in Taiwan about 40 percent below the interest rate on ordinary bank loans), the remission of indirect taxes on inputs into exports and on the exports themselves, exemption from corporate income taxes on a part of export earnings (in Taiwan, total exemption for "encouraged" products whose export exceeded 50 percent of total output), and, in Korea, export insurance and discounts on railway freight and electricity rates. The value of those practices to the exporter, expressed as a percentage of gross export receipts, is estimated at 10.7 percent in Taiwan for 1962–76 and at 8.2 percent in Korea for 1968.[19] Roughly speaking, therefore, the effective subsidy to exports was about the same in the two countries.

Both countries used a variety of additional export incentives whose value is more difficult to quantify. They include five-year tax holidays granted to foreign firms establishing manufacturing capacity in export-processing zones; accelerated depreciation on the assets of exporters; Korea's occasional cash subsidies to exporters; citations and cash awards given by Taiwan for exceptional expansion of exports and the development of new exports; the generous wastage allowance in Korea, which enabled manufacturers to import duty-free inputs into exportables far in excess of quantities actually re-exported; and the practice of allowing exporters to use all their export earnings for the purchase of imports. Other export incentives included quality control—primarily of export goods by Taiwan's Controls Bureau of Standards—and the overseas representation and information gathering for exporters by such public bodies as consular offices, the foreign branches of the Central Trust of China, the China External Trade Development Council, and the Korean Trade Promotion Corporation.

Over the period 1965–81, Korea's exports, valued in U.S. dollars, rose at an average annual rate of 35 percent, Taiwan's at 27 percent; by 1981, the proportion of the GNP exported had risen to 33.6 percent in Korea, 53.5 percent in Taiwan. Since both countries' exports have a high import content (40 percent in Korea, 58 percent in Taiwan) and also because the great expansion of exports carried with it the whole economy and rising GNP and living standards naturally lead to rising imports, the U.S. dollar value of imports—propelled even further by the rise in oil prices—rose 28.7 percent annually in Korea and 25.6 percent annually in Taiwan to reach 41.3 percent of the GNP in Korea and 52.3 percent in Taiwan by 1981. In short, imports rose more slowly than exports in both countries, enabling Korea to reduce greatly its balance-of-payments deficits and Taiwan to achieve full balance-of-payments equilibrium.

Vulnerability to World Depression

Noting those figures, one cannot help asking whether Taiwan had not overdone—or overachieved—the expansion of its foreign trade. It is natural, of course, for a small country to be more dependent on foreign trade; but even after allowing for its small size, Taiwan is more dependent on foreign trade than Korea and much more so than the average country.[20] Needless to say, there are advantages as well as disadvantages to a country's great involvement in international trade, and I know of no objective standard by which to weigh the benefits of the gain from trade against vulnerability to depression abroad. There are, however, means of reducing that vulnerability without forfeiting the gains from international specialization. One of these is the simple expedient of spreading the risks by diversifying the nature and direction of exports. Taiwan has done very well in that respect, having reduced the commodity concentration of its exports from 56 percent in 1955 to 23 percent in 1975 and their geographical concentration from 60 percent to 41 percent.[21] Korea has done almost as well, with the commodity concentration of exports at 26 percent in 1975 and their geographical concentration at 40.8 percent.[22]

The other way of reducing a country's exposure to depression abroad without losing the gains from trade is to combine an open-door policy to international trade with a limit on international capital movements. That was attempted by Korea in the 1970s, apparently with success. Most Western European countries also rebelled against having their investment activity—and with it their growth, employment, and income levels—restricted by America's restrictive high interest-rate policy of the 1970s and 1980s, but they were impotent because the openness of their capital markets prevented their pursuing an independent and less-restrictive monetary policy. Exchange control, however, enabled Korea to sustain its economy with the aid of relatively low interest rates without risking an outflow of capital. Indeed, Korea managed to engineer an inflow of capital while maintaining domestic interest rates below their U.S. level by subsidizing foreign borrowing through the payment of the differential between low domestic and high foreign interest rates. Taiwan (which also has exchange control) had no such problems because it no longer relies on capital inflows and because its persistently high interest rates still go hand-in-hand with even higher profit rates.

The Gain from Trade and Distribution

The practical and most striking evidence of the gain from trade is the universal success of the policy of export promotion. In a more narrow, strictly static, but also more rigorous sense, the gain from trading a given commodity can be expressed in dollar terms, and the measure of that gain is proportional to the difference between its prices in the importing and the exporting country before trade takes place. The gain is divided between producers, consumers, and the intermediaries between them, in proportions that depend on what the price elasticities of demand and supply are and on how trade affects the price of the commodity in the exporting and importing country.

When the exporter is a small country and the importing country or countries are large or numerous, trade has little impact on prices in the importing country, which means that the consumers' share in the gain becomes negligible and most of it is divided between producers and traders. The exporting country's share in the gain therefore depends on the nationality and domicile of the traders.

The professional literature has largely ignored or neglected the middleman, so we know very little about him and about his share in the gains from trade. Yet his role is crucial. After all, he discovers the difference in price between potential export and import markets and ascertains the scope for profitable trade. He makes potential exporters and importers aware of the gain possible from trade; establishes the contact; and makes all the necessary arrangements rendered difficult by lack of personal contact, distance, difficult communications, and often a language barrier as well. When the manufacturing firm is small, those arrangements also include the provision of financing, the procurement of inputs, arranging for transportation, insurance, and dealing with customs (or the remission of customs' duties). Middlemen also keep abreast of changing prices and market conditions abroad and, by switching trade in response to them, protect domestic exporters or importers. Those services require imagination, initiative, knowledge, experience, contacts, and familiarity with local conditions in many countries; and all that, being of value, has to be remunerated accordingly. No wonder that the firms rendering those services are often important beneficiaries of international trade and specialization.

In the eighteenth and nineteenth centuries, when Britain was the world's main supplier of manufactures, it was Britain's wholesale merchants, not its manufacturers, who attained great wealth and power and even gave their name to the period: merchant capitalism. More recently, Japan's great economic growth and export expansion is, to a large extent, credited to its general trading companies (sogo shoshas); it is they, much more than Japan's manufacturers, that attained great size, wealth, and power in the process. Between 1960 and 1973, Japan's ten largest general trading companies handled half (49.9 percent) of its exports and almost two-thirds (62.8 percent) of its imports. By that time, however, their role in Japan's foreign trade was very much on the decline because the large manufacturing firms, such as those in the automobile and electronic industries, increasingly do their own export marketing and also engage in import trade, often even beyond the importing of their own imported inputs.[23] As a result of their gradual displacement by large manufacturers in the foreign trade of their own country, the Japanese sogo shoshas are increasingly involved in international trade between third countries.

Taiwan and Korea are prominent among those third countries, but Japanese general trading companies are not the only foreigners to handle their foreign trade. In Taiwan, Japanese companies are believed to have handled about 60 percent of textile exports, but from the late 1960s onward, they were joined—and to some extent supplanted—by U.S. and European importers, who set up offices in Taipei and dealt directly with local manufacturers, including many small ones. In addition, as one analyst notes, "If the manufacturer in Taiwan was a subsidiary of a foreign company, the parent company would generally provide the marketing service. This was true, for example, of many of the electronic companies that would both have their main components supplied by the parent and return the processed and assembled goods to that parent."[24]

Unfortunately, no estimates seem to be available of the total involvement of foreign traders in Taiwan's foreign trade, nor of the money value of their services, but it is worth noting that the total contribution of domestic wholesale and retail traders to Taiwan's GNP has gradually but steadily declined, from 17 or 18 percent in the mid-1950s to 12 or 13 percent by around 1980. Since that proportion tends to be fairly stable in most countries, its secular decline in Taiwan may well be due to the secular increase of foreign trade, which crowds out domestic trade to some extent and itself makes no contribution to Taiwan's GNP when foreign companies handle it.

Korea's experience seems to have been different. Japanese general trading companies are said to have been very important in initiating, financing, and arranging Korea's foreign trade in the 1960s: according to an official of one of them (Mitsui), they probably handled about half of Korea's exports. Perhaps for that reason, the Korean government made great efforts to promote the establishment and growth of Korean general trading companies. To engage in importing and exporting required a license, the granting of which depended on the applicant's exports exceeding a progressively higher minimum value. That requirement practically forced Korean trading companies to grow rapidly, and it led to mergers when other means of growth failed. As a result, Korea now has ten very large general trading companies, each with many dozens of offices in foreign centers the world over, and most of them have controlling interests not only in the shipping, insurance, and banking companies that handle the ancillary services of foreign trade, but often also in the firms that manufacture the exports themselves, including steel mills, shipyards, construction companies, the largest automobile factory—in short, most of Korea's large manufacturing plants.

Moreover, Korea's general trading companies, in contrast to Japanese *shoshas*, are heavily involved in exercising quality control and the general supervision of the manufacturing process in the smaller and less reliable Korean manufacturing firms. They are in the habit of ferreting out profitable export opportunities, finding the Korean firms with appropriate manufacturing capabilities, and taking the initiative in persuading and helping those firms to seize hold of such export opportunities. Also, since many of the Korean trading companies control or are closely linked with large construction firms, they are often as ready to build and equip an entire manufacturing plant on a turnkey contract as they are to deliver the products of such a plant. In short, the general trading companies of Korea, again unlike their more specialized Japanese counterparts, are engaged and willing to engage in the export of such a tremendous range of goods and services that they are a powerful force for diversifying the nature and so stabilizing the volume of the country's exports.

Statistics of the value added by Korean general trading companies do not seem to be available, but national accounts show that the total contribution of wholesale and retail trade to the GDP has risen from the second half of the 1950s to the end of the 1970s by more than 5 percentage points: from an average of 11.2 percent to an average of 16.5 percent of the GDP. There is no way of knowing what part of that substantial increase reflects the transfer of export and import business from foreign to Korean trading companies and what part is due to other factors. The subject merits further study, but available information strongly suggests that Korea managed to capture for itself a good share of the gain from its foreign trade. Taiwan has also tried to encourage the establishment and growth of indigenous general trading companies, but with poor success. In 1981, her five largest trading companies transacted a mere one percent of the country's exports and barely 0.25 percent of its total imports.

Overall Growth

So far, export promotion and its successful outcome, export expansion, have been dealt with; how and why expanding exports brought about an additional expansion of the two countries' economies remains to be seen. It is true that the value of exports had risen to equal half of Taiwan's and a third of Korea's GNP, but those figures refer to gross exports, a large part of which constitutes the re-export of imported inputs. When one subtracts imported inputs from gross exports, one obtains the value of net exports, which turns out to be approximately one-fifth of the GNP in each country. The remaining four-fifths of GNP was destined for domestic use, and the question is how and why that much larger part of total output also grew at such an unprecedented rate.

Growth means increased production, due partly to a growing labor force or its increased utilization, partly to the increased productivity of labor. The latter is a more important source of growth because it is the main basis of the rise in the standard of living. Employment was growing in both countries about twice as fast as population, at an annual rate of 5 percent in Taiwan, 3.4 percent in Korea. Labor productivity was growing at an annual rate of 4.2 percent in Taiwan and 5.1 percent in Korea. Their combined effect on the real GDP was an average annual growth of 9.4 percent in Taiwan and 8.6 percent in Korea, or, on a per capita basis, 6.9 percent in Taiwan and 6.7 percent in Korea (table 4.1).

Exports increase productivity because the gain from trade means that labor engaged in producing exports enables the country to obtain in exchange more and better imports than if the same labor were engaged in producing at home the goods now imported. Accordingly, a parallel expansion of exports and imports increases labor productivity in the general sense of increasing the quantity and quality of goods and services obtained per unit of labor. Labor productivity, however, has also been increasing in the narrower engineering and technical sense, and there were at least two ways in which export expansion stimulated the rise in labor productivity in that sense too.

First of all, export expansion called for large investments in additional productive capacity in the export industries, which made it possible to reap economies of scale by putting into practice all the new techniques, economical methods of production, and better quality control that the export manufacturers learned from their foreign competitors. That benefited not only exports but the domestic consumers of exports as well.

Second, the new techniques, approaches, and habits of thought adopted by the export industries were easy to transfer to other industries and economic sectors as soon as their needs for additional productive capacity and investment provided an opportunity to do so. That opportunity was also provided by the expansion of exports because it greatly increased effective demand for domestic output. The booming export industries increased their own demand for intermediate inputs produced by other industries, and the great increase in the income they generated and paid out to their employees, owners, and stockholders increased consumers' demand as well. The increase in consumers' demand was especially great owing to the labor-intensive nature of the export industries.

The same high labor intensity of Taiwan's and Korea's rapidly expanding exports also accounts for the two countries' very low and secularly declining unemployment rates—a unique accomplishment among developing countries. Korea, with unemployment rates around 3 to 4 percent, did less well in that respect than Taiwan, where unemployment fell to 2 percent and lower, perhaps because of Korea's switch to more capital-intensive industries in the 1970s.

The expansion of the two countries' labor-intensive export industries until the 1970s and Taiwan's since then had yet another benefit: it increased the earnings of labor and so improved the distribution of income. In Taiwan the statistics show a shift of income from capital to labor among nonfarm households and a consequent reduction of inequalities in the overall distribution of income between 1964 and 1978, the period for which the requisite statistics have been collected. In Korea, too, inequalities of income declined from 1965 to 1970 but increased slightly thereafter—probably partly as the result of the switch to capital-intensive industries already mentioned, and partly of the greatly increased inequalities in the distribution of property income, which was closely connected with that changeover.

Equitable income distribution favored the expansion of effective demand and tended to concentrate it on domestically produced goods. The increase in domestic demand for domestic goods in turn called for investment, which not only created additional productive capacity and employment opportunities but by providing an opportunity for innovation and modernization led to increasing labor productivity as well.

Investment

The average proportion of the GNP devoted to gross domestic capital formation in Taiwan was—at 28.4 percent—only a little higher than Korea's 26.5 percent, but it may have been considerably more conducive to increasing productivity and productive capacity. Industrialization in Korea was accompanied by a mass migration from rural to urban areas, causing the urban population as a share of the total population to rise from 24 percent in 1955 to 48 percent in 1975. To accommodate such mass migration required much investment in new housing, new schools, new shopping facilities, and other infrastructure, which did not add to productivity and productive capacity. Taiwan was much more fortunate in that respect: although its manufacturing sector grew faster than Korea's during the same period, the migration into the cities added only 75 percent to their share in the total population,[25] because new firms and industries, attracted by lower rural wages, increasingly settled in rural areas. The proportion of workers employed in manufacturing who lived in rural areas as part of farm households and commuted daily on a seasonal or full-time basis grew steadily and constituted over half of the work force by the mid-1960s. That must have meant substantial savings in housing and infrastructure investment. Over the sixteen-year period, government investment—which is largely infrastucture—absorbed only 11.7 percent and residential construction only 10.4 percent of gross investment in Taiwan as against 14.2 percent and 13.4 percent in Korea,[26] leaving a substantially larger part of Taiwan's investable resources for public and private enterprises to invest in productive capacity.

As already mentioned, Korea also tried, through the offer of tax incentives, to induce manufacturing enterprises to settle in rural areas, but was more successful with employers than with their employees. Members of farm households, rather than staying at home and commuting to nonfarm jobs, migrated to the cities in much larger numbers than in Taiwan (see above).

Sources of Investment Funds

The directions into which investable funds were channeled in the two countries are best explained in a discussion of the way in which funds became available. Taiwan financed its entire gross domestic capital formation from 1965 to 1981 out of domestic savings; as a matter of fact, its domestic savings rate, which averaged 28.7 percent of the GNP, marginally exceeded the investment rate of 28.4 percent and even allowed for a small export of capital. Korea, on the other hand, financed less than two-thirds of its 26.5 percent average investment out of a domestic savings rate that averaged only 18.6 percent; the remainder was financed by capital imports, of which a third was aid, not quite two-thirds loans, and a negligible proportion foreign direct investment.[27]

Why was domestic savings in Korea so much lower than in Taiwan? Depreciation allowances in Korea, at 7.3 percent of the GNP, were marginally higher than Taiwan's 7.2 percent, and so was government savings: 5.8 percent in Korea as against 5.6 percent in Taiwan. On the other hand, net corporate savings of 2.3 percent in Korea was much lower than Taiwan's 4 percent, and the discrepancy was even greater between the personal savings rate of households: 5.4 percent in Korea and 12.1 percent in Taiwan.

The lower savings rate of Korean corporations seems to be largely explained by the informal pressure government put on firms to pay high dividends in an attempt to develop the stock market, and by the similarly motivated Korean system of taxes that rendered shareholders liable for income tax not only on dividends but also on half of the retained earnings of the corporations in which they held stock.[28] Corporate retained earnings, which averaged 75 percent of after-tax profits in the first four years of the 1960s, went down to an average of 56 percent of profits in the 1970s, presumably as a result of those pressures and policies, and that change explains most of the discrepancy between Korea's and Taiwan's corporate savings rate.[29]

In sum, low corporate savings in Korea seems to be the direct result of government's attempt to encourage personal savings by providing and rendering attractive yet another asset, corporate stocks, into which the individual saver can put his earnings. The attempt, however, was unsuccessful. To judge by the value of stocks issued and its relation to GNP, Korea's stock market is even more insignificant as a source of funds than Taiwan's; moreover, household saving, as already noted, is also much lower in Korea.

Household Savings

It is customary to express the rate of household savings as a percentage, not of the GNP, but of consumers' disposable income. The personal savings rate so expressed averaged 7.6 percent in Korea, 17.6 percent in Taiwan. That difference is tremendous; but surprisingly enough, no one seems to have tried to explain it. The voluminous literature on Korea's economic performance is full of discussions and explanations of why Korea's savings rate has been so very high in recent years; there is no word anywhere to explain why it has been so low—yet low it seems when contrasted to the savings rate of Taiwan. Similarly, one will look in vain for an explanation of Taiwan's very high savings rate. The closest one comes are the various explanations offered to account for Japan's comparably high personal savings rate, but they turn out not to be very helpful in explaining the great discrepancy between Taiwan's and Korea's personal savings rates.

According to the standard American theoretical explanation, the so-called life-cycle hypothesis, saving is generated by the growth of population and the rise in the standard of living, and net positive savings is proportional to their combined growth rates. The latter is half a percentage point higher in Taiwan than in Korea, which would explain approximately 1.5 percentage points of the 10 percentage point discrepancy between the two countries' personal savings rates.[30] The theory, then, does not account completely for the difference.

There are more down-to-earth explanations in Japan of the Japanese situation. The two simplest and most often advanced explanations are insufficiency of social security benefits, which forces people to save more for their old age, and the limited availability of consumer credit and mortgage loans, which renders it difficult for people without accumulated savings to dissave. The two arguments apply to Taiwan and to Korea as much as they apply to Japan. However, since they apply equally to both countries, they cannot very well explain why their savings rates are so different.[31] Equally inadequate is another explanation of Japan's high savings rate: the high proportion of older income earners in the population, who, according to the statistics, save a larger percentage of their earnings than others with the same income. But the age distribution of the employed population is almost identical in Korea and Taiwan, so this factor cannot account for the discrepancy between their savings rates either.

Yet another often-cited explanation of Japan's high savings rate is the high proportion of individual proprietorships (unincorporated enterprises) among households. The national account statistics do not separate the savings of unincorporated enterprises from those of wage and salary earners, and since the former's savings rate is believed to be quite a bit higher than the latter's, a high proportion of small businessmen among households would explain a high overall household savings rate.

In that respect, there is a difference between Korea and Taiwan. The average Korean manufacturer with more than four employees[32] employs sixty-nine people on average as compared to thirty-five in Taiwan, which implies that the number of independent manufacturing establishments in Taiwan is twice as large as it would be if their average size equaled that of Korean establishments. Accordingly, if Taiwan resembled Korea in that respect, it would have only 35,000 independent manufacturing firms instead of the 70,000 it actually has. Thirty-five thousand extra individual proprietorships seem like a large number, but they represent hardly more than 1 percent of Taiwan's 3 million households. Such a small difference in the proportion of households headed by parsimonious businessmen instead of spendthrift employees undoubtedly explains a part, but probably only a small part, of the very great difference between their overall savings rate.[33] It should also be noted that the difference between Taiwan and Korea in the proportion of businessmen households in other sectors of the economy is much smaller (e.g., in retailing) or even goes the other way around, such as in farming.

Many consider the most important explanation of Japan's high personal savings rate to be the high proportion of temporary income, because people tend to save a higher percentage of temporary than of permanent income. In Japan, half-yearly bonus payments are an important part of total wage and salary payments; they have been steadily increasing in relative importance over the years, and by now often amount to one-third of the annual wage or salary.

Taiwan and Korea share Japan's bonus-wage system for nonagricultural industries, although their bonus payments are much smaller. The two semiannual payments together average only two months' wages (or 14.2 percent) of the total annual wage. Those averages are very similar in the two countries, and at least in Taiwan, where annual data are available since 1972, show only a very small upward trend. Nonfarm employment, however, has increased relative to farm employment in both countries—and more so in Taiwan, where it now comprises 72 percent of the labor force, as compared to only 66 percent in Korea. That may account for a part of the difference between the two countries' savings rates, but probably only for a very small part. For the rest, other, less conventional explanations must be sought.

One of these may be the very high expenditure of Korean parents on their children's education, explained partly by the inadequacy of public expenditure on education, which is provided free only up to junior high school. As a proportion of household income, private expenditures on education averaged 7 percent in Korea, almost as much as the personal savings rate and more than four times the U.S. percentage. Unfortunately, comparable data seem to be unavailable in Taiwan, but there private expenditure on education is probably much lower.[34]

Another simple explanation of the difference in savings rates is that Koreans, being poorer, cannot afford to save as much as the more affluent Taiwanese. That sounds all the more plausible when one considers that the averages of the two previously quoted savings rates hide a fairly steady secular increase from about 12 percent to about 21 percent in Taiwan, which closely parallels the country's increasing affluence, and a somewhat faster but very irregular increase in Korea, with great ups and downs between a low 0.2 percent and a high 15 percent annual savings rate.

Plausible as it sounds, the explanation is distrusted by most economists because they believe that saving is mainly motivated by the need to take care of one's old age, a need just as strong among the poor as it is among the rich, and they can point to the complete lack of evidence of any correlation between savings rates and affluence in the industrial countries, where savings statistics are most reliable.

That argument, however, together with the statistical evidence, pertains to modern capitalist societies, in which mature persons are held responsible for their own welfare, both in the present and in their future old age. That was not always so, because in most primitive societies the children (eldest sons according to the Confucian ethic) took care of their parents in their old age. Accordingly, when economic development goes hand in hand with social change and the move from extended to nuclear families, it is bound to necessitate personal saving and so to raise the personal savings rate.

Such change, however, does not happen from one year to another, but is bound to be a very slow, gradual process, for two reasons. To begin with, all change in established social institutions and deeply ingrained habits is a very slow progression, initiated by the most innovating and enterprising classes and spreading slowly through different social layers toward the more tradition-bound. Further, to be able to afford to save up for one's old age, one must be either well-to-do or free from traditional financial obligations toward parents and older or disabled relatives.

In other words, causality runs both ways: personal savings free people from having to rely on their children's or relatives' support in their old age, but they themselves must also be free from old parents and relatives or the obligation to support them in order to be able to afford saving up for their own old age. That circular relationship makes it very hard to break out of the age-old tradition that views the extended family as the economic and social unit and imposes on its working members a moral obligation to support all other members who are too young, too old, or too decrepit to earn their living. Accordingly, it requires especially favorable circumstances to initiate and sustain the move from the extended to the nuclear family and the displacement of sons and relatives by accumulated savings as the source of old people's livelihood. Affluence is one such circumstance; institutions that render saving easy, safe, and attractive are another.

That brings us to the second unconventional explanation of high personal savings: high real rates of interest on savings deposits. This again is an explanation that seems to be simple common sense to the layman but is distrusted by the economist. Again, the distrust is based partly on the lack of empirical evidence of correlation between interest rates and savings rates and partly on the theoretical idea that if survival in retirement were the main purpose of people's saving, then higher interest rates would lead to less saving because the higher the interest, the less needs to be saved in order to secure a given sum or annuity for the future.

The fault with that reasoning is once again that it is anchored in the narrow institutional framework of modern capitalist society, which looks upon saving more and saving less as the only alternative ways available in which to provide for one's retirement. In countries like Taiwan and Korea, however, which are in the course of social and economic transformation, the individual's choice is the much broader one between relying on family and relying on accumulated savings as the proper means of taking care of old age, and a higher real rate of return on savings is bound to influence that choice in favor of saving.

As early as 1950, Taiwan introduced a monetary policy whose key feature was enticingly high real rates of interest on savings deposits. Taiwan stuck to that policy consistently for over thirty years, with only a single short lapse in 1974. The steady, sevenfold rise of the personal saving rate in Taiwan, from 3 percent of the disposable income in 1952 to 21 percent in 1980, may well have been due largely to the continued attractiveness of savings deposits as a means of assuring an independent and comfortable old age.

Korea adopted the same monetary policy fifteen years later in 1965, but because it was hard to reconcile with governmental control over private investment through concessionary loans, which the Korean government was anxious to retain, the monetary policy of 1965 was gradually eroded over the next six years and came to an end by 1971. From then onward, the real rate of interest on savings deposits fluctuated wildly, alternating between positive levels (in 1973 and 1977–78) and negative levels (1974–75 and 1980–81), hovering near zero in between (1972, 1976, and 1979).[35] That was hardly an inducement for the average Korean to abandon his traditional reliance on family and children in favor of the modern way of taking care of his old age through personal savings.

What could be the main explanation of the great difference between the two countries' personal savings rates has been left to the end, partly because its statistical verification is ruled out by its very nature: the need for personal savings in order to make oneself independent by starting a business. This is related to, but somewhat different from, the high propensity to save of already established businessmen; here the concern is with the savings of those who wish to become businessmen.

People start businesses not only to get a high return on savings but also and perhaps mainly because they prefer being their own bosses; standing on their own feet; and proving their ability by putting to good use their wits, skills, intuition, and knowledge of the world and people. In short, running one's own business is also a game of skill and chance, played for high stakes, and self-satisfying quite apart from the expectation of monetary gain. If that assessment of the independent businessman's motivations is correct, then he will regard his business not only as a good repository for savings, but also as a good reason to save— and to save more than if he had no business to put his savings into.

That motive for saving differs greatly between Taiwan and Korea. As mentioned, Taiwan's manufacturing sector grew primarily as a result of the fast growth in the number of its manufacturing companies. Between 1966 and 1976, 41,808 new manufacturing enterprises were created, adding more than 150 percent to the number of such enterprises (27,709) already in existence in 1966. That is an average annual increase of 9.6 percent, which is more than one-half as great as the 17.8 percent annual increase in total manufacturing production. That is very different from what happened in Korea, where manufacturing production over the same period increased at an average annual rate of 22.7 percent, but the number of manufacturing companies rose only 0.9 percent.[36]

The explanation for that striking difference between the two countries' ways of growing is simple. In Taiwan, the small size of the average firm and the large number of small firms must have made it feasible for newcomers to establish themselves on a modest scale with small initial investments. In Korea, the prevalence of much larger firms must have discouraged newcomers, especially due to the practice of granting loans on concessionary terms to already established firms, a practice that discriminated in favor of growth through increasing the size (rather than increasing the number) of firms. Accordingly, Taiwanese-style growth kept business firms small and encouraged personal saving by the newly entering or about-to-enter small businessmen; Korean-style growth discouraged new entrants and their saving, and made it easy for established firms to grow without generating their own savings.

The differences between the two countries' very different ways of expanding their manufacturing capacity and output also appears in the statistics. Capital formation financed by bank loans and by bonds issued and sold in financial markets shows up as an increase in indebtedness; the statistics reveal no increase in indebtedness when capital formation is financed by the issuing of stock, out of a firm's own undistributed savings, out of the personal savings of someone starting his own firm, or out of what he borrows in the unorganized capital market. The most widely used index of indebtedness is the debt ratio: the sum of fixed and current liabilities expressed as a percentage of the firm's net worth, reproduced in figure 4.1 for Korea, Taiwan, and the United States. The very low indebtedness of American manufacturing firms is easily explained by the importance of the New York stock market as a source of funds for investment. The stock market is unimportant in Korea and Taiwan, but Taiwanese firms are half as heavily indebted as Koreans, presumably because more than half of their new industrial capacity consists of small firms newly established by individual proprietors and financed by personal savings, supplemented when necessary by loans from friends and from the unorganized credit market.

To sum up the arguments of this long section, the much greater importance of household saving in Taiwan has a number of probable explanations. The slightly faster growth of Taiwan's GNP; the slightly faster increase in the proportion of its labor force receiving part of its income in the form of bonuses; people's lesser spending and need to spend on education; the greater proportion of people saving up to establish independent businesses; the greater number of businessmen saving up to enlarge their already established independent businesses; and people's greater willingness to save up for their old age, due partly to their greater affluence and partly to the more secure and higher returns on their accumulated savings.

The above arguments were phrased as explanations of Taiwan's high personal savings rate, but several of them could easily be reworded as explanations of Korea's low personal savings rate.

Figure 4.1   Debt Ratios in Manufacturing: Sum of Fixed and Current
Liabilities as Percentage of Net Worth

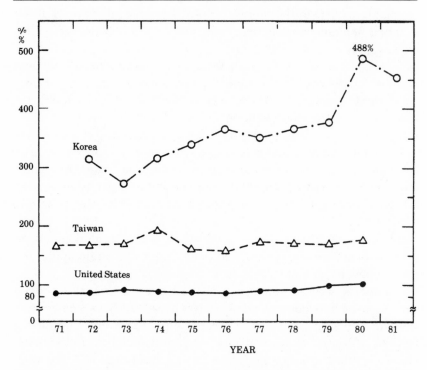

Source: Bank of Korea, *Financial Statements Analysis for 1981* (Seoul: Bank of Korea, 1982),
pp. 74, 97, 492, and 530.

Taiwan's savings rate is the exceptional one, being the second highest
(after Japan's) in the Free World; on the other hand, Korea would need
a much higher personal savings rate in order to continue its high
growth rate in the 1980s, with much less accommodating international
financial markets.

Forced Investment and Growth in Korea

It seemed standard for Korean development planners always to project,
aim for, and actively encourage more investment than seemed feasible
on the basis of expected domestic saving and expected foreign capital
inflows. The hope was that the economy would somehow accommodate itself to those overambitious plans, and the hope was usually

fulfilled—very often overfulfilled. In short, the policy worked. It is essential, however, to understand exactly how and why it worked if one wants to understand the causes of Korea's chronic inflation, its disappointing domestic savings rate, and its continued dependence on foreign capital.

Once a Five-Year Plan, or its revision, had been agreed upon and established, the Korean government encouraged investment in the desired sectors and industries by every available means, including the offer of tax concessions, credit on specially favored terms and at especially low interest rates, and a lot of informal pressure. If the inducements set in motion a sufficient volume of investment to conform with (or even exceed) the overambitious investment plans, an excess of effective demand over the available supply was the consequence. In such disequilibrium situations, something has to give in order to restore equality between supply and demand. Three things helped to restore equilibrium, mostly by raising supply, not by restricting demand: an increase in domestic supply, an additional inflow of foreign capital, and a worsening balance of payments.

Domestic supply can respond to the increase in demand through the increased utilization of existing plant capacity. That seems to have been an important source of additional supply in Korea. Statistics of capacity utilization are unavailable, but a study based on electricity use shows that the utilization rate almost doubled between 1962 and 1971, increasing at an average annual rate of 7.2 percent.[37] Unfortunately, those estimates do not go beyond 1971, but to judge by the statistics on hours worked in industry, capacity utilization seems to have continued to increase. Korea not only has the world's longest working week,[38] but is unique also in that the length of its working week increased substantially over time, while the working week has become shorter just about everywhere else. The utilization of plant capacity is very likely to have risen parallel to the lengthening of the working week (figure 4.2).

The inflow of foreign capital can also rise more than was originally anticipated and finance an additional inflow of imports to meet the excess demand. Part of that excess demand is generated by the increase in capacity utilization, which increases the need for inputs, including imported inputs. Indeed, balance-of-payments difficulties are the main reason for the underutilization of existing capacity in most developing countries. In Korea, however, the successful export drive not only relieved the foreign exchange shortages, but increased the country's credit standing as well, removing an obstacle to better capacity utiliza-

Figure 4.2   Average Weekly Hours Worked

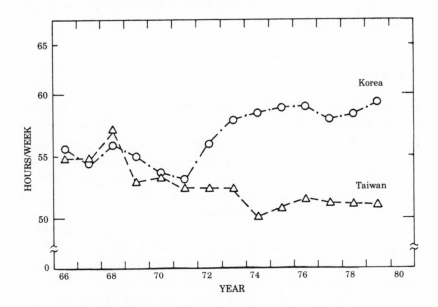

tion. In addition, the special inducements, such as tax concessions offered to investors, probably increased foreign investment.

Finally, to the extent that those two sources of additional supply were insufficient, as they usually were to fill the excess demand, the pressure of the remaining excess demand raised domestic prices and, by worsening the balance of payments and so raising the price of foreign exchange, raised import prices as well. Those price increases diverted resources from consumption to investment,[39] and those who allowed price increases to reduce the real value of their purchase to below what they had originally hoped and planned for found themselves "involuntarily financing" some of the investment in addition to the investment financed out of voluntary saving and foreign lending.

That, in a nutshell, summarizes how an aggressive economic policy causes the economy to perform beyond its apparent capacity and accommodate the excessive demand made upon it by an overambitious investment plan. Considering that in Korea the policy worked, and the overambitious projections of investment and growth were not only fulfilled but consistently overfulfilled, one is tempted to applaud that policy of forced growth. That may well be the final verdict, but the short summary just given throws more light on the sunny than on the shady side of the picture. For an objective appraisal, one must also weigh all the undesirable side effects and long-run repercussions of the excessive encouragement of investment and of the consequent inflation.

Korean Inflation

Inflation in such a case makes a positive contribution to growth because it forces the public to reduce its real purchases and so release resources needed for investment. That forced reduction of people's real purchases is best called involuntary financing or forced financing, thereby avoiding the once fashionable but misleading "forced saving." For the term "saving" conveys the idea of the saver setting aside something valuable for future use, but those whom inflation forces to reduce their real purchases have nothing to show for their sacrifice, no savings they could add to their store of assets and spend at a later date, although they involuntarily financed an investment that benefits society by improving or adding to future productive capacity. Indeed, the social injustice of the inflationary financing of investment, which causes benefits to accrue to someone other than those whose sacrifice financed it, is one of the objections to that policy.

In addition to the social injustice of inflationary financing, another injustice created by inflation is the reduction of the real value of debt for both debtor and creditor, which in effect redistributes real wealth from creditor to debtor—an injustice not without advantages. Another bad effect already mentioned was the very low, often negative, real rate of interest on savings deposits brought about by inflation. That greatly reduced the attractiveness of bank deposits, and if it is true that Korea is now in mid-transition from a traditional to a modern society, then the absence of an attractive and reliable repository for personal savings may well be the main reason for the slowness with which the habit is taking root and spreading in Korea.

The low domestic savings rate was an important reason both for Korea's extensive foreign borrowing and for its inflationary policies; the resulting inflation, in its turn, must have been an important reason that the savings rate failed to rise faster and farther than it did. In short, the policy of supplementing an inadequate supply of investable funds with inflation-induced involuntary financing created a vicious circle, because it perpetuated the situation (the low domestic saving rate) that originally had called for inflationary policies.

The well-tried and well-proven remedy of preventing the fall in real rates by raising money rates of interest in step with the inflation rate was close at hand and occasionally adopted, but since that amounted, in effect, to abandoning the whole policy of fast growth through forced capital accumulation, it was never kept very long. That alternation of inflationary with restrictive policies explains the great fluctuations in both the inflation rate and the real rate of interest, which, as mentioned earlier, may have been the root cause of the inadequacy of domestic saving.

Another undesirable effect of low and negative real rates of interest can be their supposed tendency to divert the savings of those with already well-established saving habits from more to less constructive uses. In Korea, however, that was probably not too important. The export of domestic savings (illegal in Korea) would be the most obvious form of such diversion; it is believed to have been negligible. Another channel into which savings can be diverted is real estate, whose fast rising values throughout this period must have rendered land and housing an attractive inflation hedge. Remember, however, that one person's spending is another person's receipt, so savings are misused only if real-estate speculation leads to excessive investment in residential construction. Investment in housing was much greater in Korea than in Taiwan, but so was the need for housing; it is very difficult therefore to assess the extent (if any) to which housing construction was excessive and prompted by people's desire for an inflation-proof repository for their savings.

Better known than the above, owing to the great political scandals connected with it, was the rechanneling of funds from banks into the unorganized credit market. Yet such rechanneling of funds seldom if ever constitutes a diversion of savings from more to less productive investment, although it can be a symptom of inefficient credit allocation in the organized credit market. That was the situation in Korea, where unduly low interest rates on bank deposits and bank loans swelled both the supply and demand for funds in the unorganized market. The reason for excessive supply is obvious. Excessive demand is created by cheap bank loans. They must be rationed, and such rationing inevitably leads to the accommodation of some projects with low rates of return that crowd out some others with high profitability and forces them into the unorganized market. That is why a large unorganized market can be a sign of inefficiency in the organized market's allocation of investable funds.

It is desirable, of course, that every deserving project crowded out of organized markets by their inefficiency should be accommodated by the unorganized market, but to serve as a safety valve and relieve the inefficiency perpetrated by the organized markets is not the only useful function of the curb market. Its other equally useful function is to supplement the work of the organized credit market by providing small loans to small businessmen who are creditworthy but whose creditworthiness would be prohibitively expensive for large banks to investigate. Judgments of creditworthiness based on long-term personal contacts among relatives, friends, neighbors, and between small businessmen and equally small lenders or credit brokers who live nearby can be better than those based on expensive investigation into the credit standing of an unknown applicant by a bank's loan officer. As a retailer of small loans, the unorganized market operates more efficiently and more cheaply than the small-loans window of the most efficient large bank.[40]

Once one becomes aware of the distinction between those two functions of the curb market, one also realizes that the size of the curb market cannot, by itself, indicate the inefficiency of credit allocation in the organized credit market. Only the size of the safety-valve function of the curb market could serve as such an indicator, and almost nothing is known about the relative importance of the safety-valve function and the small-loans function of Korea's curb market.

Informed guesses put the share of Korea's curb market at 40 percent of the total volume of loans processed by the entire financial system. In Taiwan, where the Central Bank publishes annual estimates of the corresponding percentages, they have fallen from 41 percent in 1965 to 21 percent in 1972 and had risen again to 33 percent by 1979–80. The curb market is not much more important in Korea than it is in Taiwan. The function of the curb market, however, is likely to be quite different in the two countries, with the safety-valve function predominating in Korea and the small-loans function predominating in Taiwan. There are three reasons for that assumption. First, in Korea there is direct and striking evidence of the inefficient rationing of bank loans, which implies a corresponding need for curb-market loans as a safety valve. Export producers in Korea had automatic access, at a concessionary 6 percent per annum interest cost, to loans much above their needs, a part of which they were able to re-lend in the curb market at an interest of 24 to 30 percent per annum, giving export producers a subsidy amounting to 4.5 percent of the value of their exports.[41]

Second, since Taiwan has many more small firms than Korea, the small-loans function of its curb market is bound to be commensurately more important than the small-loans function of Korea's curb market.

Finally, the difference seems to be reflected also by the very different attitude officials in the two countries have to their respective curb markets. While in Korea the authorities are making efforts to starve the unorganized market of funds by attracting them into the banking system, in Taiwan their much more matter-of-fact attitude seems to imply recognition of the valuable function performed by that sector of the credit market.

The Oil Crisis

Social injustice, discouragement of domestic saving, reduced efficiency in the allocation of credit, and greater need of foreign loans were the main side effects of inflationary finance. For completeness' sake, however, one must add to the list the unfortunate tendency of inflation to engender inflationary expectations and so render inflation harder to contain and the economy more prone to inflation. The oil crises, for example, and the worldwide inflation they created must have had much the same impact on Taiwan and Korea. Their governments, when they fought inflation, fought it in the same way and with the same weapons, but Taiwan, thanks presumably to its greater past stability, accomplished more, faster, and at lower cost.

The first oil-price increase led within a year (1974) to a 40 percent rise in the wholesale price index in both countries. Korea, interested in growth not stability, did nothing about it, allowing prices to rise another 40 percent the next year but managing to step up the growth rate of its real GNP from an annual average of 9 percent in the early 1970s to an average 10.8 percent from 1975 to 1979.[42] Taiwan, putting stability first, raised interest rates and restricted credit; while that slowed the growth of real GNP to 1.1 percent in 1974, it not only eliminated inflation but by 1975 rolled prices back by 5 percent. From then on, Taiwan managed to keep inflation within reasonable limits while maintaining a 9.6 percent annual rate of real GNP growth between 1975 and 1981.

The second oil-price increase, coming on top of an already inflationary situation created by devaluation and the investment policy of the late 1970s (see below), again raised Korea's inflation rate to almost 40 percent by 1979, but by that time (after President Park's assassination), Korea's new government was as stability-minded as Taiwan's and mounted much the same restrictive policies with which Taiwan responded to the first oil-price increase. Indeed, Korea raised interest rates by 5 percent at the beginning of 1980—a more drastic tightening of the monetary screws than Taiwan's 3.5 interest-rate increase six years earlier. Moreover, investment in Korea was drastically cut down by other means (for reasons to be explained), while Taiwan kept total investment up through an accelerated program of infrastructure investment. That is why real growth in Korea not only slowed, as in Taiwan, but became negative: GNP fell by 6.2 percent in 1980 and the unemployment rate went up from 3.8 percent to 5.2 percent. Nevertheless, the inflation rate came down only very gradually by Taiwanese (though not by Western) standards, from 20 to 25 percent in 1981 to around 5 percent by 1982. Accordingly, if one measures the inflationary impact of the two oil-price increases on the two countries by the rise in wholesale prices over the two-year period following each oil shock, Korea's 80 and 65 percent increases in price levels clearly testify to a larger impact than Taiwan's 35 and 39 percent price increases.

Changes in the Structure of Manufacturing Output

In the course of development, the structure of manufacturing shifted away from light industries toward heavy industries in both countries, and for much the same reasons (table 4.5). Real wages were rising, causing light industrial products to become less competitive in world markets and to lose out against developing countries whose unskilled labor was cheaper. Moreover, the developed countries became increasingly protectionist, erecting import barriers, in the beginning primarily against textiles and shoes.

In Taiwan, most of the change in the composition of output came about as the result more of businessmen's reactions to changing prices and market conditions than of governmental policies. (Indeed, it is said that government, foreseeing increasing export difficulties at an early stage, advised the textile industry to reduce or abandon investment plans, but the industry ignored the advice and went ahead expanding capacity anyway.) Exceptions to that rule were the building up of the steel, shipbuilding, and petrochemical industries, all of which are state-owned. Hand in hand with the changing structure of Taiwan's manufactured output has gone a change in the direction of its exports. Taiwan is increasingly exporting to developing countries and, as might be expected, the exports are mainly capital-intensive and skill-intensive manufactured products. It should also be mentioned that at the end of the

Table 4.5 Percentage Composition of Manufactured Output

Year	Korea	Taiwan	Korea	Taiwan
			Nonmetallic mineral products	
	Food, beverages, and tobacco		except petroleum and coal	
1960	19.3	44.5	9.2	7.2
1965	26.5	34.8	6.7	6.5
1971	24.6	20.9	6.0	4.5
1975	21.2	18.8	5.6	4.7
1979	16.5	13.0	5.8	3.9
	Textiles, clothing, and footwear		Basic metal products	
1960	28.6	14.9	2.4	3.1
1965	19.8	15.0	5.0	2.2
1971	17.5	18.0	4.7	2.9
1975	22.0	15.8	4.7	3.5
1979	19.6	15.5	7.9	6.7
			Machinery, equipment,	
	All light industry (including the above)		and fabricated metal products	
1960	70.0	71.2	10.7	8.5
1965	61.8	51.2	11.5	13.3
1971	54.7	50.7	12.2	21.2
1975	51.6	46.7	16.3	23.7
1979	44.7	44.4	24.2	26.0
	Chemicals, petroleum, and coal		All heavy industry (sum of the above)	
1960	7.7	10.1	30.0	28.8
1965	15.0	17.4	38.2	39.8
1971	23.5	20.8	45.3	49.3
1975	21.8	21.3	48.4	53.3
1979	17.4	19.0	55.3	55.6

1970s when the world depression started, investment in manufacturing capacity declined, but total investment and with it employment and the general level of activity continued to rise, thanks to greatly increased public investment in road, railroad, harbor construction, and other infrastructure projects. In Korea, there was a similar shift toward the chemical and heavy industries, but its timing was different. As is apparent from table 4.5, the development of heavy industries lagged behind Taiwan's but caught up with a sudden spurt at the end of the period, and the whole development must be attributed to deliberate government policies. The differential terms of credit and rates of taxes, which the Korean government used for stimulating investment, gave it great power to influence also the direction of investment and it used that power fully. Before investigating how and to what purpose it was used, it is well to remember that government is usually distrusted as the maker of investment decisions and to look at the reasons for such distrust.

Investment decisions must be based on predictions of future needs and availabilities, and politicians and civil servants need be no worse than businessmen at weighing all the information available for making the best predictions. People in government, however, are seldom affected quite so personally and profoundly by the outcome of their investment decisions as are businessmen, who risk the profitability and often even the survival of their businesses and therefore are under greater and more immediate pressure to weigh their investments carefully. Moreover, central planners can too easily overrule and ignore businessmen's dissent, which puts official investment plans in danger of being too monolithic, too narrowly and confidently focused on what seemed best in the planners' judgment, with little or no allowance for mistakes and unforeseen changes in circumstances. By contrast, the sum of the independent investment decisions of many businessmen reflects both differences in judgments and differences in the degree of confidence individuals attach to their judgments, and the outcome of such differences is greater dispersion of investments. It is as if the decisions, based on the majority opinion had been cautiously hedged and insured against unexpected mishaps.

In Korean practice, however, potential dangers inherent in too much central control over investment were avoided most of the time, thanks to exceptionally able and intelligent planning. Only at the end of the 1970s did the Korean government make seriously mistaken investment decisions, which would probably have been avoided under less tight governmental controls.

The initial Korean emphasis on investment in such light industries as food processing, textiles, clothing, and plywood, which were so very successful in expanding exports and providing employment for the unskilled throughout the 1960s, was gradually shifted toward investment in more capital-intensive as well as more skill-intensive products and industries by the end of the decade: steel, chemicals, shipbuilding, construction, electronics, footwear, and a shift in textile manufacturing to sports clothing and other specially and high quality items. The reasoning behind the new investment policy seems to have been the desire to exploit Korea's comparative advantage in skilled labor, to defeat U.S. import restrictions by increasing the domestic value-added content in textile exports, to diversify exports—partly by stepping into the void created by Japan's diminishing competitiveness in some sectors and by the advanced countries' own reduced output of certain products for fear of industrial pollution, and to cater to Korea's own increased domestic demand, including the demand of its export industries for intermediate goods. Finally, defense considerations, prompted by the threatened withdrawal of American forces from Korea, also played a part.

Whatever the motivation, the new investment policy was successful. The fast annual growth (10.2 percent) of real GNP during the initial years (1965–71) of export promotion continued unabated at 10.1 percent during the next six years (1971–77). Exports, which paid for 53 percent of imports in 1965 and 60 percent of them in 1971, had risen fully to equal the value of imports in 1977. That achievement was all the more remarkable in view of the greatly increased price of oil, which Korea must import.

Unfortunately, the gradual and successful shift toward greater capital and skill intensity was suddenly and greatly accelerated in 1977. At the very time when the incipient world depression led cautious businessmen in Taiwan to slow investment in manufacturing capacity, Korea's economic planners also abandoned their original investment plans as set down in the Fourth Five-Year Plan; they revised them upward by crowding into three years (1977–79) 80 percent of the total investment the plan had projected for five years, and concentrating most of it, also against the plan's original intentions, into the heavy industries. As a result, the share of investment in GNP rose from 29.4 percent in 1975 to 36.9 percent in 1977–79, and the combined share of metals, chemicals, intermediate products, machinery, transport equipment, and electronics in total investment rose from 48.2 percent to 78.9 percent.

To bring about so drastic and sudden a change in a private enterprise economy must have required tremendous governmental pressures and inducements, especially since most of that investment went into mammoth projects with productive capacities greatly in excess of domestic requirements at a time when export demand was not much in evidence. Today, with the benefit of hindsight, it is hard to understand what possible reasons could have been behind that investment program, which only led to trouble. For one thing, the great increase in investment activity raised wages and costs, thereby diminishing the competitiveness of Korean exports; for another, the cutting back of projected investments in the light industries created shortages; and the two together largely explain the reemergence, after 1977, of a trade deficit. Finally, all that investment in heavy industry created large new capacities in steel, shipbuilding, chemicals, automobiles, etc., much of which has remained greatly underutilized. The most extreme example of those overambitious investments was the building of a large complex for the manufacture of atomic, thermo, and hydroelectric power generating equipment, equipped with the most up-to-date computer-controlled machinery, having a capacity that is five times estimated domestic requirements, but with a present utilization rate of only 40 percent of that capacity.

Yet much of Korea's new heavy industry is highly competitive, thanks to the combination of modern technology with low labor costs. For example, Korea manages (as does Taiwan) to export steel to Japan, although Japan's own steel capacity is greatly underutilized, and both countries' shipyards are busier and have more orders than most other countries' shipyards. Indeed, the underutilization of manufacturing capacity is a worldwide phenomenon in the present global depression; Korea's problem is that many of its newly built plants seem condemned from the outset to indefinite underutilization.

Korea's New Economic Policy, 1980–81

The mistakes of Korea's investment policy of the late 1970s were fully recognized as such by 1979, and the huge investment program was stopped in its tracks. In addition, a restrictive policy of high interest rates was instituted in January 1980. As a result, real investment, which had been rising uninterrupted for fifteen years, fell in 1980, leading to a reduction in real GNP—the first since the Korean War—and investment remained low in the following year. Inflation, however, continued, given further impetus by the second oil crisis and also by the successive devaluations of 1980 with whose aid the authorities tried to restore the competitiveness of exports. The annual rate of inflation reached almost 40 percent in 1980, and it took two years of restrictive policies to bring it down to around 5 percent.

The sustained application of those restrictive policies and the policies instituted since the inflation has been controlled all suggest that the new Korean regime of President Chun is determined to approach economic problems in a new spirit. The new policies include the offer of high real rates of interest on personal bank deposits, the elimination of the interest-rate differential between ordinary loans and what used to be concessionary loans, the change in character of the latest (and fifth) Five-Year Plan from an obligatory to an indicative plan, and various measures (in addition to the high interest rate on bank deposits) designed to starve the curb market of funds. They all seem to aim at making greater use of market incentives and the allocating function of market prices, and at relying on the organized financial market to stimulate domestic saving and channel funds to where rates of return are the highest. The government has also announced its intention to denationalize the banks as a means of increasing efficiency and cutting down favoritism in the allocation of loans.

Most of those changes bring Korea's approach to economic problems closer to Taiwan's, and they can only be welcomed, although the denationalization of banks may create as many problems as it solves. In view of the economy's very great dependence on bank credit, the sale of the banks to private parties, presumably to the large conglomerates, would substantially and dangerously increase the latter's economic power and may merely substitute their favoritism for governmental favoritism—unless the bank debt of manufacturing businesses is substantially reduced and funded first and Korea's stock and bond markets are developed and expanded much beyond their present state.

Present State and Future Prospects

Until now, the development of most developing countries hinged on their ability to exploit their comparative advantages and capture the gains from international specialization. World depression, however, breeds a spirit of protectionism, which can stifle international specialization; that raises the question how the developing and newly industrializing countries will fare in today's world. Both Korea and Taiwan are poor in natural resources, but rich in the human resources of labor, labor skills, education, and ingenuity. They have no choice but to depend heavily on foreign trade in their further development. Furthermore, Korea has the additional problem of insufficient domestic saving and the need to borrow abroad if it is to continue to grow at a rate anywhere near its past growth rate. The world depression, however, which has brought so many countries to the brink of bankruptcy, is also rendering foreign borrowing more difficult.

The debt problem is easier to discuss and may well be dealt with first. Korea has accumulated an external debt that, as a proportion of the

Table 4.6   The Burden of Foreign Public Debt in 1980

	Debt outstanding as percentage of GNP	Debt service as percentage of export earnings
Korea	28.8	12.2
Taiwan[a]	12.1	4.2
Mexico	20.6	31.9
Brazil	16.4	34.0
All middle-income, oil-importing countries (average)	15.4	11.9

a. Data refer to 1979.

GNP, is not only much higher than Taiwan's, but higher than that of most industrializing countries and even higher than Mexico's (table 4.6). However, thanks to Korea's very high export earnings, its debt-service ratio (interest payments and repayments of principal as a percentage of export earnings) is about average at 12.2 percent and considered to be reasonable. It certainly is much lower than that of Mexico or Brazil. In view of that reasonable debt-service ratio, Korea's ability to borrow has not yet been impaired, but it probably depends crucially on its current and expected future ability to grow and to make exports grow. Therefore, any judgment concerning Korea's growth prospects will also serve as a judgment concerning Korea's prospective ability to borrow for the purpose of financing such growth.

In that respect, Taiwan has the great advantage of a high domestic savings rate, which renders continued fast growth independent of foreign borrowing. As to Taiwan's and Korea's dependence on foreign trade, both are small enough and their exports diversified enough for changes in their exports to make no significant impact on world trade. The total exports of each are less than 1 percent of total world trade, which partly explains why both were able, even during the depressed 1979–81 period, to increase the value of their exports by almost 19 percent annually.

For the future, both countries are trying, first of all, to limit the growth of their import bill by various energy-conservation methods, by slowing the domestic development of energy-intensive industries such as nonferrous metal refining, by joint investments in resource-rich countries to secure cheaper raw material supplies (e.g., aluminum), by offshore prospecting for oil and gas (Taiwan), by the expansion and modernization of coal mining (Korea), and by greater reliance on nuclear power for electricity generation (Korea).

Furthermore, both countries are trying to expand exports, and their efforts are aimed at three targets. One is to recapture, through modernization, automation, and improved control, the competitiveness of their light industries, which was lost owing to the rise in wages. The two countries are trying to accomplish that in diametrically opposite ways. The Korean government seems to be abandoning its past excessive favoritism toward large firms and is now stressing financial and managerial assistance to small and medium-sized firms through such agencies as the Small and Medium Industry Promotion Corporation and the Korea Production Technology Service Corporation. Taiwan, on the other hand, is now discovering the benefits to be had from the economies of scale and is encouraging mergers and the growth of very small firms in the interests of greater efficiency.

Textiles is one industry receiving a lot of attention; it is hoped not only that costs will be lowered by modernizing and automating productive methods, but also that quality will improve through more sophisticated design and better dyeing techniques. Quality improvement is especially important, because import restrictions are a response mostly to price competition, very seldom to quality competition. Another industry whose exports Korea plans to expand is the one producing nuts, bolts, and other machinery parts and components (spare parts). They seem to be superior in quality to American products, and Korea hopes to increase their export partly through production in joint U.S.-Korean ventures, again an area where imports are unlikely to be restricted.

Another important aim of both countries is to compensate for the lost comparative advantage of their light industries (once based on cheap manpower) by gaining a comparative advantage in electronics and other emerging industries based on cheap brainpower. In the past, both countries have been heavily engaged in the assembly of consumer electronics; they are attempting to shift into the production of semiconductors, large-scale integrated circuits, computer terminals, microcomputers, electronic switching systems, and telecommunications equipment, much of which they need for automation in their own industries, as well as for export. Being a new industry, electronics has the advantage of a rapidly growing market that is unlikely to be protected by import restriction; it also has the disadvantage that its established members are reluctant to license their know-how and permit its spread to competitors and foreign countries. Partly to deal with this problem, both Taiwan and Korea are soliciting more direct investment from abroad, with Korea allowing multinational companies to set up wholly owned subsidiaries; both countries are increasing public and encouraging private expenditures on research and development as well. In that respect, Korea is ahead of Taiwan, thanks principally to the size of many of her manufacturing firms, more than fifty of which already have their own research and development institutes. Plans are for total research and development expenditures to rise in Korea by 12 percent per annum to 2 percent of the GNP in 1986 and in Taiwan by 15 percent per annum to 1.2 percent of the GNP in 1985. (United States expenditures on research and development were 2.3 percent of GNP in the late 1970s.)

Brainpower in both countries is very cheap. Young electronics engineers earn one-half or less of what their counterparts earn in Japan, who in turn again earn only one-half of what they would in the United States. The supply is plentiful in both Taiwan and Korea, thanks to the importance attached to education. Taiwan graduates 50 percent more engineers in proportion to its population than does the United States, and while previously most of them emigrated to the United States, they increasingly find challenging and promising jobs at home. Korea's engineers are trained in a number of institutes of science and technology, which are largely manned by a U.S.-trained faculty who is paid a competitive salary, often supplemented by consulting for private industry. Both countries, however, have ambitious plans to upgrade their educational systems and put more emphasis on scientific and technical training—especially Korea, which plans to extend compulsory education through senior high school, establish ninety-three new technical high schools and twenty new junior colleges, and increase public spending on education from 3 percent of the GNP in 1980 to 5 percent by 1986.[43]

In addition to the two countries' efforts to revive their light exports and establish a comparative advantage in the newly emerging high technology industries, Korea's new export drive also has a third target: the developing countries' need for intermediate and capital goods, heavy equipment, and manufacturing and infrastructural facilities. That part of import demand, far from being restricted by the new protectionism, is enhanced by it. The two countries' cost advantage in heavy industry has been demonstrated by the export successes of their steel and shipbuilding industries, and they are well equipped to cater to demand for heavy equipment from later developing countries. Korea is especially well placed for capturing such demand with its newly built and still underemployed heavy industries, its large construction industry whose reputation abroad is well established, and the worldwide presence of its trading companies.

The one ingredient Korea lacks for exports of this type is the ability to grant large, long-term export credits on favorable terms, and one of the main uses to which it hopes to put a part (estimated at 12.5 percent) of the funds it expects to borrow in international credit markets is to re-lend them as export credits to developing countries that become customers. In this section an attempt has been made to rationalize the two countries' projected and hoped for export drives, as they are spelled out in Korea's Five-Year Plan for 1982–86 and Taiwan's Four-Year Plan for 1982–85. The rates at which they expect their respective GNP and exports to grow are almost identical. They count on exports to continue expanding as fast as during the past three years (1979–81), and both countries plan to stick with their outward-looking policies and rely on further export expansion to lead the growth of their economies.

5

LAWRENCE J. LAU

The Economy of Taiwan, 1981–1988: A Time of Passages

With an annual gross national product (GNP) per capita in excess of US$6,100, the Republic of China on Taiwan is today on the verge of becoming a developed country. Taiwan will soon be joining the exclusive club of advanced industrialized countries such as the United States, Japan, Italy, and others. The economy, under the leadership of the late president Chiang Ching-Kuo, current president (and former vice president) Lee Teng-Hui, Premier Yu Kuo-Hwa,[1] and Senior Presidential Adviser Li Kwoh-Ting, has been and continues to be a top performer. Annual growth of real GNP has averaged more than 9 percent since 1965. Over the same period, unemployment has averaged 1.2 percent and never exceeded 1.9 percent. In addition, despite the robust economic growth and the two oil shocks, economic policymakers have managed to maintain a relatively low inflation rate—6.3 percent according to the GNP deflator—while achieving a distribution of income that is among the most equitable in the world. Taiwan, with a combined volume of exports and imports in excess of US$110 billion in 1988, is now the thirteenth largest trading nation in the world. The current-account surplus, which reached almost US$18 billion in 1987, remained high at US$10 billion in 1988. Official foreign-exchange reserves held by the central bank totaled US$76 billion as of early 1989. Foreign debt is a negligible US$1.4 billion, and the New Taiwan dollar is strong. This combination of growth, price stability, equity, and freedom from foreign debt is almost unique among developing countries and the success of

Taiwan is often described as a miracle in the annals of economic development.

But this success is no miracle. Rather, it is the fruit of the collective wisdom and hard work of economic policymakers, entrepreneurs, consumers, and workers in Taiwan.[2] What is remarkable about Taiwan's experience is that more than 70 percent of the average annual growth of real output has come from increases in the capital input, and the remainder has come from increases in the labor input and technical progress. In other words, most of Taiwan's economic growth can be attributed to high rates of savings and investment.

If the Taiwanese economy continues to grow at its historical average rate, real GNP will approximately double every seven and a half years. By the beginning of the next century, Taiwan's real GNP will reach approximately US$500 billion in 1988 prices, and real GNP per capita will reach US$20,000. The prospects are bright and rosy indeed.

Yet profound economic, political, and social changes have also been occurring in Taiwan. On the economic front, beginning in 1981, Taiwan has been running a string of increasingly higher trade and current-account surpluses, especially with the United States. This in turn put upward pressure on the exchange rate and growth of the money supply and fanned protectionist sentiments abroad.

In response, the government embarked on an import liberalization program: lowering tariffs and abolishing restrictions on thousands of commodities. It eliminated remaining direct and indirect export subsidies and essentially switched from a policy of promoting exports to a policy of encouraging imports. The New Taiwan dollar was allowed to appreciate against the U.S. dollar beginning in 1986, and by 1989 it had increased more than 40 percent. In July 1987, the Statutes of Foreign Exchange Regulations were extensively amended to permit citizens and firms of the Republic of China to hold foreign exchange and to remit up to US$5 million abroad per year without government approval. The rule governing the inward remittance of foreign exchange by nongovernment entities remained.[3]

In 1988, in a further attempt to make productive use of the abundant foreign-exchange reserves, the government established the International Economic Cooperation and Development Fund with capital of NT$30 billion (approximately US$1.2 billion at the current exchange rate). The purpose of the fund is to assist developing countries through the extension of loans and grants-in-aid. This marked a significant milestone for Taiwan's foreign aid program: previously the government had sent only technical assistance teams to developing countries but never significant amounts of monetary aid.

With the rising value of the New Taiwan dollar, many traditional industries, such as textiles and shoes, became uncompetitive in the world market, and firms were forced to either close down or contract drastically. Other industries, especially agriculture, became threatened by potential imports. The necessity of industrial upgrading became obvious, and the government, which had previously largely eschewed an industrial policy, dramatically increased its funding of large-scale industrial research and development (R&D) projects. Such government support may well be necessary given Taiwan's particular mode of industrialization, which relies on a large number of diverse but relatively small firms. The advantages of this mode of industrialization are an equitable distribution of income, social mobility, and flexibility.[4] The disadvantage is that few firms are large enough and financially strong enough to undertake long-term and high-risk investments, especially in R&D.

Simultaneously, the government undertook efforts to increase domestic aggregate demand so as to reduce reliance on the export sector. In addition to accelerating the completion of the fourteen major infrastructural projects already under way, a further sixteen projects were planned. Progress on some of these, however, was stalled by environmental opposition and land condemnation disputes. In the long run, growth in domestic aggregate demand must come from the private sector, as the government has had to run budget deficits, even in the boom years of 1984 and 1986.

There were also signs of worrisome developments in the financial sector. Because of the growth in real income and hence in saving and the de facto moratorium on the issuance of new bank licenses, the assets of the nonbank financial institutions, including credit cooperatives and investment trust companies, expanded rapidly. They were not adequately supervised however, and several collapsed as a result of fraudulent loan practices and the depositors had to be bailed out by the government. By the late 1980s, underground "finance companies," many of which appeared to be no more than pyramid schemes in which early depositors were paid with later depositors' money, have come to the fore. By offering rates of interest of up to 4 percent per month, they have managed to garner a significant share of the savings deposits in Taiwan. These underground finance companies were also intricately bound to the fortunes of the highly speculative and volatile stock market in Taiwan. Some decisive actions, however painful, may be necessary in order to avert a full-fledged financial crisis.

On the political and social fronts, there was an almost total sea change. On July 14, 1987, martial law, which had been in place for almost forty years, was lifted in the Republic of China. In addition, the bans on new political parties and newspapers were also removed by the late president Chiang Ching-Kuo. These actions indicated significant progress toward democracy and respect for human rights in Taiwan. Later that year, the ban on travel to mainland China was also removed, allowing hundreds of thousands of Taiwanese residents to visit their relatives in mainland China for the first time in forty years.

Important new government institutions were established in the meantime, signaling new priorities and directions. The Environmental Protection Bureau, for example, was elevated to cabinet level and renamed the Environmental Protection Administration in August 1987. The Labor Department of the Ministry of the Interior was upgraded to an independent ministerial level labor commission, reporting directly to the premier. The Labor Standards Law was passed, strengthening protection of the rights of workers.

In January 1988, President Chiang Ching-Kuo passed away and was succeeded by his constitutional successor, then vice president Lee Teng-Hui. Power, which had been concentrated in a single person, has since become more diffused. Many new political parties and interest groups have been formed in the newly liberalized political climate. With the lifting of martial law, labor unions have become more active and militant in their wage and other demands. Environmental and other special interest groups have also become more active. There is increasing public concern about public goods and externalities, particularly the environment, public health, and culture, brought about partly by the rising affluence and education of the citizens and partly by the liberalized political climate. The legislatures—the Legislative Yuan, the Control Yuan, and the National Assembly—have become more assertive and independent. Gone are the days in which a single authoritarian figure can make decisions on behalf of all the groups in society. This evolution toward political pluralism has made the resolution of disputes, economic and otherwise, between opposing groups difficult. What is needed in Taiwan is the development of an effective and efficient process for social decision making.

Given the new domestic and international environment, can the Taiwanese economy continue to grow and prosper as it has in the past?

This issue is explored throughout the chapter. In the next section the historical performance of the Taiwanese economy is briefly reviewed. Significant economic developments in the 1980s are examined, and then the major challenges facing the Taiwanese economy are analyzed. Finally, the future prospects for the Taiwanese economy are discussed.

Review of Historical Performance

Gross National Product. The real GNP of the Republic of China on Taiwan grew at an average annual rate of approximately 9 percent between 1965 and 1988.[5] This is one of the highest growth rates of real output achieved by any country over a sustained period. The only economy with a comparable record is that of the Republic of Korea (South Korea). Taiwan has managed to maintain this high growth rate despite the two oil shocks of 1973–74 and 1979–80 as well as the political turmoil and uncertainty caused by the derecognition of the Republic of China on Taiwan by the United States in the late 1970s. Nominal GNP (GNP at current prices) grew at an annual rate of 16 percent between 1965 and 1988, with less than 40 percent of this, or 6.3 percent per year, representing inflation. In the 1980s, inflation in Taiwan has averaged less than 2 percent. Figure 5.1 shows that, except for the two slight decelerations caused by the two oil shocks (and the resulting worldwide recessions), real GNP grew more or less continuously with small year-to-year fluctuations. The growth of real GNP per capita followed an essentially similar pattern.

Although part of the fluctuations in the growth rate of real GNP was undoubtedly caused by the internal dynamics of the Taiwanese economy, a substantial proportion of the fluctuations can be traced to the influence of external factors—changes in the price of oil, growth of world trade, and the economic health of the major purchasers of Taiwan's exports—factors largely beyond Taiwan's control. Thus, to a considerable extent, the development of the Taiwanese economy has become vulnerable to occurrences in the rest of the world.

In figure 5.2 the annual growth rate of real GNP is plotted against the annual growth rate of real exports for 1952 to 1988. It shows a clearly positive correlation between the two growth rates. (The outlier is 1954.) This correlation shows how dependent the growth of the Taiwanese economy has become on the export sector. To reduce the vulnerability to an abrupt decline in real GNP growth, an expansion in domestic

Figure 5.1 Growth of Real GNP and Real GNP per Capita, 1953–1988 (percent per year)

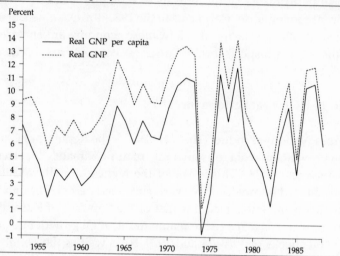

Council for Economic Planning and Development, Republic of China, *Taiwan Statistical Data Book*, various issues (Taipei).

Figure 5.2 Real GNP Growth and Real Export Growth (percent per year)

Source: Data for the annual growth of real GNP and real exports are taken from Council for Economic Planning and Development, Republic of China, *Taiwan Statistical Data Book 1989* (Taipei), pp. 26 and 45.

aggregate demand as a proportion of total aggregate demand is desirable.

Inflation. Between 1965 and 1988, one measure of inflation, the GNP deflator, grew at an average rate of 6.3 percent per year. During the same period, the consumer price index grew at an average rate of 6.4 percent per year. By contrast, the comparable deflators for South Korea and the United States grew at respective average rates of 14.4 percent and 5.7 percent per year over the same period.[6] It is clear from figure 5.3 that Taiwan's inflationary experience since 1965 can be unambiguously divided into two distinct periods. The first of these, from 1965 to 1981, had significant inflation (as measured by the GNP deflator), which peaked at over 32 percent in 1974 and averaged over 8 percent. By contrast, in the second period, from 1982 to 1988, the inflation rate declined to less than 2 percent per year.

The decrease in inflation after 1981 was primarily attributable to fiscal restraints practiced by the Taiwanese Government, sterilization of increases in foreign-exchange reserves, the liberalization of imports (including the reduction of tariffs and the elimination of restrictions), and the appreciation of the New Taiwan dollar since 1986, though the decline in the price of oil and general worldwide price stability undoubtedly helped.

Between 1965 and 1988, the money supply of Taiwan expanded at the average annual rate of 24.5 percent, which is higher than the growth rate of real GNP (9 percent) and the growth rate of the GNP deflator (6.3 percent) combined.[7] This means the velocity of circulation of money, defined as the ratio of nominal GNP to the money supply, has declined significantly during this period, by approximately 10 percent per year (see figure 5.4). Thus, the simple quantity equation of money does not have much predictive power for Taiwan during this period.

The Interest Rate and Wage Rate. The real interest rate on secured bank loans, calculated as differences between the nominal rates and the rate of change of the consumer price index, was relatively low by the standards of developing countries, but nevertheless positive since 1960—except in 1974, 1980, and 1981 (see figure 5.5). Moreover, there was a consistent positive spread between the real interest rates on lending and three-month time deposit rates. Thus, the banking system does not need to be subsidized or otherwise assisted by the government. The

Figure 5.3   Inflation and Money Growth, 1953–1988 (percent per year)

Source: *Taiwan Statistical Data Book 1989*, pp. 26, 151, and 181.

Figure 5.4   Velocity of Money, 1953–1988
             (GNP as a proportion of money supply, 1980=1)

Source: see Figure 3.

Figure 5.5　　Real Interest Rates, 1953–1988 (percent per year)

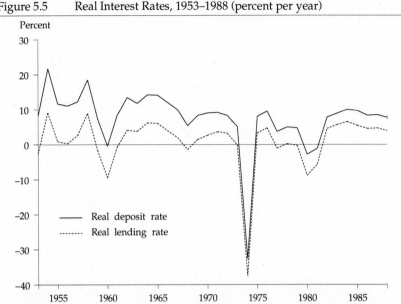

Note: These rates are calculated as differences between the nominal rates and the rate of change of the consumer price index.
Source: Council for Economic Planning and Development, Republic of China, *Taiwan Statistical Data Book 1978* (Taipei), p. 177; and *Taiwan Statistical Data Book 1989*, p. 199. Data for the consumer price index are taken from *Taiwan Statistical Data Book 1989*, p. 181.

positive real interest rate on savings deposits undoubtedly encouraged saving in Taiwan.

The real wage rate grew with the economy. Between 1965 and 1988, the real wage rate (average earnings per employee in manufacturing deflated by the consumer price index) rose almost fourfold, approximately matching the increase in labor productivity (real GDP per unit labor employed). (See figure 5.6.) Growth of the real wage rate lagged behind the growth of productivity until 1980. Since then, the growth of the real wage rate has exceeded the growth of productivity.

Consumption and Saving. Growth in real private consumption per capita has not kept pace with the growth in real GNP per capita. Between 1965 and 1988 real GNP per capita increased almost fourfold, and private real consumption per capita increased less than threefold. Private nominal consumption per capita was approximately US$140 in 1965 and US$3,000 in 1988, while nominal GNP per capita was approximately US$220 in 1965 and US$6,100 in 1988.

Figure 5.6   Real Earnings and Labor Productivity (1980=100)

Source: Data on monthly earnings per employee in manufacturing are from *The Statistical Yearbook of the Republic of China*, p. 160; and Council for Economic Planning and Development, Republic of China, *Taiwan Statistical Data Book 1989* (Taipei), p. 18. Data on employment are from *Taiwan Statistical Data Book 1989*, p. 15. Data on real GDP are from *TSD 1989*, p. 44.

In figure 5.7 it is clear that there is a positive, linear relationship between the savings rate (gross national savings divided by GNP) and real GNP per capita at low levels of real GNP per capita—NT$50,000 in 1980 prices or approximately US$1,250 at the 1980 exchange rate. As real GNP per capita increases beyond the threshold level, the savings rate stabilizes at approximately 35 percent, a remarkably high rate by world standards.

Investment and Capital Formation. As the savings rate rose, domestic investment grew by leaps and bounds. In the late 1960s and early 1970s, domestic investment was almost entirely financed by national savings. There was no foreign aid and relatively little foreign investment. Since 1981, however, national savings consistently exceeded domestic investment (reflected by the export surplus), sometimes by a wide margin (see figure 5.8). The growth rate of real fixed capital stock fell perceptibly in the 1980s (see table 5.1). There are many reasons for the slowdown in investment and it is worrisome that the slowdown occurs exactly when Taiwan should be investing to upgrade its industrial structure. Despite the slowdown, real investment remained high in absolute terms and in fact resumed its growth in 1987 and 1988.

Figure 5.7   Savings Rate and Real GNP per Capita

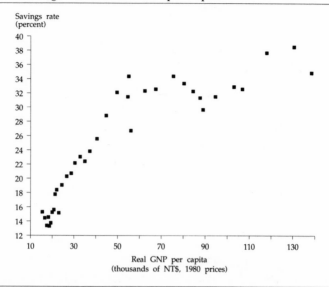

Note: Savings rate is equal to gross national savings as a percentage of GNP.
Source: Data for savings rate are taken from Council for Economic Planning and Development, Republic of China, *Taiwan Statistical Data Book 1989* (Taipei), p. 56.

Figure 5.8   Domestic Investment and Saving, 1952–1988 (1980 prices)

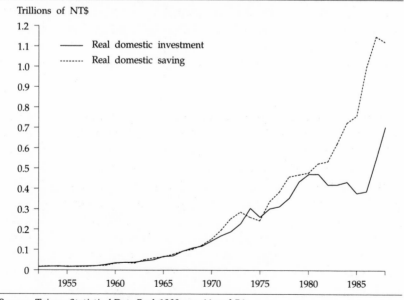

Source: *Taiwan Statistical Data Book 1989*, pp. 44 and 56.

Table 5.1   Growth of Total Factor Productivity and Its Components, 1953–1988 (percent)

| Year | Growth rates | | | | Labor's share of GDP |
	Total factor productivity	Real GDP	Real capital stock	Labor force	
1953	6.87	9.3	3.25	1.01	34
1954	5.48	9.5	5.30	1.87	38
1955	3.69	8.1	5.58	2.51	38
1956	2.83	5.5	3.61	1.15	38
1957	3.64	7.4	4.38	2.63	37
1958	3.01	6.7	3.81	3.52	37
1959	3.50	7.7	5.10	2.53	37
1960	1.33	6.3	6.96	1.60	37
1961	1.15	6.9	8.55	1.05	38
1962	2.33	7.9	8.34	1.09	38
1963	3.79	9.4	8.06	1.54	38
1964	5.78	12.2	9.24	1.92	39
1965	5.09	11.1	8.79	1.75	39
1966	1.69	8.9	10.55	2.18	40
1967	1.54	10.7	12.51	4.25	41
1968	−0.80	9.2	14.35	3.69	41
1969	−1.86	8.9	15.51	4.09	41
1970	1.01	11.4	14.83	4.02	42
1971	2.96	12.9	14.70	3.55	44
1972	2.37	13.3	16.07	4.21	43
1973	0.34	12.8	16.17	7.43	41
1974	−8.94	1.2	15.21	3.26	44
1975	−4.03	4.9	14.99	1.53	46
1976	4.13	13.9	16.06	2.05	45
1977	0.30	10.2	13.52	5.46	45
1978	5.16	13.6	12.07	4.04	45
1979	0.30	8.2	12.19	2.75	46
1980	−0.26	7.3	12.49	1.87	47
1981	−1.57	6.2	12.99	2.04	49
1982	−4.36	2.9	11.50	2.88	50
1983	0.69	7.8	9.73	4.41	49
1984	4.05	9.6	7.96	3.10	50
1985	−0.37	4.4	7.32	2.14	50
1986	5.83	10.6	5.70	3.84	49
1987	7.74	12.4	6.19	3.00	49
1988	2.64	6.8	7.46	0.78	50

Source: *Taiwan Statistical Data Book*, various issues.

With the high investment rate, the capital stock of Taiwan grew rapidly between 1965 and 1988—at an estimated 12.1 percent annually. With the labor force growing at an average annual rate of 3.3 percent, the capital intensity, or capital-to-labor ratio, rose at an average annual rate of slightly less than 9 percent.[8] By comparison, the capital stock of the advanced industrial economies as a group grew at an average annual rate of less than 5 percent during the same period.[9]

Labor Force and Employment. Between 1965 and 1988, employment grew faster than the labor force, 3.4 percent versus 3.3 percent per year. The labor force, in turn, grew much faster than the population, which grew at only 2 percent per year.[10] Unemployment was almost negligible, with an average rate of less than 1.1 percent.

During the same period, the labor force also became better educated. The proportion of the population above the age of six with at least a primary education rose from 72.9 percent to 91.3 percent; the proportion with at least a secondary education rose from 17.5 percent to 54.3 percent; and the proportion with higher education rose from 2.3 percent to 10.1 percent.[11] The labor force is highly skilled and eminently trainable.

Total Factor Productivity. In table 5.1, data on real gross domestic product, real fixed capital stock, the labor force, and the share of labor (total compensation of employees as a ratio of gross domestic product) are presented. We note that the share of labor in Taiwan has never exceeded 50 percent. An index of real output per unit of labor and an index of total factor productivity, computed with the usual total factor productivity formula, are presented in figure 5.9.[12] After a rapid rise between 1952 and 1965, total factor productivity was virtually stationary between 1965 and 1985, after which time it resumed its upward climb. The sources of economic growth are analyzed in table 5.2. It is clear that capital input is by far the most important source of growth, accounting for almost 75 percent of the growth in real output, followed by the labor input, with total factor productivity (technical change) taking a distant third.

The Government Budget. The government budget was in deficit in the late 1960s and for much of the 1980s, but for most of the 1970s the government ran healthy surpluses (see figure 5.10). The deficit never exceeded 2 percent of GNP, reflecting the fiscal restraint of the

Table 5.2 Sources of Growth, 1965–1988

	Growth rate (%)	Contribution to output growth	Percentage of output growth
Output	9.0	N.A.	100
Source of output growth			
Capital	12.1	6.7	74
Labor	3.3	1.4	16
Total factor productivity	0.9	0.9	10

Source: Table 1.

government. Even this modest deficit, however, was frequently masked by the accounting practice of including the proceeds from government sales of bonds, other government borrowing, and "withdrawals" from accumulated surpluses from prior fiscal years as revenue items in the budget. Only very recently did the government begin to publish data on the "real" surplus (deficit) systematically, and this is the data presented in figure 5.10.

International Trade. The growth of exports in both nominal and real terms is nothing short of phenomenal. Between 1965 and 1988, the value of exports in U.S. dollars increased by 24 percent annually and real exports increased by 15 percent annually. These increases were the result of the export-promotion policy, which consisted of preferential tax treatment and credit subsidies, rebates of customs duties for reexported intermediate goods and raw materials, and maintenance of an appropriate exchange rate.

The export sector has grown from less than 10 percent of GNP in the 1950s to over 50 percent in the 1980s (see figure 5.11). This is classic export-led growth.

Imports consist of capital goods, intermediate goods including raw materials, and more recently, consumer goods. Since 1981, Taiwan has been running a string of increasingly high trade and current account surpluses. The New Taiwan dollar was revalued upward by almost 40 percent against the U.S. dollar, from approximately NT$40 per U.S. dollar to NT$25; import tariffs were lowered, and many import restrictions were lifted. As a result, imports have grown much faster than exports in recent years. In figure 5.12, the phenomenal growth of real exports and imports is apparent. In *real* terms, the trade balance turned from a

Figure 5.9   Total Factor Productivity (1952=100)

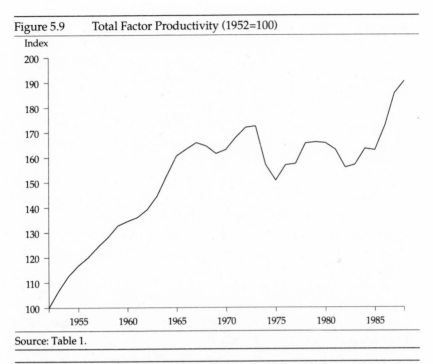

Source: Table 1.

Figure 5.10   Government Budget Surplus as a Percentage of GNP, 1963–1988

Note: For fiscal year ending on June 30 of indicated year.
Source: *Taiwan Statistical Data Book 1989*, pp. 42 and 168.

Figure 5.11　　Exports as a Share of GNP, 1952–1988

Percent

Figure 5.12　　Foreign Trade of Taiwan, 1952–1988 (1980 prices)

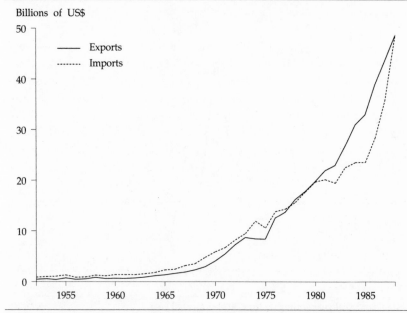

Billions of US$

——— Exports

---------- Imports

Figure 5.13   Taiwan–United States Trade, 1952–1988

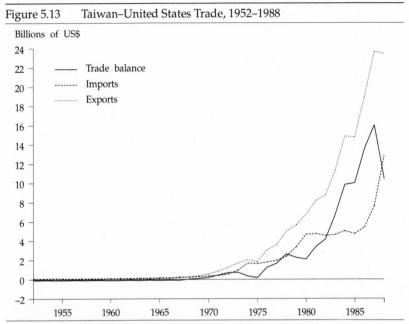

Source: Council for Economic Planning and Development, Republic of China, *Taiwan Statistical Data Book 1989* (Taipei), p. 215.

deficit to a surplus position around 1980; however, by 1988, the trade gap closed once more.

The trade surplus of Taiwan with the United States became very large in the early 1980s and continued to grow (see figure 5.13). It has become a principal source of friction between Taiwan and its most important trading partner. Taiwan has been under a great deal of pressure from the United States to open domestic markets further and to revalue the New Taiwan dollar, both of which were done. There is still some question whether the *merchandise* trade between Taiwan and the United States can ever be balanced, on a current basis, at any exchange rate. The best hope for balancing the current account between the two countries lies in trade in services—including banking, insurance, tourism, transportation, and technology. The effective protection of intellectual property rights becomes an extremely important issue.

The increasingly large trade surpluses led to rising foreign-exchange reserves at the Central Bank of China, initially because private individuals and firms were not allowed to hold foreign exchange; they had to sell it all to the central bank in return for New Taiwan dollars. Subsequently, even after the restrictions were lifted,

Figure 5.14   Nominal and Real Exchange Rates, 1952–1988

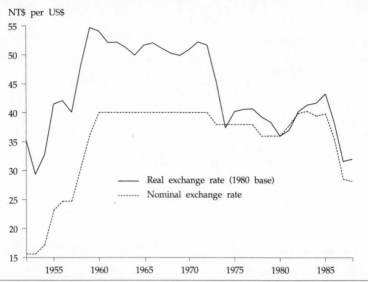

Source: Exchange rate data from *Taiwan Statistical Data Book 1978*, p. 177; and *TSD 1989*, p. 199. GNP deflator data from *TSD 1989*, pp. 42 and 44; and *International Financial Statistics Yearbook*, various issues.

expectations of a revaluation of the New Taiwan dollar, due to the continuing trade surpluses, discouraged private individuals and firms from holding any foreign exchange, especially the U.S. dollar. Total foreign-exchange reserves held by the Central Bank of China reached US$76 billion in early 1989.

The Exchange Rate. In the 1960s, Taiwan adopted a system of floating exchange rates that turned out to be de facto a managed system. The exchange rate was maintained within a 10 percent band for more than two decades. Since September 1985, however, the New Taiwan dollar has continuously appreciated, from NT$40.40 per U.S. dollar to almost NT$25.00 currently. The nominal exchange rate and the real exchange rate, calculated as the nominal exchange rate in NT$ per U.S. dollar times the GNP deflator of the United States (1980=100) divided by the GNP deflator of Taiwan (1980=100), are presented in figure 5.14. The real exchange rate measures the change in the terms of trade between Taiwanese and U.S. real output. Figure 5.14 shows that it was approximately constant during the 1960s, but turned against the United States beginning in 1972. One unit of real U.S. output can now be exchanged

Figure 5.15   Gini Coefficients of Taiwan, 1964–1988

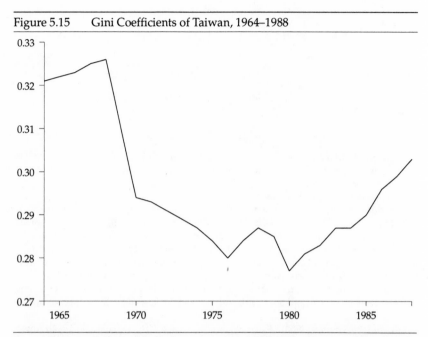

Source: Directorate-General for Budgets, Accounts, and Statistics, Executive Yuan, Republic of China, *Report on the Survey of Personal Income Distribution in Taiwan Area* (Taipei), various issues.

for approximately 40 percent fewer units of real Taiwanese output than in 1965. In other words, in real as well as in nominal terms, the New Taiwan dollar has appreciated by approximately 40 percent against the U.S. dollar since the 1960s. In terms of absolute purchasing power, however, there is evidence that in 1989 the New Taiwan dollar is already overvalued with respect to the U.S. dollar.

Distribution of Income. In the 1970s, the Gini coefficient of income inequality was lower in Taiwan than in the United States, Japan, or South Korea, but it has deteriorated slightly since then.[13] Nevertheless, the income distribution still remains highly egalitarian by world standards. In figure 5.15, the Gini coefficients of Taiwan during the last quarter of a century are plotted against time. Table 5.3 shows that the income distribution of Taiwan has been and remains more equitable than that of selected other countries.

The Financial System. The Central Bank of China has all the customary and normal functions of a central bank, such as control and

Table 5.3   The Gini Coefficients of Income Distribution
               in Selected Countries

	1965	1970	1975	1980	1985
Taiwan	0.322[a]	0.294	0.284[b]	0.277	0.290
Japan	0.344[c]	0.355	0.360	0.346	
U.S.		0.362[d]			
S. Korea	0.344	0.332	0.381[e]	0.389[f]	0.356[g]

a. Interpolated between 1964 and 1966. Data for Taiwan from the Directorate-General of Budget, Accounts and Statistics, *Report on the Survey of Personal Income Distribution in Taiwan Area*, various issues.
b. Interpolated between 1974 and 1976.
c. Data for Japan from M. Bronfenbrenner and Y. Yasuba, "Economic Welfare," in K. Yamamura and Y. Yasuba, (eds.), *The Political Economy of Japan, Vol. 1: The Domestic Transformation* (Stanford: Stanford University Press) pp. 93–136. For the period 1962–1970, Bronfenbrenner and Yasuba rely on T. Mizoguchi and N. Takayama, *Equity and Poverty under Rapid Economic Growth: The Japanese Experience* (Tokyo: Kinokuniya, 1984) p. 12. I am grateful to Professor Charles Horioka for bringing these references to my attention.
d. 1972. Data for the United States and South Korea from T. Scitovsky, "Economic Development in Taiwan and South Korea, 1965–1981," Chapter 4, table 3, this volume.
e. 1976.
f. 1980 and 1984 data for South Korea from S. Y. Kwack, "The Economy of South Korea, 1980–1987," Chapter 6, table 10, this volume.
g. 1984.

management of the money supply, credit, and foreign-exchange reserves. It determines the interest rate and the exchange rate. It also sets guidelines and issues directions on the allocation of credit.

There are three major nationwide commercial banks—First Commercial Bank, Chang Hwa Commercial Bank, and Hua Nan Commercial Bank—all of which have the government as the majority shareholder. The government has, in principle, approved their privatization, but has set no firm schedule for doing so. Other banks include the Bank of Taiwan (also government-owned), the International Commercial Bank of China, and several smaller banks. In addition, there are specialized government banks such as the Export-Import Bank and the Bank of Communications, which functions as a national development bank. There are approximately fifty branches of foreign banks. There are also credit cooperatives, investment trust companies, insurance companies, and short-term finance companies. These financial institutions as well as the Postal Savings System provide the depository for household savings. With the exception of the Postal Savings System, they also supply credit to the business sector.

Growth in the nonbank financial sector has been extremely rapid, partly because of the rapid growth in domestic savings. As a result, many underground finance companies came into being in the late 1980s. Illegal and unsupervised, these finance companies used extremely high rates of interest, up to 4 percent per month, to attract deposits from the public. Such high rates of interest in an essentially noninflationary environment cannot be sustained in the long run, although in the short run they seem to be supported by the inflow of new deposits, the recycling of old deposits, and the explosive stock market. There is, however, the potential of a financial crisis if these underground finance companies fail.

There is also a fledgling commercial paper market and a developing short-term money market. Most of the financial activity, however, is currently on the Taiwan Stock Exchange. The Taiwan Stock Exchange, founded in 1956, has 167 companies listed.[14] The daily turnover averages US$4.75 billion, the third highest in the world, after Tokyo and New York. The total market capitalization of more than US$200 billion probably puts Taipei as the fourth or fifth largest market in the world. The market value of each of the four listed commercial banks exceeds the market value of Citicorp; however, the market has become highly speculative: the average holding period has been estimated at twenty-three hours! The market index has risen more than 1,000 percent over the last two years. The average price-to-earnings ratio is approximately 100, which even exceeds that of the Tokyo Stock Exchange. There is a need to tighten supervision and curb abuses on the market, but the most urgent task is to increase the available supply of securities perhaps through privatization of public enterprises, through new issues by successful companies that are already listed on the exchange, and by allowing well established foreign firms to issue debt or equity instruments on the exchange. There should also be an intensified effort to open channels for overseas investment, both direct and portfolio, by Taiwan investors.

At this time, foreign investors can participate in the Taiwan Stock Exchange only through mutual funds specializing in Taiwanese stocks. These funds are listed on U.S. and European exchanges and have been doing well, often selling at considerable premiums to their net asset values. The restrictions on portfolio investment by foreigners must be lifted if Taiwan is to become an international financial center. In the long run, the foreign funds, with their professional management and long-term outlook, would prove to be a major stabilizing force for Taiwan's stock market.

With the rapid growth of the financial markets and the dismantling of barriers to capital movement, Taiwan has the potential of supplanting Hong Kong as an international financial center of the region. Whether this potential can be realized depends on the size and strength of Taiwan's financial institutions, the degree of freedom of movement of capital, and the credibility and stability of financial markets, including their regulators. None of these conditions are going to be fulfilled overnight; they will require many years of effort. Since Taiwan is likely to be a net capital exporter for years to come, it is in a good position to play an important role in East Asian regional finance. The liberalization and internationalization of financial markets are the necessary first steps in this direction.

Significant Economic Developments in the 1980s

Emergence of Persistent Trade Surpluses. Since 1981, when the price of oil finally stabilized and then began to decline, Taiwan's trade and current-account surpluses became persistently large. At the peak, the trade surplus amounted to some US$18 billion. The largest bilateral trade surplus, approximately US$16 billion, was with the United States. The foreign exchange earned through these current-account surpluses, which had to be sold to the Central Bank of China until the law was changed in 1987, boosted the official foreign-exchange reserves of Taiwan to approximately US$76 billion at the end of 1988. As the Central Bank had to purchase the foreign exchange with New Taiwan dollars, this led, in turn, to a very rapid growth of money supply. As a result, the Central Bank had to engage in extensive sterilization operations through the issuance of bonds.

Revaluation of the New Taiwan Dollar. In the face of mounting trade and current-account surpluses and pressure from Taiwan's trading partners, especially the United States, it was inevitable that the New Taiwan dollar would appreciate, and in 1986 this was allowed to happen gradually. In 1987, in an attempt to reduce the pressure on the central bank to purchase U.S. dollars, the restrictions on capital exports and private holding of foreign exchange were lifted. Nevertheless, foreign-exchange reserves continued to grow because of the public's perception that further appreciation of the New Taiwan dollar was likely. Not only was the public reluctant to hold U.S. dollars, but speculative money began to flow into Taiwan, seeking to take advantage of potential currency appreciation. By 1989 the New Taiwan dollar had risen more than 40 percent against the U.S. dollar. This represents a very drastic change, considering that between 1960 and 1986 the New Taiwan dollar was pegged to the U.S. dollar and the exchange rate was maintained within a range of NT$36 to NT$40 per U.S. dollar.

Industrial Adjustment. The appreciation of the New Taiwan dollar (as well as the market-opening moves to be discussed below) has caused many industries in Taiwan—including automobile manufacturing, electronic assembly, shoemaking, and textiles—to be uncompetitive. As a result, many firms went out of business, and those that remained had to cut back drastically to survive. Many traditional light industries, such as shoemaking and textiles, have relocated manufacturing to developing countries with low labor costs, such as the Philippines, Thailand, and even mainland China. This adjustment is one of the three challenges of the 1990s discussed in the next section.

Trade Adjustment. The export-promotion policy may have outlived its usefulness because of the inherent distortions it has introduced to the economy and the persistent balance-of-payments imbalance it has caused. Indeed, the government has switched from a policy of promoting exports to a policy of encouraging imports. Tariff barriers have been drastically reduced since 1986. Imports of consumer goods have increased markedly. Even with the reduction in tariffs, total customs revenues have increased as a result of the rising imports.

The government is also making a serious effort to increase procurement abroad, especially from the United States. There has been some discussion of a possible Taiwan-United States free trade area, but it has remained at a very preliminary stage. What looms large are two issues: intellectual property rights and agricultural imports. Satisfactory resolution of the first issue is in sight, but the second is politically less tractable. In this area, Taiwan would do well to learn from the mistakes of others, such as the United States and Japan, and adopt an income support program for *existing* farmers rather than a protective price-support program for farm output. Of course, there are legitimate national security concerns about over-reliance on imports for staple food crops. For this reason, there must be some assurances made by potential agricultural exporters that there will be no embargo.

Import expansion, in addition to reducing the trade surplus and thus partly accommodating protectionist critics in the United States and other developed economies, offers some real benefits: Lower-cost goods, reduced monopolistic power of domestic enterprises, less pressure on the money supply and exchange rate, moderated domestic price increases, increased incentive for innovation and adoption of more efficient management practices by domestic industry. Import expansion also permits focusing resources in areas in which Taiwan may have a comparative advantage. Nor should import expansion be limited to goods; it should also be extended to imports of services, including overseas studies, consultancies, tourism, banking, insurance, and other financial services. Import expansion can only bring benefit to domestic consumers.

As of mid-1989, the trade surplus seems to have stabilized, although it still stands near the US$10 billion mark.

Labor and the Environment. With the relaxation of political controls came a new militancy on the part of the labor movement and environmental groups. Strikes and work stoppages became commonplace in 1988 and 1989. Labor demands include not only wages, but also social services and working conditions. The environmental groups have become very vocal about air and water pollution and toxic waste. The petrochemical industry, which had not invested sufficient resources in waste treatment and cleaning up the environment, was identified as a principal culprit. As a result of opposition by environmental groups, the development of nuclear power was suspended indefinitely, as was the development of thermal power. As a result, a shortage of power for both households and industry looms on the horizon.

The Savings-Investment Gap. With the rapid increase in real GNP per capita, savings rose as well. The savings rate reached almost 40 percent during this period. At the same time, traditional industries were no longer attractive candidates for new investment, but many entrepreneurs were reluctant to venture into new and unfamiliar industries because of real and perceived risks. In addition, they were faced with the uncertain exchange rate and political uncertainties created by the illness and death of the late president Chiang Ching-Kuo. Environmental and labor disputes further contributed to the uncertain business climate. Domestic investment thus remained stagnant, and gross national savings far exceeded gross domestic investment since the early 1980s. Since 1987, however, real investment resumed some growth.

A Low Inflation Era. The economy of Taiwan continued to perform well during this period. Between 1981 and 1988, annual real GNP growth averaged 8.2 percent. The annual inflation rate, as measured by the GNP deflator, averaged 1.5 percent, much lower than in earlier periods, in spite of the high rates of growth of the money supply (see figure 5.3). The consumer price index increased 3 percent per year whereas the wholesale price index only registered 0.2 percent per year.

Reorientation Toward Domestic Demand. One way to reduce the trade surplus is to increase domestic aggregate demand. In a market economy the government does not have many levers on private consumption and investment, although liberalization of imports of consumer goods will stimulate private consumption. What the government of Taiwan can and has been trying to do is invest in infrastructure projects such as airports, subways, environmental preservation and cleanup, and even education and culture. Unfortunately, some of these projects have been slowed down by environmental disputes. Moreover, the government has a budget deficit for much of the 1980s, and new resources are limited.

Housing, especially private residential housing, would be a good sector to expand because it can be funded privately and is investment rather than consumption. More housing provides long-term benefits by raising the standard of living and improving the quality of life. Housing must be promoted in a way that prevents landowners from appropriating all of the economic rent. In particular, the government should make use of the vast public holdings of land to keep housing prices affordable. Widespread occupant ownership of residential housing at all levels of society will also give everyone a stake in economic stability and continued prosperity.

Financial Scandals. Early in 1986 Taiwan was rocked by a series of banking scandals that jeopardized public confidence, posed a serious economic threat to the nation, and resulted in the resignation of two Cabinet ministers. The executives of several large credit cooperatives and trust companies, including the Tenth Credit Cooperative, Cathay Investment and Trust Company, Ltd., and Asia Investment and Trust Company, Ltd., had violated banking laws and regulations through illegal borrowing and lending, forgeries, or writing of bad checks. To prevent further damage to the financial system, the Ministry of Finance promptly reorganized the failing financial institutions and, in effect, covered any possible losses to the depositors. A deposit insurance corporation patterned after the U.S. Federal Deposit Insurance Corporation (FDIC) was formed. Deposit insurance, however, has its own well known problems of moral hazard, and Taiwan must take special care not to repeat the mistakes made by the United States with regard to savings and loan associations. This care includes stringent net capital requirements, separation of the transactions function from the credit function of the bank, and securitization of loans, in addition to tighter regulations and closer supervision. Privatization of the banks should help if the equity requirement is increased to a high enough level to deter moral hazard.

The Bull Market. The Taiwan stock market, which has been small and dormant for years, suddenly sprang to life in the mid-1980s, fueled by the excess national savings as well as the massive inflows of hot money attracted by the prospects of revaluation of the New Taiwan dollar. It is marked by excess speculation and volatility, and increased institutional ownership rather than individual ownership is needed to help stabilize the market. For example, only 20 percent of the shares on the Tokyo Stock Exchange are held by individuals; the rest are held by institutions. This provides the market with a great deal of stability. Thus, foreign institutions, such as insurance companies, mutual funds, and pension funds, with long-term investment goals should be welcomed to invest in the Taiwan stock market, subject to regulations that preserve orderliness when funds are withdrawn from Taiwan. The regulators of the Taiwan Stock Exchange must ensure safety and stability for investors while promoting competition.

The Challenges of the 1990s

The economy of Taiwan faces three major challenges that place it at a critical turning point. The first is to adjust and upgrade Taiwan's industrial structure in response to the changed domestic and international environments. The second is to improve the total quality of life while maintaining a rapid rate of economic growth. The third is to preserve social harmony and political stability as Taiwan moves into an era of political pluralism.

The First Challenge. The first challenge is adjusting and upgrading Taiwan's industrial structure. Domestically, Taiwan faces environmental concerns and rising labor costs, with the latter due partly to the disappearance of surplus labor and partly to the increased militancy of the labor movement. Internationally, Taiwan is hampered by a revalued currency and increasing protectionism abroad, both of which make continual expansion of exports difficult.

Superficially, the economy of Taiwan appears to have weathered these changes quite well. Despite an appreciation of the New Taiwan dollar by almost 40 percent since 1986, the economy continued to grow rapidly. Inflation however, remained low, despite the extremely rapid rate of growth of the money supply, which was primarily caused by the increases in the trade surplus. Short-term growth in exports owes much to the diversion of demand for goods produced in other countries and to forward foreign-exchange operations by Taiwanese exporters.[15] Neither of these causes can be replicated or sustained now that the New Taiwan dollar has reached its new height and new regulations have been introduced in the foreign-exchange market. Adjustment and upgrading of the industrial structure is necessary to maintain competitiveness abroad and full employment and a rising standard of living at home.

There are two dimensions to the necessary structural adjustments. The first dimension is macroeconomic—adjusting the mix of final output between exports and domestic demand to increase the proportion of the latter. The second dimension is microeconomic—phasing out the traditional industries that are no longer competitive under the new exchange and wage rates and switching into higher value-added industries in which Taiwan may have a potential comparative advantage. Import liberalization can facilitate this process by increasing domestic consumption and focusing domestic resources on industries with long-term viability. These adjustments have already begun to occur in Taiwan. It is important that the government resist the politically appealing temptation to protect, through subsidies or tariffs, the declining industries and do no more than provide temporary and transitional income and retraining support for displaced workers.

Taiwan must begin to move in the direction of higher value-added industries. With a small population and resource base, Taiwan must upgrade industries to remain internationally competitive and maintain full employment; however, industries that are capital intensive or have significant economies of scale, such as automobile manufacturing, are probably not appropriate for an economy of Taiwan's size. Rather, knowledge- and technology-intensive industries have far greater potential. Already, the government of Taiwan has increased its funding of large-scale industrial R&D projects.

Establishing a new industry requires the combination of three factors: technology, capital, and labor. Neither technology nor labor appears to be a potential bottleneck: Taiwan has a broad and deepening base of R&D institutions and scientific and technical manpower and can also draw on the many scientists and engineers of Chinese ancestry in the West. In addition, Taiwan has good access to foreign technology, especially now that it has adopted tough intellectual property protection measures. The critical factor is capital, which may seem paradoxical, as Taiwan is currently awash with liquidity—the national savings rate of over 35 percent far exceeds the domestic investment rate—however, what is required is not just money, but capital that is large and lumpy, patient, and not afraid of bearing risks.

First, the higher value-added industries that Taiwan must establish to upgrade the economy, such as semiconductor manufacturing, will have a high capital requirement per project, unlike the simple processing or assembly industries that rely on low labor costs and have relatively low economies of scale. Second, the break-even period for the capital will be longer—seven to ten years compared with the more customary two to four years for garment or shoe factories. Because of the longer return period and the larger and more lumpy amounts of initial investment greater risks are involved. In addition, the investor faces technological uncertainty in a new industry.

This kind of capital is in short supply. Generally, commercial banks are not in a position to supply the long-term capital required, even less so given the risks involved. In any case, this kind of capital should be predominantly in the form of equity rather than debt. Only investors with a long-term perspective—a development bank, private investment banks, venture capitalists, and pension funds—are likely to back these projects. A broadening of the existing capital market may be necessary to increase the potential supply of this kind of capital.

Information is crucial for the capital market to perform its function of allocating the right capital to the right people efficiently. Getting reliable information to investors, bankers, and entrepreneurs would involve a substantial effort and require new and enforceable regulations on audits and disclosures.

A second consideration is that Taiwan does not have the concentration in wealth and economic power that South Korea has. In South Korea, the top five or six *chaebols* (Korean conglomerates) dominate the economic landscape, while in Taiwan this is far from the case: there are some very large firms but many more medium-sized and small firms that employ fifty or fewer workers. This diversity in size gives the economy a great deal of adaptability and vitality and allows a great deal of innovation and competition. At the same time, the absence of dominant firms makes the organization and financing of large and risky projects very difficult. In order to remain competitive, it may be necessary for Taiwan to adopt a more activist industrial policy by financing and supporting R&D projects that, for reasons of risk, appropriability, size, or lengthiness of the time horizon, cannot be undertaken by private firms.

The Second Challenge. The second challenge is improving the total quality of life. There is almost universal agreement that the real standard of living in Taiwan has increased substantially over the years. At the same time, it is beyond dispute that in some important aspects the quality of life has deteriorated: the air is more polluted, the traffic congestion is worse, and so on. As affluence and education rise, citizens are no longer satisfied with economic development at all costs, and they have higher standards and greater demands with regard to the environment and public health. Policymakers in Taiwan have responded to these demands by establishing the Environmental Protection Administration to deal with these problems.

However, everyone prefers clean air, clean water, and safe electric power; but not everyone is aware of the costs involved, some of which may be invisible or unobservable. Moreover, not everyone is willing to bear the costs voluntarily, and there are likely to be many conflicting interests. Two questions are important: The first is one of social costs and benefits—how to strike a balance between conflicting goals such as industrial growth and pollution. The second is one of cost allocation—how to share the burden of undertaking (or not undertaking) a project. The second question also involves the more fundamental issue of the boundary between individual and social responsibility.

Answering the first question requires a comprehensive and impartial social benefit and cost analysis for any proposed project. There are very few projects that are all benefit and no cost; if there were any they probably would have been undertaken a long time ago. The issue is whether the benefits outweigh the costs, and this requires a careful assessment of the benefits and costs not only to private individuals, but also to society as a whole. For example, one must balance the costs of a power shortage against the costs of the pollution that an additional power plant may cause. It may well turn out that the total social benefits of the power plant are exceeded by the total social costs, but the assessment should be made in the most objective manner possible.

The second question addresses the issue of how to share the burden—who pays the costs? It is important to realize that when the government pays for something, everyone pays and that sometimes the cost may not be direct. For example, if a power shortage causes factories to be shut down and workers thrown out of work, should these workers be compensated? If so, who should pay for it: the government, the electric utility, the factory owners, or those who oppose the building of additional power plants? There are no easy answers. The question is further complicated by the fact that such things as clean environment and public safety are public goods with significant externalities.

Taiwan needs to institutionalize social benefit and cost analysis and establish basic principles of social cost sharing. Requiring an identifiable polluter to pay for polluting, for example, is one way of allocating costs. Only in this way can there be some assurance that Taiwan will stay on the development path that improves the total quality of life, not just real GNP per capita or the environment.

The Third Challenge. The third challenge—preserving social harmony and political stability—has arisen because of the increasing public interest and participation in the political processes of Taiwan, especially since the lifting of both martial law and the ban on the formation of new political parties. Labor unions have also become much more assertive about their demands not only on wages, but also on social issues. Many, sometimes conflicting, demands have been put forth for new social welfare programs, services, subsidies, regulations, and greater government intervention in the economy in general.[16] How are harmony and stability to be promoted amidst all this contentiousness? Again, efforts should be undertaken in two directions. First, an attempt must be made to develop a consensus on a basic vision for the country—a set of national principles and values, if you like—with regard to the boundary between individual and social responsibility. This boundary, moreover, has a significance beyond the simple question "who pays?" it also defines the limits of government action and individual choice. Second, a mechanism or process should be developed for the effective, expeditious, orderly, and peaceful resolution of social disagreements.

Where does individual responsibility end and public responsibility begin? This is a complex question whose answer depends very much on the cultural, historical, and institutional background of the economy. In addition to equity and social welfare aspects, incentive effects on individuals and groups must be examined. We consider three examples, the first of which is unemployment insurance. The basic issue is whether the individual or society is responsible when someone is out of work. In some countries, unemployment insurance serves a useful, short-term purpose of tiding people over. In others, it may actually discourage some people from working. If the unemployment benefit is made too attractive, the incentive to work may be seriously eroded; if it is made too low, it fails to provide a needed social safety net. The ideal solution is to make the net strong enough to cushion a fall, but not comfortable enough to lie in.

The second example is the stock market. Most academic economists believe that the stock market is efficient for the allocation of investments and risks. It is supposed to provide capital to the most deserving firms and distribute risk to those investors most willing and able to assume them. In order for the stock market to perform its function investors must be well informed. If the investors know little or nothing about the firms whose shares they buy and sell, the stock market becomes no different from a casino, and cannot fulfill the function of efficient allocation of investments and risks. In 1987, government banks in Taiwan, were, for a while, called upon to support the price level of the Taiwan Stock Exchange by purchasing shares. Such action makes little sense for the economy as a whole (even though it does help existing shareholders bail out at the expense of the taxpayers) and has very negative incentive effects on the investors. If there is in fact an implicit no-loss guarantee by the government, many investors will not be motivated to do the homework necessary to invest wisely—and make gains while avoiding losses. Moreover, asking the government and hence the taxpayers to bail out investors is the same as asking everyone to pay for the bad investments of a selected few, which is hardly equitable and provides the wrong incentives. A boundary must be drawn between individual and social responsibility, and investment in the stock market should be an individual responsibility.

The third example is pollution. Here the question is: Who should pay? To the extent that the polluter can be identified without incurring too much cost, the polluter should be made to pay for the costs of eliminating or reducing the pollution. If the individual consumer directly impacted or the public pays, not only does it seem inequitable but the polluter is not deterred from further pollution. In general, public payment of pollution abatement costs is not incentive-compatible.[17]

It will take time to reach a national consensus on the proper division of responsibility between the individual and society, but the debate and discussion have already begun. With a clearer delineation of the boundary, many potentially contentious disputes on pet programs, pork barrel projects, and special interest legislation may be avoided.

On the basis of such a consensus, the remaining social disagreements may be resolved through an agreed-upon mechanism or process. Such a mechanism or process must, of course, be consistent with the principles of rule of law (due process), majority governance, and respect and protection for the rights of the minority. To the extent that it provides expeditious, orderly, and peaceful resolution of social disagreements, it facilitates social decision making and thus helps to preserve social harmony and stability in the long run. The mechanism or process itself is most likely to evolve through democratization, and this is the direction in which Taiwan is clearly heading.

Concluding Remarks

While the economy of Taiwan faces major challenges, there are reasons to be cautiously optimistic about the future. First, Taiwan has an extremely good track record in responding to adversities and crises: the oil shocks of 1973 and 1979, the derecognition of the Republic of China by the United States in 1978, and the financial scandals of 1986. In every case, the economy came out unscathed or stronger. Second, there is now an enlightened and far-sighted leadership, a high-caliber government bureaucracy, and a well-educated electorate. Taiwan should be able to evolve a way of solving the problems caused by rapid development and demonstrate to the rest of the world how to organize a society that provides incentives for individual innovation, saving, and hard work while preserving the environment and taking care of its poor and unfortunate.

Third, while labor strife and special interest group militancy have become almost constant fixtures in the economy, there is no need for despair. In this regard the Japanese development experience offers hope: management-labor relations in Japan have not always been as cooperative or smooth as they may now appear. In the early 1960s, strikes, work stoppages, lockouts, and other forms of conflict between management and labor were routine.[18] Eventually, however, both Japanese management and labor came to realize the commonality of their long-term interests and devised ways of working together. Today, Japanese management-labor relations are widely admired. The labor strife in Taiwan, serious as it may appear, will pass as management and labor discover new modes of operation and cooperation.

Finally, Taiwan's most important asset lies not in foreign-exchange reserves, but in the people. The labor force is now one of the best educated in the region. Universities and university enrollments are expanding at a rapid rate. R&D expenditures are being stepped up. Taiwan has access to an enormous pool of distinguished scientists and engineers in the West who are originally from Taiwan. In the long run, the quality of human capital will enable Taiwan to adjust and upgrade its industrial structure to meet the new challenges.

6

SUNG YEUNG KWACK

The Economy of South Korea, 1980–1987

At the turn of the decade, the Korean economy experienced a severe setback. In 1980, Korea's real GNP declined by 5.2 percent; inflation soared to 29 percent; and the current-account deficit enlarged to US$5.3 billion, equivalent to 9 percent of GNP. The savings rate fell from 28.1 percent in 1979 to 20.8 percent in 1980, and outstanding external debt nearly doubled during the two years of 1979 and 1980. Among the factors behind this setback were sharp increases in the prices of oil and international interest rates, and the recession of industrial economies. In addition to these external shocks, two domestic developments—poor harvests and the assassination of President Park—added to deterioration in economic performance.

In dealing with this situation, Korea placed greater emphasis on reducing inflation and the current-account deficit than on boosting economic growth. Among the measures taken to this end were tight monetary and fiscal policies, depreciation of the Korean exchange rate, and initiatives to reduce the rate of growth of wages and the intensity of energy use. The growth of the money supply (defined as M_2) decelerated from 25.0 percent in 1981 to 7.7 percent in 1984. The deficit of the government budget as a ratio of GNP was also cut back sharply from 4.6 percent in 1981 to 1.4 percent in 1984. The nominal exchange rate was depreciated in small magnitudes with a range of 4 to 6 percent on an annual basis during the period of 1981–85 following a 36 percent devaluation against the U.S. dollar in 1980. This nominal exchange rate depreciation, together with a remarkable reduction in inflation, resulted in a real exchange rate depreciation amounting to about 15 percent from 1980 to 1985. The annual growth rate of wages declined from 23.4 percent in 1980 and 20.2 percent in 1981 to 10.1 percent in 1985.

The favorable external developments in the prices of oil, interest rates, and economic activity, together with these measures started to substantially reduce inflation and the current account deficits. Inflation in terms of the consumer price index declined from 21.3 percent in 1981 to 2.6 percent in 1985, while the current account deficit was reduced from $5.3 billion to $0.8 billion, which is about 1.0 percent of the GNP. Despite tight monetary and fiscal policies cum exchange rate depreciation, Korea did not experience a disruptive recession. The growth of Korea's GNP averaged 6.0 percent during the period of 1981–82 and then picked up to 10.2 percent for the subsequent two years followed by a moderate 5.4 percent rate in 1985.

Two points are noteworthy. The first is that Korea did successfully minimize the trade-offs between growth and price stabilization. One factor behind this was the decline in import prices and costs that served to minimize the adverse effects the contractionary monetary policies might have on the growth of the GNP. The second point is that the GNP growth rates fluctuated from year to year. In a trade-dependent economy such as Korea, external factors are very influential on the variations in the growth rates. The high growth in Korea's GNP for 1983–84 coincided with the economic recovery in the OECD countries (especially the United States). As the United States and other OECD economies began to slow down from mid-1984 onward, Korean exports suffered and GNP growth faltered, as indicated by the 2.1 percent growth in real exports of goods and services and 5.4 percent growth in GNP in 1985.

To achieve three interrelated goals—price stability, reduction in the current account deficits, and sustained high growth during the 1980–85 period—Korea has not only realigned its macroeconomic policies, but has also attempted to restructure the economy. The thrust of the structural adjustment policies which are still under way is deregulation conducive to allowing market forces to play a larger role in resource allocation. Trade liberalization was aggressively pursued, and the result was a steady rise in the ratio of the number of items that were allowed to be imported without government permission to the number of total imported items (the import liberalization ratio). This figure rose from 68.6 percent in 1980 to 87.7 percent in 1985. The average tariff rates were also brought down from 31.7 percent in 1982 to 21.9 percent in 1984. By the year 1988 the import liberalization ratio is scheduled to rise to 95.4 percent, while the average tariff rates will fall to 18.1 percent. The policy to have firms more exposed to external competition was accompanied by the policy to strengthen the base for internal competition through allowing entry to more segments of the industry.

The financial sector has also undergone a series of reforms. The Korean government took measures to denationalize commercial banks by disinvesting its share and reducing its control over banking operations. It also discarded the complicated preferential lending rate system and unified all lending rates to 10 percent. The government eased restrictions on entry into the non-banking sector, and as a result the number of non-banking financial institutions increased and their share in total deposit liabilities increased from 26.7 percent in 1980 to 42.4 percent at the end of 1984.

The most remarkable development since 1985 has been the emergence of a surplus in the current account, simultaneously with high economic growth (12 percent) and low inflation (3 percent). During 1986 the current account surplus was $4.6 billion, and for 1987 the surplus was $9.7 billion. As a result of the continuing surplus, Korea's gross and net external debts were reduced to $35.6 and $22.4 billion, respectively, by 1987. Thus, Korea became a high growth country with low debt. There are many factors that have contributed to this remarkable achievement. Among them, the external causes are low oil prices and interest rates, and exchange rates and economic growth of developed economies, notably the United States and Japan. In addition, the domestic factors are the government fiscal and monetary policies to reduce the monetary growth and thereby to decrease domestic sources of inflation.

The current account surplus brought an excessive growth of money stock and inflation pressure into the economy. Simultaneously, Korea has been under pressure to appreciate the exchange rate and reduce import restrictions. To meet the internal need and the external demand, the exchange rate was appreciated and import restrictions and tariff rates were substantially reduced. Further, on the assumption that continuous surplus in the current account at an excessive level is undesirable, the government is currently designing policies to expand Korea's imports that are helpful for housing investment and research and development.

In December 1987, the Korean people elected Mr. Roh Tae Woo as their president. This event symbolizes Korea's desire to run the

Table 6.1   Structural Change in Production (percentage shares)

	Value added				Employment			
	1970	1975	1980	1985	1970	1975	1980	1985
Agriculture	29.6	24.0	14.4	14.2	50.2	41.4	32.0	25.5
Mining	2.1	1.9	1.4	1.4	1.1	1.1	1.1	1.1
Manufacturing	15.5	22.6	29.6	30.7	12.4	19.2	21.7	22.9
Construction	7.0	6.7	8.3	8.7	3.7	4.0	5.3	6.1
Services	45.8	44.8	46.3	45.0	32.5	34.3	39.8	44.4

Source: Bank of Korea, *National Accounts* and *Input-Output Tables.*

government according to the will of the people. Consequently, Dr. Rha Woong Bae, Deputy Prime Minister, and his economic team are attempting to sustain economic growth with equitable distribution through a well-functioning market system. To assist the operation of the market system, the reform of the tax system, assistance for low-income and rural groups, and the reform of the banking system are in process, in addition to measures for the promotion of free trade and capital movement. Thus, the focus of economic policies is placed on the achievement of balanced growth and internationalization of its economy.

Growth and Structure

During the period of 1981–87, Korea's real GNP registered an annual average growth rate of 7.5 percent, increasing the nominal GNP to US$118.6 billion and per capita GNP to US$2,826 in 1987. The manufacturing sector grew 10.9 percent annually, while the social overhead capital and service sector grew 8.5 percent annually. The agricultural sector grew 2.4 percent during 1982–87 following 22.4 percent growth in 1981— a repercussion to the severe crop failure in 1980. Reflecting different rates of growth between manufacturing and agriculture, the structures of production and employment continued shifting from agriculture to manufacturing, albeit to a lesser degree than in the 1970s (table 6.1). The share of agriculture in real value added declined slightly from 14.4 percent in 1980 to 14.2 percent in 1985, while the share of manufacturing increased from 29.6 percent in 1980 to 30.7 percent in 1985.

The growth of the manufacturing sector was led by heavy and chemical industry, particularly metal products and machinery. During the period of 1980–85, the share of heavy and chemical industry in GNP increased from 14.5 percent in 1980 to 17.0 percent in 1986, while the share of light industry remained stagnant at a level of 13.0 percent. The substantial rise in the output of heavy and chemical industry has at least two important implications. First of all, Korea's push for heavy and chemical industry in the 1970s started to pay off. On completion of the push, the industry met severe difficulties originating from both internal and external causes. Internally, the macroeconomic policies were severely misaligned and externally the second oil shock depressed demand in both domestic and world markets. Facing up to this situation, Korea implemented restructuring plans featuring mergers and capacity reduction at the same time. This contributed to the industry gaining export competitiveness. Second, as the heavy and chemical industries have increasingly supplied intermediate inputs to domestic user industry, import dependency as a share of imported intermediate inputs in total inputs, including value added, has declined considerably. Import dependency in heavy and chemical industry declined from 31 percent in 1980 to 28 percent in 1985, while that in light industry remained at 13 percent in 1985. What are the factors behind the rapid growth of the heavy and chemical industry? Export expansion played a more significant role than domestic market expansion. According to World Bank estimates, the contribution of export expansion to output growth in heavy and chemical industry accelerated over time from 35.9 percent in 1970–75 to 41.3 percent in 1975–80 and then to 54.1 percent in 1980–83 (table 6.2). In metal products and machinery, export expansion contributed 48.8 percent to output growth in 1980–83. The residual 51.2 percent comprised domestic market expansion of 48.6 percent and technical development of 2.6 percent.

There are many factors behind how this export expansion was made possible. Among them is a global strategy of multinational firms in industrial economies. This is particularly true in the machinery industry. Some firms in the West engaged in production of machinery, including automobiles, machine tools, and electrical machinery, are increasingly facing fierce competition from Japanese firms. For instance, in the case of the computer numerically controlled lathe industry, Japan increased its share of world production from about 15 percent in 1975 to nearly 45 percent in 1981. In the case of the automobile industry, Japan captured 20 percent of the market share in the United States, the largest single market for automobiles. To compete against these aggressive Japanese firms, some firms in the West recognized a need to collaborate with foreign firms capable of producing quality parts and components

Table 6.2   Sources of Output Growth in Manufacturing

	Consumption expansion	Investment expansion	Export expansion	Import substitution	Changes in I-O coefficient
1970–75					
Heavy and chemical industry	24.0	23.5	35.9	3.6	13.0
Chemical and chemical products	37.7	9.7	30.6	2.4	21.6
Primary metal manufacturing	8.6	31.1	45.3	8.5	6.6
Metal products and machinery	13.0	41.8	39.8	3.1	2.2
Light industry	57.8	7.9	32.5	-0.8	2.6
Total industry	54.8	15.5	27.3	-1.3	3.7
1975–80					
Heavy and chemical industry	25.6	22.7	41.3	7.1	3.3
Chemical and chemical products	44.3	7.9	34.9	5.6	7.3
Primary metal manufacturing	7.0	29.8	57.2	12.7	-6.7
Metal products and machinery	9.9	39.9	40.8	5.8	3.6
Light industry	51.7	13.1	31.7	1.4	2.0
Total industry	48.1	21.2	27.3	1.7	1.8
1980–83					
Heavy and chemical industry	30.5	14.6	54.1	7.9	-7.1
Chemical and chemical products	55.6	15.9	52.8	-3.7	-20.5
Primary metal manufacturing	18.7	-2.7	74.2	19.6	-9.8
Metal products and machinery	17.5	19.2	48.8	12.0	2.6
Light industry	55.6	6.7	37.0	-1.2	2.0
Total industry	45.8	19.8	32.9	3.7	-2.2

Source: World Bank estimates, July 1986.

Table 6.3   Gross Fixed Capital Formation and Savings Rate
(percentage of GNP)

	1980	1981	1982	1983	1984	1985	1986
Gross fixed capital	32.2	28.7	30.5	31.3	31.3	30.8	30.4
Savings	20.8	20.5	20.9	25.3	27.9	28.6	32.6
Private	15.4	14.9	14.8	18.1	20.9	21.7	25.8
(Household)	6.6	6.9	6.8	7.6	9.9	10.6	13.0
(Corporate)	8.8	8.2	8.0	10.5	10.0	11.1	12.7
Government	5.4	5.6	6.1	7.2	7.1	6.9	6.8

Source: BOK, *Economic Statistics Yearbook.*

or assembling imported parts and components at lesser costs. Thanks in part to this strategy, Korea emerged as a manufacturing base for machinery products and thus its exports of machinery increased rapidly.

Investment and Savings

Brisk investment activities are essential not only to support sustained economic growth but to facilitate industrial restructuring. In 1981–87, Korea's real fixed capital investment growth averaged 8.8 percent with wide fluctuations from year to year. Investment reduced 4 percent in 1981 and picked up to 17.1 percent in 1983. It again slowed down to 4.4 percent in 1985 and rose to 13.6 percent in 1986. The ratio of nominal fixed capital investment to nominal GNP remained at more or less the 30 percent level during 1981–87 (table 6.3).

The ups and downs in real investment growth coincided with the business cycle in OECD economies. This means that Korea's investment is highly responsive to the prospects for exports growth rather than other factors such as interest rates and credit availability. In 1983–84, as the OECD recovery accelerated, the prospects for exports brightened and thus investment grew rapidly despite the tight monetary policy. Beginning in late 1984, investment started to falter, reflecting the gloomy prospects for exports as OECD economies slowed down.

The tight monetary policy did not act to dampen investment activities seriously—contrary to our expectations. The growth of money supply (M_2) plummeted from 26 percent in 1981–82 to 8 percent in 1984 and then moved to 19 percent in 1987. Thus credit availability for investment at banks was obviously tightened during 1984 and 1985.

However, non-banking financial institutions (NBFI) took up an increasing role to supply credit to the corporate sector. As noted earlier, the number of NBFIs increased quickly and their deposit liabilities and lending capacity increased sharply. While the growth of credit supplied through banking systems was being reduced, the credit supply of NBFIs was not contracted in parallel. In fact, NBFIs' credit increased 37 percent in 1981 and then continued to increase, albeit decelerated, at annual rates of 32 percent during 1982–84 and at 20 percent per year from 1985 to 1987. This level of credit supply was not short to meet demands for credit, as indicated in the sharp drop in the curb market interest rates, which are considered to reflect supply of and demand for credit. The rise in domestic savings backed up investment, with less reliance on foreign savings. Domestic savings in Korea have recovered steadily from the sharp decline in 1980 caused by the negative income growth and the loss in external terms of trade. In 1979, domestic savings as a percentage of GNP reached 27.8 percent and then plummeted to 20.8 percent in 1980. Since then, the savings rate has gradually increased to 32.6 percent in 1986 (table 6.3).

Domestic savings consist of three components: household, corporate, and government. The household savings as a percentage of GNP have shown a steady increase from 6.6 percent in 1980 to 7.6 percent in 1983, followed by a large jump to 9.9 percent in 1984 (table 6.3). Two factors contributed to this growth in household savings. One is the steady growth of household income and the other is the sharp rise of real deposit interest rates. The real deposit interest rates rose by almost 10 percent between 1980 and 1987, largely due to the drastic reduction in inflation. The corporate savings remained stagnant during the period of 1980–82, then increased to 10.5 percent in 1983, and since 1983 have risen to 12 percent in 1987. The change in corporate savings relates to changes in profit levels as well as tax and depreciation allowances. Considering that there was no significant change in the tax burden, though the corporate tax rate was brought down from 38 – 40 percent to 30–33 percent in 1983, the increase in the corporate savings rate in recent years was largely due to the increase in profit levels reflecting economic boom. The government savings rose from 5.4 percent in 1980 to 7.2 percent in 1983 and since then remained at the 7 percent level. The tight controls on government expenditure were conducive to the increase in government savings. There was little increase in tax burden; the ratio of tax revenue to GNP remained 18.1 percent over the period 1981–87.

Table 6.4   Noneconomically Active Population in Housekeeping and
Attending School (thousands)

	Housekeeping			Attending School		
Year	Total	Male	Female	Total	Male	Female
1970	4,694	393	4,301	1,920	1,135	785
1975	5,099	348	4,751	2,860	1,711	1,149
1980	5,410	276	5,134	2,873	1,725	1,148
1981	5,565	285	5,280	3,105	1,848	1,257
1982	5,604	292	5,312	3,146	1,895	1,251
1983	5,926	377	5,549	3,267	1,979	1,288
1984	6,216	411	5,805	3,738	2,214	1,524
1985	6,108	393	5,715	3,925	2,280	1,645
1986	6,069	411	5,658	4,074	2,358	1,716

Source: Economic Planning Board, *Yearbook of Labor Statistics*, 1985 and 1986.

Labor, Wages, and Prices

Labor Market. During the period of 1981–87, employment in Korea grew 2.77 percent annually, while the population 15 years of age and over grew 2.55 percent annually. Despite the resulting increasing discrepancy in supply of and demand for labor, the unemployment rate remained virtually unchanged at the 4 percent level during this period. The explanation for this pattern is the increase in the non-economically-active population attending school and in housekeeping (table 6.4). The population attending school did not show a sharp increase during the period of 1980–84. Table 6.5 shows that the increase in population attending school registered 940,000 and 845,000 respectively in 1970–75 and 1975–80, while in 1980–87 it registered 1,200,000. Given the moderate increase in the population attending school, the sharp increase in the non-economically-active population is mostly ascribed to the increase in population in housekeeping. The population in housekeeping increased 12.2 percent in 1980–86 compared to 6.3 percent in 1975–80. This is largely due to the rapid rural-urban migration that took place between 1982 and 1985. During this period migration took place at an annual rate of about 600,000, which is much higher than annual migration of about 350,000 during the period of 1977–80. New migrants are older and less educated than those in the 1970s, and thus may find it harder to enter the labor market. Considering that it is not an easy job to clearly discern between the unemployed and the non-economically-active population, there appears to be a considerable number of the

Table 6.5   Changes in Price Indices and Exchange Rate (percentage)

	1981	1982	1983	1984	1985	1986	1987
Wage rate	20.2	14.6	11.9	7.7	10.1	9.2	11.3
Labor productivity	16.9	7.2	13.0	10.0	6.9	12.7	9.9
Wholesale prices	20.4	4.7	0.2	0.7	0.9	-1.5	0.5
Consumer prices	21.3	7.3	3.4	2.3	2.4	2.8	3.0
Import prices	2.4	-5.3	-4.2	0.3	-2.7	-6.7	10.9
Export prices	3.0	-3.6	-2.9	1.8	-2.3	-0.4	8.3
Nominal exch. rate (Won/US$)	6.2	6.9	6.2	4.0	7.6	-0.3	-0.7

Source: Bank of Korea, *Economic Statistic Yearbook*. Ministry of Labor, *Report on Monthly Labor Survey*.

disguised non-economically-active population who are both willing and able to enter the labor market when its situation improves. The point here is that though the unemployment rate is fairly low, Korea's employment has not improved in recent years.

Wages. Nominal wage growth has decelerated sharply from a rate of 20.2 percent in 1981 to about 7.7 percent in 1984. Thereafter the wage rate has tended to rise gradually to 11 percent in 1987 (table 6.5). Wage growth in the public sector has been decelerating since 1981 and was effectively frozen in 1984, followed by a 4 percent growth in 1985. During this period, the government tried to have an influence on wage settlements in the private sector by setting low growth in public sector wage rates. This form of wage guidelines has not had a great influence on private wage settlements. During the same period of 1982–87, labor productivity grew 10 percent annually. The development in real wage rates and labor productivity resulted in reducing unit labor cost and thus exerting downward pressure on inflation. Wage structure has been improved. Wage differences between managers and production workers have been greatly reduced and so have wage differences between college graduates and middle school graduates and less. Managers earned on average 3.70 times more than production workers in 1980. In 1986, the difference was reduced to 3.18 times. College graduates earned 3.32 times more than middle school graduates and less in 1980. In 1986, this ratio was slightly reduced to 2.86 times.

Prices. The most remarkable economic achievement in the post-1980 period is the sharp reduction in inflation. The rate of increase in wholesale price index (WPI) decelerated from 20.4 percent in 1981 to 4.7 percent in 1982 and 0.5 percent in 1987, while that of consumer price index (CPI) decelerated from 31.3 percent in 1981 to 7.3 percent in 1982 and 3 percent in 1987. One factor behind these low rates of inflation is continuing declines in the prices of oil and other imported commodities as well as low inflation in Korea's major industrialized trading partners. Import prices in U.S. dollars declined by 5.3 percent in 1982 and 6.7 percent in 1986, followed by an 11 percent rise in 1987. Export prices followed a similar pattern; they dropped by 3.6 percent in 1982 and then picked up to 8.3 percent in 1987. There has been continuous significant depreciation of Korea's won until 1986. This, by and large, offset the pulling-down impact of the decline in import prices on domestic inflation.

Money, Interest Rates, and Financial Markets

Money and Financial Markets. Due to tight monetary policy and rapid growth of NBFIs, Korea's financial structure has seen a rapid change in the period 1980–87. The most prominent change is that the share of the banking sector in the financial market has shrunk rapidly. In terms of the share in total financial credits, the bank's share was 63 percent in 1980 but dropped to 49 percent by 1987 despite a 14 percent increase in the ratio of bank credit to GNP (table 6.6). NBFIs accordingly took up more share in both credits and deposits of all financial institutions.

What are the factors facilitating the rapid development of NBFIs? NBFIs comprise investment and finance companies and insurance and investment trust companies. Investment and finance companies deal in short-term commercial paper, whereas insurance and investment trust companies attract longer term funds that are again used to invest in corporate bonds or loan directly to business. In the early 1980s the investment and finance companies were encouraged to grow in the expectation that they would serve as a bridge between the curb market and the organized financial market. In an effort to attract curb market funds into the organized financial markets, interest rates on the commercial papers offered by investment and finance companies were allowed to be determined freely depending on the market situation and have been higher than deposit rates in the banks. Further, banks guaranteed commercial papers in an effort to reduce risk and facilitate the growth of this asset. For insurance and investment trust companies, interest rates have been set at

Table 6.6　　　Financial Sector Development (percentage)

	1975	1980	1981	1982	1983	1984	1985	1986	1987
M1/GNP	12.0	10.0	9.0	11.0	12.0	10.0	10.0	10.0	10.0
M2/GNP	31.0	34.0	34.0	38.0	39.0	37.0	39.0	39.0	40.0
M3/GNP[a]	36.0	48.0	51.0	60.0	65.0	68.0	75.0	82.0	92.0
Bond/GNP[b]	—	4.0	5.0	6.0	8.0	10.0	10.0	10.0	10.0
Bank Credit/GNP	39.0	43.0	44.0	49.0	51.0	51.0	56.0	50.0	49.0
NBFI Credit/GNP	10.0	25.0	28.0	33.0	37.0	44.0	50.0	47.0	50.0
Credit Share Banks									
Banks	79.4	63.2	61.1	59.8	58.0	54.0	53.0	1.0	49.0
NBFIs	21.4	36.8	38.9	40.2	42.0	46.0	47.0	49.0	51.0
Bond yields	20.1	30.1	24.4	17.3	14.2	14.1	14.2	12.8	12.8
Bank lending rate	15.5	20.0	17.0	10.0	10.0	10.0	10.0	10.0	10.0

Source: The Bank of Korea, *Economic Statistics Yearbook*, various issues.
a. M3 is defined as the sum of M2 plus deposits at non-bank financial institutions and commercial bills sold and certificates of deposits and debentures issued by deposit money banks.
b. Value of listed corporate bonds.

two to three points higher than bank rates. These higher interest rates served to increase NBFIs' rapid deposit liabilities. On the user's side, firms had to have access to NBFIs or the direct credit market due to the tight control on domestic credit of the banking sector.

What are the implications of the increasing share of NBFIs in the development of the financial market? First, the curb market has been successfully incorporated into the organized financial market. Second, a great financial deepening took place. Total credit of all financial institutions measured by the money supply M3 increased sharply from 36 percent of GNP in 1980 to 92 percent in 1987. Further, the ratio of M2 to GNP increased slightly from 34 percent in 1980 to 40 percent in 1987. That of M1 remained unchanged at about the 10 percent level. The rapid growth of NBFI deposits accounted for much of the growth of the M3 to GNP ratio. Third, though associated with financial deepening, it was not difficult for firms to borrow funds despite the tight bank credits, meaning that overall liquidity was not so strained as the bank's liquidity. Without having increased bank credits, a firm's needs for funds were largely met through the loans from NBFI and issuing corporate bonds.

Interest Rates. In recent years the level of interest rates has fallen sharply and their structure has been rearranged markedly. As inflation decelerated, nominal interest rates dropped in parallel. In nominal terms bank lending rates fell from 20.2 percent in 1980 to 10.0 percent in 1982 and then remained between 10 and 11.5 percent. The real rate of interest, however, has been kept positive since 1981. Average real rates during 1981–84 were about 6 percent, increased to around 7–10 percent in 1985, and remained at that level thereafter. This is compared with the negative real rates prevalent throughout most of the 1970s. This movement in bank rates was by and large in line with the movement in yields on corporate bonds, which are determined by market forces. The yields on corporate bonds fell from 30.1 percent in 1980 to 17.3 percent in 1982, 14.2 percent in 1983, and then down to the 13 percent level by 1987. The difference between bank rates and yields on corporate bonds has narrowed from 7.2 percent in 1980 to 5.3 percent in 1982, 4.2 percent in 1983, and then 2.7 to 4.2 percent during 1985–87. The tendency that the gap between bank rates and bond yields has been narrowing indicates that bank rates are approaching market rates. Helped by this trend, in 1984 the government introduced a system that permits banks to lend at rates with larger margins, presumably depending on the assessment of the borrower. This is understood as a first step toward complete liberalization of the interest rate in the future.

Balance of Payments, Trade Structure, and External Debt

Korea's current account has seen a remarkable improvement during the period 1980–87. The current account changed gradually from a deficit of US$5.3 billion in 1980 (8.9 percent of GNP) to a surplus of US$9.8 billion in 1987 (8.3 percent of GNP). Merchandise trade balance reached equilibrium in 1985 from the deficit of US$4.4 billion in 1980, and then grew gradually to US$7.7 billion in 1987 (table 6.7). The improvement in the trade balance can be greatly ascribed to reduction in oil prices and depreciation of Korea's real exchange rate. During 1980 through September 1985, Korea's won was depreciated against the U.S. dollar by 84.2 percent and the real exchange rate was depreciated by 29.8 percent, taking into account Japanese and U.S. prices and exchange rate changes. From September 1985 to 1987, the Korean exchange rate against the U.S. dollar was appreciated by 9 percent. But the real exchange rate still depreciated by 13.8 percent, owing to the sharp appreciation of the yen relative to the

Table 6.7   The Korean Balance of Payments (billion $U.S.)

	Current account	Trade balance			Invisibles	
		Net	Exports	Imports	Net	Interest
1978	−1.1	−1.8	12.7	14.5	0.2	1.0
1979	−4.2	−4.4	14.7	19.1	−0.2	1.5
1980	−5.3	−4.4	17.2	21.6	−1.4	2.6
1981	−4.6	−3.6	20.7	24.3	−1.5	3.5
1982	−2.6	−2.6	20.9	23.5	−0.6	3.6
1983	−1.6	−1.8	23.2	25.0	−0.4	3.2
1984	−1.4	−1.0	26.3	27.4	−0.9	3.8
1985	−0.9	−0.0	26.4	26.4	−1.4	3.6
1986	4.6	4.2	33.9	29.7	−0.6	3.2
1987	9.8	7.7	46.2	38.6	1.0	2.7

Source: The Bank of Korea, *Economic Statistics Yearbook*, various issues.

U.S. dollar. Invisible balance improved, largely due to a strong turn-around in the balance for shipping and transportation that more than offset the increased payment of interest on the external debt and reduced earnings from overseas construction.

Trade Structure. Korea's export structure has continued to change in the last five years (table 6.8). Manufactured exports have increased their share from 84.6 percent in 1980 to 96.5 percent in 1987. The most significant change is that light industry exports have declined in relative terms as heavy industry products have increased their share by more than 6 percent from 49.0 in 1980 to 55.5 percent in 1987. This increased share of heavy industry products is largely attributable to the increase in the shares of electrical and electronics from 12.3 percent in 1980 to 23.0 percent in 1987. In addition, the export of automobiles has increased rapidly, contributing to the increased share of the heavy industry products.

On the import side, two developments are noteworthy. One is that the share of oil in import value dropped sharply from 25.2 percent in 1980 to 9.0 percent in 1987, largely due to the decline in the prices of oil, as well as strong energy conservation efforts since 1981. The other is that the share of capital goods in imports increased sharply from 20.2 percent in 1980 to 35.5 percent in 1987.

Korea's market diversification has decreased since 1980. The United States and Japan, Korea's principal trading partners, accounted

Table 6.8   Composition of Exports by Major Firms (percentage)

	1975	1980	1984	1987
Primary products	17.6	5.4	3.4	3.5
Manufacturing products	81.6	84.6	96.6	96.5
Light	56.5	48.4	36.4	41.0
Textiles & garments	36.2	28.2	21.6	21.4
Heavy and chemical	26.1	49.0	60.2	55.5
Electrical & electronics	8.7	12.3	15.6	23.0
Machines	—	3.4	2.5	3.4

Source: Korea Trade Association, *Annual Trade Statistics*, various issues.

for over 56.6 percent of its exports and 54.6 percent of its imports in 1987, while the combined share in exports was 44 percent and the share in imports was 48 percent in 1980. To some extent, the importance of the two countries is unavoidable because they have been the main source of global incremental demand recently, and most developing countries have been in stagnation since the early 1980s. Moreover, Korea's bilateral trade has shown increasing imbalances. With the United States it is in surplus, which increased from only US$280 million in 1982 to US$9.5 billion in 1987; and with Japan it is in deficit, which increased from US$1.9 billion in 1982 to US$5.0 billion in 1987. These increasing imbalances in bilateral trade are largely due to the rise in the value of the dollar against yen, the difference in the growth of GNP, and Korea's high import dependence of its production on Japanese capital goods and components. The exchange rate appreciation since 1986 and Korea's effort to reduce its trade surplus with the United States are expected to change the pattern of bilateral imbalances considerably in the future.

External Debt. Korea's external debt has increased from US$27 billion in 1980 to US$46.7 billion in 1985 and then declined to $35.6 billion in 1987. Deducting foreign assets Korea possesses in the form of deposits in foreign banks and export credits, net external debt increased from US$19.6 billion in 1980 to US$22.4 billion in 1987 (table 6.9). The continuous reduction in external debt is the result of the decrease in the current account deficit and the surplus in the latter years. In addition, the maturity structure has improved. Short-term debt has declined from a third of total debt in 1981–82 to less than a quarter in 1985–1987. Although the debt-service ratio has remained around 20–30 percent during this period,

Table 6.9   External Debt Developments

	1981	1982	1983	1984	1985	1986	1987
Total external debt							
($ billion)	32.5	37.1	40.2	43.1	46.8	44.5	35.6
Medium- and long-term							
debt (%)	68.5	66.5	69.9	73.2	77.0	79.2	73.9
Short-term debt (%)	31.5	33.5	30.1	26.8	23.0	20.8	26.1
Total external assets ($ billion)	8.0	8.8	9.5	10.1	11.2	12.0	13.2
Net debt ($ billion)	24.5	28.3	30.9	32.9	32.6	32.5	22.4
Debt ratio service (%)	21.2	22.6	20.9	22.6	21.8	22.7	30.8
Debt/GNP ratio (%)	48.3	52.4	53.4	52.5	56.2	46.7	30.0

Source: Ministry of Finance.

Korea's debt position has significantly improved as shown by the debt/GNP ratio of 30 percent in 1987.

The most significant changes in the sources of external financing are that bonds have become an important source of external finance, and that direct and portfolio foreign investments, while still minor sources, have risen rapidly. Bond-type instruments such as promissory notes and floating rate notes and certificates of deposit accounted for only 6 percent of the gross financing requirement in 1982, but rose to 24 percent in 1985. The advantage in more reliance on bonds is that sources of funds are more diversified and the transaction costs are lower. But more importantly, bonds have no restrictions regarding the use of funds in general. Direct foreign investment in terms of its cumulative amount has doubled since 1982 as government has eased restrictions on foreign investments. The government announced its plan to open up at least 90 percent of Korea's industries to direct foreign investment by 1988. Portfolio foreign investment has increased as well. Since 1981 foreigners have been allowed to buy Korean securities indirectly through special investment trusts. Six such trusts are now in operation. Korea also allowed domestic companies to issue convertible debentures and depository receipts, which are another source of portfolio foreign investment.

Social Welfare and Income Distribution

Of the welfare programs the Korean government has implemented since the early 1980s, the health programs deserve special attention. The

Table 6.10   Gini Coefficient

	1970	1976	1980	1984
All households Gini coefficient	0.3322	0.3908	0.3891	0.3567
Non-Farm households Gini coefficient	0.3455	0.4118	0.4053	0.3655
Farm householdsGini coefficient	0.2945	0.3273	0.3555	0.2992

Source: Korea Development Institute estimates, July 1986.

population covered by medical aid or insurance has increased remarkably from 29.6 percent of total population in 1980 to 51.4 percent in 1985. In Korea, medical insurance is compulsory in the sense that firms with a certain number of employees are required to join the insurance program. This compulsory coverage has been expanded as an outcome of the government's measure to lower the required number of employees from 300 in 1979 to 16 in 1983. The Korean government recently announced its plan to raise the coverage to 100 percent by 1988. Then the workers in small firms and the population in rural areas will benefit from medical insurance. Fiscal expenditure for health has remained small as indicated by a mere 0.3 percent of GNP in 1983, compared to 7.8 percent in Australia and 11.0 percent in the Netherlands in 1984.

Korea's income distribution has improved in the post-1980 period. The Gini coefficient for all households dropped from 0.3891 in 1980 to 0.3567 in 1984. Similarly the Gini coefficient for farm households declined (table 6.10). The reasons for improving income distribution are many. Among them, notable are the decreasing wage disparities between skilled and unskilled, price stability, and government policy to abolish preferential loans for strategic sectors largely related to large firms and heavy and light industry.

The Fifth and Sixth Five-Year Economic and Social Development Plans

The Fifth Five-Year Plan (1982–1986) launched in 1982 was revised in 1983 due to rapid changes in external assumptions and a need to realign priorities. The revised Fifth plan stressed that top priority should be given to achieving price stability at the 1–2 percent level, and to realizing a small surplus in the current account in the final year of the plan period. The plan also emphasized sustaining 7–8 percent of GNP growth. To achieve these goals, the plan suggested a series of industrial and financial reforms to promote competition. By and large, all of these goals were achieved. In addition to an average inflation of 3.6 percent and sustained GNP growth at an average rate of 8.7 percent during the plan, the current account for 1986 is a surplus of US$4.6 billion. The changes in industrial and financial policies envisaged in the Fifth plan have by and large been made. However, export performance was not up to expectations largely because of growing protectionism abroad and slower recovery of OECD economies than expected. The employment situation also did not improve as expected. Despite the sweeping deregulation measures, de facto government intervention is still heavy, hampering the development of the market economy, and thus limiting private initiatives in resource allocation and decision making.

The Sixth Plan (1987–1992), which is under revision, gives top priority to a reduction in Korea's net external debt and completion of trade and financial liberalization. The plan is forecasted to eliminate its net debt by 1992 and achieve net assets of $0.4 billion. Thus Korea will be transformed from a high growth/debt country to a high growth/asset country. Domestic savings will increase to a level to more than finance the required investments for 7.5 percent GNP growth, and the ratio of current account surplus to GNP will be reduced from 8.3 percent in 1987 to 2.3 percent in 1992. Korea's exports will increase at an annual rate of 10 percent. One of the characteristics of the Sixth plan is that domestic demand will play a greater role in leading GNP growth, while the role of exports will be relatively reduced. In addition, by completing trade and financial liberalization, the plan envisages that the Korean economy will be more market-oriented and play a leading role for the promotion of free trade among the nations of the world.

Economic Issues for the Future

In December 1987, Korea elected Mr. Roh Tae Woo as its president. The Roh government is expected to govern the country in a more democratic manner than before. Thus, the people will actively participate in the decision making of the government. Further, the role of the private sector will be enhanced in the management of the economy and in economic policy making.

Dr. Rha Woong Bae, deputy prime minister and minister of the Economic Planning Board, and his team have faced and will continue to face both internal and external demands. Internally, the public wants to sustain economic growth and the current account surplus, and at the same time it—especially labor and low income groups—wants to equitably share the fruit of economic growth with others. Externally, the United States and other countries are asking for Korea to open its market to foreigners, leading to keeping Korea's current account surplus at levels satisfactory to both Korea and other countries. The government is likely to establish economic policies that are consistent with a market-oriented economy, namely market forces themselves solving economic problems. For example, the government did not intervene in strikes and production stoppages by workers pushing for higher wages and improved benefits. To reduce Korea's current account surplus and trade friction between Korea and the United States, the exchange rate was appreciated substantially despite high wage hikes, which are equivalent to real appreciation in the exchange rate. The government will design the policies to supply housing for low-income groups, improve rural economic conditions, and expand medical programs. It is hoped that these policies will raise the welfare level of the country.

There are three important economic issues that Korea has to tackle. The first issue is how to cope with continuing protectionism in the United States and OECD countries. In the last five years, between 35 percent and 43 percent of total Korean exports have been under one form of restriction or another. For some products such as footwear, textiles, and silk goods, restrictions have typically covered over two-thirds of total exports. In the 1970s, most light industrial products were subject to restrictions, but restrictions now extend to heavy industrial items such as steel products and high technology items including television sets and other electronic products. OECD countries have had increasing recourse to bilateral agreement as well as anti-dumping and countervailing actions. To cope with mounting protectionism, Korea has made efforts to diversify both markets and products. More importantly, Korea has pursued and expanded import liberalization. But if the effects of these policies will not immediately be realized, what are the policies Korea needs in order to satisfy the external demand?

The second issue is how to increase the competitiveness in domestic markets through the promotion of two key forms of competition: internal competition and competition among Korean exporters in foreign markets. The export rivalry with insufficiency of internal competition turned out to be less effective in ensuring the dynamic efficiency. In recognition of the need for more dynamic efficiency, a series of reforms were made to lift restrictions on imports as well as allow new firms to enter monopolized segments of the industry. However, there are still many segments of the industry that enjoy monopolistic status. Thus, concerted efforts to reduce the monopolistic status need to be made through eliminating restrictions and reducing tariff rates.

The third issue is how to reduce the high financial leverage of Korean firms. Korean firms have excessively high financial leverage compared to those in the United States and Japan. The ratio of equity to total value of equity plus debt in Korean firms stood at 20 percent in 1984, while those in Japan and the United States stood at 31.7 percent and 49.1 percent, respectively, in 1981. The most important causes for the weak financial structure are frequent bailouts of large corporations and shortcomings in the corporate and personal income tax systems. Frequent bailouts have not only created moral hazard problems but given firms a strong incentive to maximize borrowing. This, together with the large tax advantage of borrowing, has weakened the financial structure. In the corporate tax system, corporate interest payments are tax deductible, whereas returns to stockholders are not. Since tax deductibility of interest payments reduces the after-tax cost of debt, debt has more tax advantage than equity. In the personal tax system, the tax rate on interest income is substantially smaller than the tax rate from stocks, the average of dividend tax and capital gains tax. This makes holding equities disadvantageous relative to debt securities. The corporate tax system encourages firms to borrow, and the personal tax system makes investors prefer debt securities to common stocks. Thus, the tax system needs to be revised in such a way that both supply of and demand for equity capital are encouraged.

7

LAWRENCE J. LAU

Conclusion

Over the past quarter century, the economies of both Taiwan and South Korea have been successful beyond what anyone dared dream in the mid-1960s. In Taiwan, gross national product (GNP) per capita in 1988 was more than twenty-seven times higher than in 1965, and in South Korea it was almost thirty times higher.[1] In real terms, GNP grew at an average annual rate of approximately 9 percent in both economies over this period.[2] To put this performance in perspective, we may note that during the two decades of most rapid economic growth in the history of the United States (approximately 1870–1890), real GNP grew at a rate of less than 5 percent per year.[3] Of all other countries, only Japan, from 1955 to 1976, has ever experienced a comparable rate of real economic growth.[4] No other economies have ever had as high a rate of real economic growth over as long a period.

The international trade of both economies has also grown by leaps and bounds—a direct consequence of their export promotion policies. For Taiwan, total two-way trade on a free on board (f.o.b.) basis rose from US$974 million in 1965 to US$107 billion in 1988.[5] For South Korea, the comparable figures are US$591 million in 1965 and US$108 billion in 1988.[6] Both Taiwan and South Korea are now among the top trading nations in the world. Their trade deficits of 1965—US$72 million for Taiwan and US$240 million for South Korea—have turned into trade surpluses by 1988—US$13.8 billion for Taiwan and US$11.4 billion for South Korea. External debt for Taiwan is currently a mere US$1 billion or so, and for South Korea it is approximately US$30 billion and declining rapidly. Official foreign-exchange reserves now total US$75 billion for Taiwan and US$15 billion for South Korea. Since 1985, the exchange rate of Taiwan has appreciated more than 40 percent against the U.S. dollar, and that of South Korea has appreciated 25 percent.

What are some of the reasons behind the phenomenal economic successes of Taiwan and South Korea? From a growth accounting point of view, more than half of the increases in real output per capita can be attributed to increases in inputs, especially capital inputs. The savings rates (measured by the ratio of nominal gross national savings to nominal GNP) of both Taiwan and South Korea have always been high by the standards of developing countries. Since 1965, the savings rate of Taiwan has averaged 30 percent, has never fallen below 20 percent, and reached a peak of 38.5 percent in 1987. The Korean savings rate was somewhat lower at the beginning of the period (7.3 percent), but nevertheless averaged higher than 25 percent over the whole period, peaking at 37.7 percent in 1988. As a result of these high savings rates, there has been rapid capital accumulation—net real capital stocks grew at average annual rates of 12.15 percent and 14.5 percent respectively in Taiwan and South Korea.[7] There has also been significant growth of the labor force in both economies—3.3 percent per year in Taiwan and 3.0 percent per year in South Korea.

The rates of growth of total factor productivity, however, (growth in real output net of growth in inputs), have not been exceptionally high for either of these two economies. They may be estimated at between 0.75 and 0.9 percent per year for both Taiwan and South Korea between 1965 and 1988.[8] These rates are comparable in magnitude to those of advanced industrial economies. For example, the average rate of growth of total factor productivity in the United States over 1948–1979 has been estimated at 0.8 percent per year by Jorgenson, Gollop, and Fraumeni.[9] Unlike the situation in advanced industrial economies, however, the growth in total factor productivity, or as some may prefer, technical progress, accounts for only a relatively small, though not insignificant, proportion of the growth in real output in both economies.

But there are countries with similarly high savings and investment rates, such as mainland China, that failed to take off economically because they did not utilize their inputs efficiently. Thus the growth in inputs alone is a necessary but not sufficient condition for the superior economic performance of the two economies; one must look for additional explanations elsewhere.

From the point of view of economic policies, the replacement of import substitution with export promotion, together with the maintenance of realistic interest rates, deserves a great deal of credit.[10] The latter policy undoubtedly helped to encourage saving. However, many other countries, such as Brazil and Mexico, also tried export promotion, and some even succeeded for a while, but most failed to take off into sustained growth. Thus, export promotion and maintenance of realistic interest rates alone cannot be the whole story.

There have also been claims that it was the authoritarian nature of the governments of Taiwan and South Korea that was responsible for their successes.[11] Obviously, stability and continuity of policies encourage investment, other things being equal. There is doubtless a considerable advantage in having a government or government leader with enough authority and security to make the critical, difficult, and contentious decisions in an expeditious manner, without having to wait for a consensus to form. But among the world's economic "basket cases" are countries governed by well-entrenched authoritarian regimes. One need not look very far or very long to see that authoritarianism is associated more often with economic backwardness and stagnation than with economic growth. Both Taiwan and South Korea were fortunate enough to have able and dedicated bureaucrats spearheading the development process.[12]

One important factor common to the development experiences of both Taiwan and South Korea is the prominent role accorded private enterprise. Early in their development drive (the late 1950s for Taiwan and the early 1960s for South Korea), the respective governments decided that firms to be established in the new (initially mostly export-oriented) industries were to be private rather than government-owned, except in naturally monopolistic industries such as utilities. This choice turned out to have enormous economic significance. First, private enterprise means that the firms, most run by owner-managers, are motivated to make profits. Second, the owner-managers of these private firms often have to put their own equity capital at risk, because no one, including the government, is going to make good any losses that they may incur. The owner-managers of these firms thus have the incentive to maximize profit and minimize loss and, most important, to pay careful attention to the consequences of what they do and do not do, unlike the managers of government-owned enterprises. There is, moreover, little or no incentive incompatibility problem as long as firms remain essentially family affairs.[13]

A second important factor common to both Taiwan and South Korea is the establishment of the rule of law in the economic sphere.

This implies not only the fair and timely enforcement of contract laws but also the guarantee of due process and the reduction of administrative discretion in routine economic matters. The rule of law enhances predictability and security of returns from investments. It also means that any profit made legally will not be arbitrarily taken away, either directly by the government or indirectly by other enterprises with special privileges or good government connections. The government intervenes directly or indirectly on behalf of particular private firms only very sparingly. Thus, the rewards of economic success will ordinarily go to the efficient, not to the merely politically powerful or well connected, and not to the government.

This is not to say that the governments of Taiwan and South Korea have not been interventionist. They have been, but at the same time they have also been largely content to let owner-managers run their firms without interference and retain any profits they make. On the whole, however, South Korea seems to be more intrusive than Taiwan in directing the activities of private firms.[14]

A third important factor is the presence of competition. Both Taiwan and South Korea have generally refrained from creating or supporting domestic monopolies, except those operated by the governments for revenue and other reasons, such as increasing returns to scale. Even in South Korea, with its high degree of industrial concentration, there is usually more than one firm in a given line of business. Moreover, the governments do not compete with private firms through unfair means. The export orientation of the economies means that most firms have to compete internationally with firms of other nations, in third-country markets, over which neither they nor their governments have much control. The discipline imposed by the fiercely competitive world market keeps the firms lean, mean, and honest. With the increasing openness of the domestic markets of Taiwan and South Korea, the firms will be subject to even more intense competitive pressure to be efficient.

Perhaps the critical difference between the policies of import substitution and export promotion lies in the fact that under import substitution there is little or no competitive pressure on the firms, whereas under export promotion firms in one country have to compete with firms all over the world. While it is true that inefficient export firms can still be subsidized, it is more noticeable and more difficult to sustain in the long run than an import tariff or restriction. There is also much less rent to be sought and appropriated on the open world market.

The combination of all three factors—private enterprise, rule of law, and competition—has been essential to the successes of Taiwan and South Korea. Private enterprise without competition will result in private monopolies with possibly far worse consequences for allocative efficiency than public monopolies. Without the rule of law, there will be a great deal of rent seeking and other similarly socially wasteful, but nevertheless privately profit-maximizing, activities. Private enterprise provides the profit motive, but the competition and rule of law are also necessary to ensure the efficient allocation of resources. It is only because of real or potential competition that private owner-managers must strive for efficiency in order to make a profit. For firms in both Taiwan and South Korea, there has been adequate competition, if not from domestic rivals, then from the open international marketplace.[15]

In many other aspects, the economies of Taiwan and South Korea remain different. Taiwan continues to have more control than South Korea over inflation, which has been consistently higher in South Korea than in Taiwan. There are many reasons for this: First, South Korea is not as competitive as Taiwan; Korean firms are in general larger and more monopolistic. Second, imports are also less liberalized in South Korea. By and large, Korean imports still consist of mostly capital goods and not consumer goods. Third, there is greater polarization between management and labor in South Korea, which results in less downward flexibility in the real wage rate. Finally, and more recently, the appreciation of the Korean won is not quite up to the level of the New Taiwan dollar. There are also factors favoring South Korea, however: the South Korean current-account surplus is lower, and the rate of increase of the money supply is consequently also lower. The rate of growth of the money supply in South Korea was just over 20 percent per year in early 1989, while it was 25 percent in Taiwan at the end of 1988. Actual inflation, however, has been lower in Taiwan.

But there also seems to be a partial convergence in the economic policies of Taiwan and South Korea in the 1980s. Both Taiwan and South Korea have allowed their currencies to appreciate; but Taiwan's has appreciated more than South Korea's. More recently, however, there is once again discussion of a possible devaluation of the Korean won as a way of maintaining international competitiveness. South Korea has, since the early 1980s, begun to pay more attention to income distribution and social welfare, and Taiwan has recently begun to pursue a more active industrial policy through the government funding of major research-and-development projects. Both Taiwan and South Korea have embarked on a process of liberalizing their financial markets.

Taiwan and South Korea also face many common problems, and both are now at critical crossroads: they no longer have low labor costs; strikes have become commonplace; exchange rates have appreciated significantly, affecting their international competitiveness; they must transform and upgrade their industrial structure to remain competitive in the world market; they face environmental opposition at home and protectionism abroad; and they also have to face the thorny problem of how and whether to continue supporting their farmers at home in the face of U.S. pressure to open up their economies to agricultural imports.

What are the prospects for future growth in Taiwan and South Korea? Despite the existence of many problems at home and abroad, such as the environment, labor, trade surplus and protectionism, and the even bigger issues of working out an orderly mechanism for resolving social conflicts and achieving a consensus on social policies, this author remains optimistic. Most of the people in Taiwan and South Korea are pragmatists. They will realize soon enough that confrontation and noncooperation work against the interests of everyone and that accommodation and cooperation are "positive-sum" strategies. In this regard the Japanese development experience provides hope. Contrary to public conception, Japan has not always been a shining example of successful management–labor relations. As late as the early 1960s, there were constant strikes and bitter conflicts between labor and management in Japan, not unlike those in Taiwan and South Korea today. Only since then have Japanese management and labor begun to see that their long-term interests were interrelated, and that they would be better off working together. Today, Japanese management–labor relations are widely admired. The labor strife of the 1960s now seems distant and largely forgotten. Thus, there is no need to despair about the labor strife occurring in Taiwan and South Korea now. It too will pass with the maturation of the labor movement, and when it does the economies will become so much stronger.

In addition, the high and rising level of human capital in both economies will help raise their technological levels and enable the upgrading of their industrial structures in response to rising labor costs and exchange rates.[16] Already, labor costs in Taiwan are no longer low compared with other newly industrialized economies and would-be NIEs, and they are creeping higher in South Korea. The inevitable major restructuring of the industries has already begun.

Where can Taiwan and South Korea go from here? The two economies should attempt to find their own respective ways, taking into account their own histories and cultures. Taiwan and South Korea have moved beyond basic subsistence and have established a solid foundation for continued capital accumulation and real output growth. Now is the time for the citizens of both countries to reflect on the composition of outputs to be produced, on the quality and way of life, and on the shape and form of the society desired for the future. The social welfare states of Western Europe, such as the Scandinavian countries, West Germany, and the United Kingdom, do not provide a good model for emulation. They do not allow sufficient incentives for individuals to assume responsibilities and risks. When workers have no incentive to work, consumers have no incentive to save, entrepreneurs have no incentive to be efficient, and investors have no incentive to invest wisely, and more generally, when people do not have the incentive to take responsibility for their own well-being, the economy and the society will be in serious trouble. Japan does not provide a good model either. While there is no question that in terms of U.S. dollars, Japan has a higher per capita income than the United States, in terms of real standards of living, most Japanese will readily acknowledge that they have a long way to go before achieving parity with the Americans. This situation has been brought about by serious distortions in the allocation of resources in the Japanese economy; distortions that cannot be easily corrected now because of the immense networks of vested interests built up over so many years. These distortions are manifested in the high prices of food, housing, and other consumer goods relative to prices in the rest of the world. It is important for Taiwan and South Korea to avoid introducing and perpetuating the same distortions. A real danger for Taiwan and South Korea is to end up like today's Japan, with a high per capita nominal income but a low real standard of living for the average citizen.

Appendix

Profiles of Policymakers in the Republic of China and the Repubic of Korea

The Republic of China—Ramon H. Myers

Taiwan is widely cited as a notable example of a country that has provided a continually rising standard of living for its people. Many studies document Taiwan's so-called miracle in transforming a backward economy into a prosperous one, and many development economists believe that strong and stable leadership is a prerequesite to economic success in developing countries.

Who were the principal architects of Taiwan's success? During the past decade, Chiang Ching-kuo, as president of the Republic of China, provided Taiwan with strong, stable leadership. Before becoming premier of the Republic of China in Taiwan in 1972 and president in 1978, Chiang served in many important government postions, both in mainland China and in Taiwan. Among them were: administrative commissioner for South Kiangsi in mainland China from 1939 to 1945; special foreign affairs commissioner for northeastern China from 1945 to 1947; deputy economic control supervisor for Shanghai in 1948; chairman of the Vocational Assistance Commission for Retired Servicemen from 1957 to 1964; minister of the National Defense Ministry from 1964 to 1969; and vice premier and chairman of the Council for International Economic Cooperation and Development from 1969 to 1972.

With the experience gained from his long successful government service and his natural gift as a leader, Chiang was immensely popular among both mainlanders and native Taiwanese. As premier and later as president of the Republic of China on Taiwan, Chiang forged a team of able and dedicated economic planners and administrators from a diverse group of professionals. He passed away in January 1988 and was succeeded as president by Lee Teng-Hui.

Taiwan's present success can also be attributed to a number of other distinguished figures. Most of these policymakers were trained in developed countries, but they also are well versed in the doctrines of Confucius and Sun Yat-sen. Yu Kuo-hwa and Li Kwoh-ting have been particularly influential in Taiwan's economic development during the past two decades.

Yu Kuo-hwa was educated at Tsinghua University, Harvard University, and the London School of Economics. From 1936 to 1944 he served as a personal secretary to the late President Chiang Kai-shek and in this capacity became very familiar with the inner workings of the government. From 1947 to 1950 he served as an alternate executive director of the International Bank for Reconstruction and Development (World Bank) and from 1951 to 1955 as an alternate executive director of the International Monetary Fund, representing the Republic of China in both organizations.

In 1955, Yu became the president and managing director of the Central Trust of China, which has an extensive network of offices all over the world and handles banking, trust, insurance, and trading functions. He served in that post until 1961. From 1961 to 1967 he served as the chairman of the Bank of China. From 1967 to 1969 he served as the minister of finance. In that capacity, he represented his country as a governor of the International Bank of Reconstruction and Development and the International Development Association.

The Central Bank of China in Taiwan plays a very important role in the field of monetary policy and in formulating economic and financial policies. From 1969 to 1984 Yu served as the Central Bank's governor, one of the most influential posts in the country. In this position, he has represented his country as the governor of the International Monetary Fund and the Asian Development Bank. His influence in Taiwan's economic matters grew even greater when he also served as the chairman of the Finance and Economic Committee from 1974 to 1977 and became the chairman of the Council for Economic Planning and Development in 1977, one year before Chiang Ching-kuo assumed the presidency of the Republic of China. In 1984, Yu was asked by President Chiang to lead the new government as premier during his second presidential term. Chiang's successor, Lee Teng-Hui, asked him to continue as premier, in which capacity he still served in 1988.

Li Kwoh-ting is another important figure with an international reputation. Surprisingly, he is a physicist by training. Educated at the Central University in Nanking and at Cambridge University, he was a professor at Wuhan University from 1937 to 1940. From 1951 to 1953 he was the president of Taiwan Shipbuilding Corporation. Li's career in government is illustrious: from 1953 to 1958 he was a member of the Industrial Development Committee under the Economic Stabilization Board; from 1958 to 1963 he was the secretary-general of the Council for U.S. Aid (CUSA); from 1963 to 1973 he served as the vice chairman of the Council for International Economic Cooperation and Development (CIECD); from 1965 to 1969 he was the minister of economic affairs; from 1969 to 1976 he was the minister of finance, and in this capacity, he was also a governor of the International Bank for Reconstruction and Development. From 1978 to 1988, Li served as a minister without portfolio and a member of the National Science Council. In July 1988 Li was appointed a senior adviser to the President of the Republic of China, Lee Teng-Hui. In recognition of his many contributions to Taiwan, Li was awarded the Ramon Magsaysay Award for Government Service in 1968.

Finally, one should also mention Lee Teng-Hui, president of the Republic of China on Taiwan since January 1988. Lee was born in Taiwan and was educated at Kyoto University and National Taiwan University, where he received his B.S. degree. He received his M.A. and Ph.D. degrees from Iowa State University and Cornell University respectively. From 1948 to 1978, he was a professor of agricultural economics and economics at National Taiwan University. Between 1957 and 1972, Lee held major research positions in the Sino–American Joint Commission for Rural Reconstruction and was responsible for the formulation and implementation of the agricultural sector policies in Taiwan during that period. From 1972 to 1978, he served as a minister without portfolio in the executive yuan (cabinet) and was given a variety of important assignments in addition to his general responsibility for the agricultural sector. He was appointed mayor of Taipei in 1978 and governor of the Province of Taiwan in 1981. In 1984, he was asked by President Chiang Ching-Kuo to serve as the vice president of the Republic of China on Taiwan during Chiang's second term. In January 1988, Lee succeeded Chiang as president upon the latter's death.

The Republic of Korea—Sung Yeung Kwack

Of the many factors that have contributed to Korea's economic progress, we cannot underestimate the role of policymakers. The late president, Park Chung Hee, was the principal architect of the so-called Korean miracle. The son of a peasant, his first job after graduating from normal school was as an elementary school teacher from 1937 to 1940. He then entered the Japanese Military Academy. Graduating in 1945, Park served as a Japanese army officer until the liberation of Korea, when he joined the Korean Army and established a reputation for being a strong general "of pure heart and clean hands." In May 1961, Park, by then a major general, ousted the civil government in Korea by a military coup—the first since the country's liberation. Officially installed as president in 1963, he retained power until his assassination in 1979.

Despite the limited freedom that generally characterized the political side of his government, the leadership of President Park has been credited as an important factor in promoting Korean economic growth. Unlike his predecessors, President Park took full charge of economic policy and was responsible for all final decisions in this area. Although he had no formal education in economics, his decisions have been shown to be generally correct. A capable manager himself, President Park significantly reformed Korean public administration by introducing a modern managerial system (based on American procedures) to government bureaucracy. Use of the staff system was an important element in this reform. President Park set up his own secretariat of economic specialists, which became in essence a cabinet above the formal cabinet. He relied heavily on his secretariat in the decision-making process.

Many professional economists, particularly those educated in the United States, participated in policymaking. Minister Nam Duck Woo was the most outstanding figure among these. Following an initial career at the Research Department of the Bank of Korea, he received his Ph.D. in economics at the University of Oklahoma in 1960. From 1963 to 1969 he taught at various universities in Korea. He was then appointed as Korea's minister of finance. In 1974 he was promoted to deputy prime minister and minister of the Economic Planning Board. He served in that post until 1978. Nam is regarded by the public as a proponent of freemarket mechanisms and an outward-looking national policy. He was instrumental in achieving a policy shift from government intervention to activation of market mechanisms in Korea.

Another important policymaker, Chang Key Young, served as deputy prime minister and the minister of the Economic Planning Board from 1964 to 1967. Under his supervision, Korea's First Economic Plan was launched. Chang graduated from a commercial high school in 1934, entered the Research Department of the Bank of Korea, and was promoted to vice president of the Bank in 1950. From 1952 to 1964 he was president of two newspaper companies.

Kim Hak Yol became deputy prime minister and minister of the Economic Planning Board in 1969 and remained in that position until 1972. He graduated from law school in Japan in 1944 and passed the highest-level Korean civil service examination in 1950. During the early 1950s, Kim studied economics at the University of Missouri and Akron University, under a government-sponsored training program. After serving capably on the senior staff of the minister of finance, he was promoted to minister of finance in 1966.

Tae Wan Sun succeeded Kim Hak Yol as deputy prime minister in 1972 and served until 1974. Tae graduated from law school in 1936, and served as congressman from 1950 to 1954. Prior to Park's ascension to power in 1961, Tae held the position of minister of commerce and industry under the Jang Myon government. During the 1960s he was a member of the opposition party. In 1961, however, he was selected by President Park to be minister of construction.

Kim Jon Pil, President Park's right-hand man at the time of his military coup, served as the first director of Korea's Central Intelligence Agency and then as prime minister until 1975. Although Kim's impact on the country was felt more in the political arena, he did play two important roles in the formulation of economic policy. First, he contributed to the adoption of economic development as the primary policy objective of the military government in the early 1960s, popularizing the terms "modernization," "industrialization," and "take-off." Second, Kim was instrumental in normalizing relations with Japan during the 1950s.

Kim Chung Yom studied economics in a Japanese junior college and worked at the Bank of Korea until 1956, when he entered the Ministry of Finance. He was promoted to minister of finance in 1966 and appointed minister of commerce and industry the following year. In 1969, he was made chief of the presidential secretariat, a position he held for ten years. Although not well known to the public during his career, Kim was nevertheless very influential in policymaking.

Kim Mahn Je received his Ph.D. in economics from the University of Missouri in 1964 and served as professor at Seogang University from

1965 to 1970. He was appointed the first president of the Korea Development Institute (KDI) in 1971. Kim directed the Institute until 1982, and under his direction it participated in the design of the Fifth Year Economic Plan and also supplied the government with long-term economic research. During Kim's tenure, KDI became the "think tank" of the Korean government for economic policy.

Notes

1. Lawrence J. Lau: "Introduction"

1. The comparison with Japan is a little misleading, however, because Taiwan nationals were not permitted to hold foreign assets without government approval prior to 1987. Thus, the official foreign reserves held by the Central Bank of China in Taipei represented the total amount of foreign assets held by the nationals of Taiwan. By contrast, private Japanese holdings of foreign assets are many times the official foreign reserves held by the Japanese government through the Bank of Japan.

2. Among the proponents of this theory of the "new authoritarianism" are the advocates of economic reform in mainland China, who use it to justify the centralization (and recentralization) of economic and political power there.

3. See, for example, the discussion by L. J. Lau, "A Comparative Analysis of Economic Development Experiences in Chinese Societies," in Y.C. Jao, V. Mok and L. S. Ho, *Economic Development in Chinese Societies: Models and Experiences* (Hong Kong University Press, 1989).

2. Ramon H. Myers: "The Economic Development of the Republic of China on Taiwan, 1965–1981"

1. Ramon H. Myers, "The Economic Development of Taiwan," in Hungdah Chiul (ed.), *China and the Question of Taiwan: Documents and Analysis* (New York: Praeger, 1973), pp. 33–41; Samuel P.S. Ho, *Economic Development of Taiwan, 1860–1970* (New Haven, Conn.: Yale University Press, 1978), chapter 3.

2. About two-fifths of the residents in both large and small cities in 1973 supposedly came from rural areas. See Ming-cheng Chang, "The Economic Adjustment of Migrants in Taiwan," *Industry of Free China*, Vol. 51:3 (March 25, 1979), p. 29.

3. Tsay Ching-lung, *Employment and Earnings of City-Ward Migrants: A Study on Individual Outcomes of Migration to Taipei* (Nankang, Taipei: The Institute of Economics, Academia Sinica, 1981), No. 18, Monograph Series, p. 14.

4. Charles Robert Roll, Jr., *The Distribution of Rural Incomes in China: Comparison of the 1930s and 1950s* (New York: Garland Publishing, 1980) pp. 204–6.

5. *Taiwan Statistical Data Book 1983*, p. 36. Hereafter *TSD*.

6. Ibid., p. 189.

7. Ibid., p. 16.

8. Teng-hui Lee, *Agriculture and Economic Development in Taiwan* (Taichung, Taiwan: Ta-Kung Printing Co., 1983), Vol. 3, pp. 1834–35.

9. Shirley W. Y. Kuo, *The Taiwan Economy in Transition* (Boulder, Colo.: Westview Press, 1983), pp. 246–47.

10. Ibid., p. 249.

11. Bank of Taiwan, *T'ai-wan chin-jung, t'ung-chi yueh-pao (Taiwan Financial Statistics Monthly)*, No. 61 (December 1956), pp. 29–30.

12. Ibid.

13. Ibid., December 1965, p. 62.

14. Ibid., June 1984, p. 76.

15. Ibid.

16. Ibid., December 1965, p. 68.

17. Ibid., December 1975, p. 72.

18. Ching-Yuan Lin, *Industrialization in Taiwan, 1946–72: Trade and Import-Substitution Policies for Developing Countries* (New York: Praeger, 1973), p. 105.

19. Walter Galenson, "The Labor Force, Wages, and Living Standards" in Walter Galenson (ed.), *Economic Growth and Structural Change in Taiwan: The Postwar Experiences of the Republic of China* (Ithaca, N.Y.: Cornell University Press, 1979), p. 386.

20. *TSD 1983*, p. 256.

21. Chieh-chien Chao, "Economic Growth, Trade Development, and Foreign Investment in Taiwan, ROC," *Industry of Free China*, Vol. 63:3 (March 25, 1985), p. 22.

22. Ibid., p. 23.

23. Ibid., p. 256.

24. Shirley W. Y. Kuo, op. cit., pp. 202–3.

25. Ibid., p. 206.

26. *TSD 1983*, p. 238.

27. *Wall Street Journal*, May 6, 1985, p. 37.

28. *TSD 1983*, p. 235.

29. Gustav Ranis, "Industrial Development," in Walter Galenson (ed.), op. cit., p. 230.

30. Ibid., p. 236.

31. *TSD 1983*, p. 151.

32. A. James Gregor with Maria Hsia Chang and Andrew B. Zimmerman, *Ideology and Development: Sun Yat-sen and the Economic History of Taiwan* (Berkeley, Calif.: Center for Chinese Studies, Institute of East Asian Studies, University of California, 1981), chapter 1.

33. Wei Wo, "Ming-sheng chu-i ti ching-chi mo-shih" (The economic model for people's livelihood), *Chung-hua hsueh-pao*, Vol. 8:2 (July 1981), p. 134.

34. Anthony Y. C. Koo, *The Role of Land Reform in Economic Development: A Case Study of Taiwan* (New York: Praeger, 1968), chapter 3.

35. Ching-Yuan Lin, op. cit., p. 79.

36. Ibid., p. 93.

37. Ibid., p. 104.

38. *TSD 1982*, pp. 23, 39.

39. *Statute for Investment by Foreign Nationals*, Development and Investment Center, Republic of China, June 1973.

40. F. J. Eu, "The Present and Future of Artificial Fiber Industry in Taiwan," *Industry of Free China*, Vol. 12:2 (August 25, 1959), pp. 5–18.

41. Kwei-jeou Wang, "Economic and Social Impact of Export Processing Zones in the Republic of China," *Industry of Free China* (December 25, 1980),pp. 7–28.

42. K. T. Li, "Up-grading of Science and Technology in Taiwan," *Industry of Free China*, Vol. 54:2 (August 25, 1980), p. 3.

43. W. A. Yeh, "The Ten Major Development Projects and Taiwan's Economic Development," *Industry of Free China*, (April 25, 1979), pp. 8–23.

44. Council for Economic Planning and Development, "Highlights of the 12 New Development Projects," *Industry of Free China*, Vol. 52:3 (March 25, 1980), p. 35.

45. *TSD 1983*, p. 161.

46. *Fortune*, August 22, 1983.

47. Council for Economic Planning and Development, "Wou-kuo tien-tzu kung-yeh-hsien-k'uang you p'ing-ku" (The current conditions and an assessment of Taiwan's electronics industry), *Tzu-you chung-kou chih kung-yeh*, Vol. 54:2 (August 25, 1980), p. 17.

48. John H. Y. Yu, "Man-Made Industry in Taiwan," *Industry of Free China*, Vol. 33:2 (February 25, 1970), pp. 29–37.

49. Cited from an unpublished work by Gustav Ranis and Chi Schive. I am grateful to Dr. Schive for sharing this information with me.

50. Andrew Tanzer, "Asia Plugs into the Computer," *Far Eastern Economic Review*, July 21, 1983, p. 60.

51. Chi Schive, "Technology Transfer Through Direct Foreign Investment: A Case Study of Taiwan Singer," Proceedings of the Academy of International Business Asia-Pacific Dimensions of International Business, Honolulu, December 18–20, 1979, p. 114.

52. Shih Chi-tseng, "Nung-kung pu-men-chien kung-tzu ch'a-i yu lao-li i-tung" (Manpower Mobility and the Wage Differential Between the Agricultural and Industrial Sectors), Proceedings from the Conference on Taiwan Manpower, December 21–23, 1977, Institute of Economic Research, Academia Sinica, Nankang, Taiwan, p. 389.

53. Shirley W. Y. Kuo, op. cit., p. 244.

54. Ibid., p. 271.

55. *TSD 1983*, p. 55.

56. *Basic Agricultural Statistics, Republic of China, 1983*, p. 39.

57. These monetary estimates of rice-in-kind subsidies to rice-growing farmers have been provided to me by Miss Ch'en.

58. T. H. Shen, *The Sino–American Joint Commission on Rural Reconstruction: Twenty Years of Cooperation for Agricultural Development* (Ithaca, N.Y.: Cornell University Press, 1970), p. 45.

59. T. H. Shen (ed.), *Agriculture's Place in the Strategy of Development: The Taiwan Experience* (Taipei: Joint Commission on Rural Reconstruction, July 1974), pp. 42–44.

60. Ibid., p. 283.

3. Sung Yeung Kwack: "The Economic Development of the Republic of Korea, 1965–1981"

1. For useful and detailed descriptions of the development and modernization process, see Soon Cho, *Direction of Korean Economic Development* (Seoul: Bi Pong Publishing Co., 1981); Charles R. Frank, K. S. Kim, and L. Westpal, *Foreign Trade Regime and Economic Development: South Korea* (New York: Columbia University Press, 1975); Kim and Michael Roemer, *Growth and Structural Transformation* (Cambridge: Harvard University Press, 1979); and Edward S. Mason, et al., *The Economic and Social Modernization of Korea* (Cambridge, Mass.: Harvard University Press, 1981).

2. Bank of Korea, *Analysis of Productivity*, May 1982.

3. Economic Planning Board, *Summary Draft of the Fifth Five-Year Economic and Social Development Plan, 1982–1985*, August 1981.

4. Ibid.

5. Chung Woong Lee and H. J. Yoo, "Differential Behavior Between Wholesale and Consumer Prices," *Monthly Economic Research of the Bank of Korea* (September 1979), pp. 4–15.

6. This point is documented fully in Paul W. Kuznets', *Economic Growth and Structure in the Republic of Korea* (New Haven, Conn.: Yale University Press, 1977).

7. Economic policies in Korea have been intended to assist Korea's export-led growth strategy, which was advocated by, among others, Bela Balassa in *The Newly Industrializing Countries in the World Economy* (Elmsford, N.Y.: Pergamon Press, 1981).

8. The financial reform of 1965 can be regarded as an implementation of the view of Ronald I. McKinnon in *Money and Capital in Economic Development* (Washington, D.C.: The Brookings Institution, 1973). By making regulated interest rates more realistic in a financially repressive economy, financial institutions can mobilize savings and stimulate growth. For detailed descriptions of the reform measures and process, see Robert F. Emery, *The Korean Interest Rate Reform of September 1965* (Washington, D.C.: Board of Governors of the Federal Reserve System, 1966).

9. David C. Cole and Y. C. Park, *Financial Development in Korea, 1945–1978*, Korea Development Institute Working Paper No. 7904, 1979.

10. Suk Mo Koo, S. Y. Hong, and J. M. Shin, *A Study in Informal Financial Markets in Korea* (Seoul: Korea Economic Institute, 1982).

11. Ibid.

12. Sung Y. Kwack and M. Merced, "A Model of Economic Policy Effects and External Influences on the Korean Economy," SRI/Wharton EFA World Economic Discussion Papers, No. 9 (April 25, 1980).

13. For detailed examination of Korea's distribution of income and its relationship to economic growth, see Irman Adelman and S. Robinson, *Income Distribution Policy in Developing Countries, A Case Study of Korea* (Stanford: Stanford University Press, 1978); and Hakchung Choo and Daemo Kim, *Probable Size Distribution of Income in Korea: Over Time and by Sectors* (Seoul: Korean Development Institute, 1978).

4. Tibor Scitovsky: "Economic Development in Taiwan and South Korea: 1965–1981"

Most of the data cited in this paper are from the *Statistical Yearbooks* of Taiwan and Korea. References will be given only for data from other sources.

1. The five are Japan, South Korea, Taiwan, Singapore, and Hong Kong. The comparison is based on data from the World Bank's *World Development Report, 1982*, Appendix table 1, p. 110, supplemented with the World Bank's unpublished computer printout for Taiwan.

2. For convenience, South Korea is referred to as "Korea" throughout. The article does not consider economic change in North Korea.

3. Kwang Suk Kim and Michael Roemer, *Growth and Structural Transformation: Studies in the Modernization of the Republic of Korea: 1945–75* (Cambridge, Mass.: Harvard University Press, 1979), p. 147; I. M. D. Little, "An Economic Reconnaissance," in W. Galenson (ed.), *Economic Growth and Structural Change in Taiwan* (Ithaca, N.Y.: Cornell University Press, 1979), p. 455.

4. Little, op. cit., p. 461.

5. The striking similarity of both land reforms to the Japanese land reform carried out under the directive of the Allied Occupation Authorities attests the strong influence of the American expert, the late Wolf Ladejinsky, who served as land-reform adviser to all three countries.

6. World Bank, 1972; Little, op. cit., p. 458.

7. The average is calculated from M. Scott, "Foreign Trade," in W. Galenson, op. cit., p. 370.

8. That average, quite a bit lower than estimates occasionally quoted elsewhere, is calculated from data given in Anne O. Krueger, *The Development Role of the Foreign Sector and Aid: Studies in the Modernization of the Republic of Korea: 1945–75* (Cambridge, Mass.: Harvard University Press, 1979), tables 18 and 30, pp. 67 and 109, respectively.

9. From the review of Krueger's above-cited book by Jayati Datta Mitra, in *Economic Development and Cultural Change*, Vol. 30 (1981), p. 199.

10. Krueger, op. cit., pp. 145–47; I. M. D. Little, "The Experience and Causes of Rapid Labour-Intensive Development in Korea, Taiwan Province, Hong Kong, and Singapore and the Possibilities of Emulation," in Eddy Lee (ed.), *Export-Led Industrialization and Development* (Singapore: International Labour Organization, 1981), pp. 37–39.

11. See, however, H. E. Arndt, "Two Kinds of Credit Rationing," in *Banca Nazionale del Lavoro Quarterly Review*, No. 143 (December 1982), for an interesting contrary view.

12. Note that the rise in wages does not discourage the use of labor-intensive methods of production because it raises the costs of both labor and of goods made with labor (which include capital goods) in approximately equal proportions. Nor, for that matter, do rising interest rates raise the price of capital goods in relation to other prices. What they do instead is raise the cost of payments due before production starts in relation to payment made concurrently with

production, whatever the nature of the resources so paid for. It is the relative cost of those two kinds of payments that determines the labor- or capital-intensity of the methods of production chosen; and it, in turn, is determined by the interest rate alone.

13. President Park assumed power in 1961 and was assassinated in 1979.

14. The quotation and much of the argument of this part comes from E. S. Mason et al., *The Economic and Social Modernization of the Republic of Korea* (Cambridge, Mass.: Harvard University Press, 1980), chapter 8.

15. The ratio of acreage harvested to total farmland. The ratio has fallen quite a bit since 1964, probably because of increased livestock feeding and production of perennial crops, especially fruit.

16. I wish to thank Professor Irma Adelman and Mr. Yoon Je Cho for information on that subject.

17. I owe the information to Dr. Avishay Braverman.

18. The data in this section are from E. Thorbecke, "Agricultural Development," in W. Galenson (ed.), op. cit. and S. H. Ban, P. Y. Moon, and D. H. Perkins, *Rural Development: Studies in the Modernization of the Republic of Korea: 1945–1975* (Cambridge, Mass.: Harvard University Press, 1980).

19. Bela Balassa and Associates, *Development Strategies in Semi-Industrial Economies*, World Bank Research Publication (Baltimore, Md.: Johns Hopkins University Press, 1982).

20. There is a formula according to which it is "natural" for a smaller country's export and import ratios to exceed a larger country's trade ratios by the fourth root of the ratio in which that country's population exceeds its own—see Hans Linnemann, *An Economic Study of International Trade Flows* (Amsterdam: North-Holland Publishing Co., 1966), p. 206; Scott, op. cit., p. 350. By that reckoning, Taiwan's exports and imports would have to be around 45 percent of GNP for its trade dependence to match Korea's rather than around 50 percent as they are today.

21. Balassa and Associates, op. cit., p. 314, table 10.13.

22. The concentration ratio is the square root of the sum of the squared proportions that each commodity or each country destination forms of a country's total exports; and it ranges from 0 to 100 percent. For example, the 40.8 percent geographical concentration of Korea's exports shows that 56 percent of its exports is destined for the United States and Japan and the remainder is well dispersed among other countries. (The concept was introduced by Albert Hirschman. For the formula and its explanation, see the note to the table referred to in the text.)

23. Honda, for example, imports oranges to Japan, needing their bulky freight for ballast on the return trip of the boats in which it ships its cars for export.

24. Scott, op. cit., p. 367.

25. The definition of urban areas is different in the two countries, which makes it impossible to compare their degrees of urbanization precisely.

26. Korea's large investment in residential housing may have had another reason as well, which will be presented shortly.

27. Yet another way in which a good export performance helps also the rest of the economy to grow is worth mentioning: it enhances the country's credit- worthiness and renders foreign loans more easily accessible. Both countries enjoyed that advantage; the interesting question is why Taiwan had no need for it.

28. That tax is additional to the corporate income tax, which both countries levy on the corporation's total net profits.

29. The percentages are calculated from Yung Chul Park, "Export-Led Development: The Korean Experience 1960–78," in Eddy Lee (ed.), *Export-Led Industrialization and Development* (Singapore: International Labour Office, 1981), p. 90.

30. The customary simple numerical model of the life-cycle hypothesis shows that each percentage point of annual growth in income gives rise to 3 percentage points of positive net saving expressed as percentage of income. See F. Modigliani and R. Brumberg, "Utility Analysis and the Consumption Function: An Interpretation of Cross-Section Data," in K. K. Kurihara (ed.), *Post-Keynesian Economics* (New Brunswick, N.J.: Rutgers University Press, 1954).

31. For an English language summary of the several explanations of Japan's high savings rate, see M. Shinobara, *Industrial Growth, Trade, and Dynamic Patterns in the Japanese Economy* (Tokyo: University of Tokyo Press, 1982), chapter 10.

32. Korea collects no statistics on manufacturing establishments with four or less employees. The data used are from *The Report of 1976 Industrial and Commercial Censuses of Taiwan-Fukien District of the ROC*, Vol. 3, bk. 1, p. 118; and *Korea Statistical Yearbook* 1979, p. 155.

33. All of the data used in this paragraph refer to 1976, the year of Taiwan's last industrial census; and they come from the sources cited in the previous footnote.

34. I want to thank Mr. Yoon Jer Cho for suggesting that explanation for Korea's relatively low household savings rate.

35. Needless to say, the fluctuations in the real rate of interest resulted not from adjustments in the interest paid on savings deposits, but from failure to adjust it in response to fluctuations in the rate of inflation, which resulted from sudden and drastic changes in economic policies. The personal savings rate also fluctuated, but in no systematic relation to fluctuations in the real rate of interest. Indeed, the fluctuating savings rate is best explained as the result of the public's attempt to maintain its real consumption on a steady course, in the face of great fluctuations in incomes and prices.

36. Although Korean statistics refer only to enterprises employing at least five employees, it is not unreasonable to assume that their rate of increase was more or less the same as the rate of increase of *all* enterprises. Note also that the very small increase in the number of companies is a net increase: the difference between the number of new companies established and the number of old companies that have disappeared through merger or something else; and a look at the annual data suggests that the number of mergers must have been quite large. It would be more appropriate to use gross figures, but they are not available. One must bear in mind that the Taiwanese figures are also net and not gross.

37. Balassa and Associates, op. cit., p. 264.

38. International Labour Organization, *International Yearbook of Labour Statistics* (Geneva: ILO, 1983).

39. Resources could also have been diverted from other sources and types of investment, in which case total investment would not have increased. In Korea, however, to judge by the statistics, that does not seem to have happened to any significant extent.

40. The saving in processing costs, however, benefits the middlemen more than the borrower and lender; and that, of course, is the objection to curb markets.

41. The estimate refers to 1968 and is quoted in Mason et al., op. cit., p. 335.

42. Luck had something to do with that. Alone among the oil-importing countries, Korea saw its balance of payments improve at the time and as a result of the oil-price increase, because its construction industry won US$2.5 billion worth of contracts in 1976, mainly from the oil countries. Construction has been Korea's main source of foreign-exchange earnings since then, the gross value of foreign contracts averaging US$2.5 billion worth of contracts in 1976, mainly from the oil countries.

43. Taiwan spent 3.9 percent of the GNP on education in 1980, and the United States 5.2 percent.

5. Lawrence J. Lau: "The Economy of Taiwan, 1981–1988"

The author wishes to thank Masahiko Aoki, Charles Horioka, K. C. Fung, S. W. Kung, Kuo-Shu Liang, Jia-Dong Shea, and Eric T. Wu for very helpful discussions and Paul Lau for invaluable research assistance. This research has been supported in part by a grant from the World Journal Culture Foundation, Inc. to the Center for Economic Policy Research of Stanford University, which is gratefully acknowledged.

1. In May 1989, Premier Yu Kuo-Hwa resigned and was succeeded by Premier Lee Huan.

2. See, for example, J. C. H. Fei, G. Ranis, and S. W. Y. Kuo, *Growth with Equity: The Taiwan Case* (New York: Oxford University Press, 1979); W. Galenson (ed.), *Economic Growth and Structural Change in Taiwan* (Ithaca, N.Y.: Cornell University Press, 1979); S. W. Y. Kuo, *The Taiwan Economy in Transition* (Boulder, Colo.: Westview Press, 1983); K. T. Li, *The Evolution of Policy Behind Taiwan's Development Success* (New Haven, Conn.: Yale University Press, 1988); and S. C. Tsiang, "Taiwan's Economic Miracle: Lessons in Economic Development," in A. C. Harberger (ed.), *World Economic Growth* (San Francisco: ICS Press, 1984), pp. 301–25.

3. This rule has been gradually liberalized. As of September, 1989, the limit for remittances into Taiwan is US$500,000 per person per year.

4. See T. Scitovsky, "Economic Development in Taiwan and South Korea, 1965–1981," chapter 4, this volume.

5. This is real GNP before adjustment for terms of trade. See Council for Economic Planning and Development, Republic of China, *Taiwan Statistical Data Book 1989* (Taipei), p. 26. Hereafter *TSD*.

6. For South Korea, the deflator is for GDP between 1965 and 1987. International Monetary Fund, *International Financial Statistics Yearbook 1989*, pp. 456–59. For the United States, the deflator is for GNP. Ibid., pp. 720–25.

7. Data for the money supply are taken from *TSD 1989*, p. 151. The money supply includes net currency and net checking account, passbook, and passbook savings deposits. Real GNP and GNP deflator are from *TSD 1989*.

8. Data on labor force are taken from *TSD 1989*, p. 13.

9. See Organization for Economic Cooperation and Development, *Flows and Stocks of Fixed Capital, 1960–1985* (Paris: OECD, 1987).

10. *TSD 1989*.

11. *TSD 1989*, p. 7.

12. The rate of change of total factor productivity is, under the assumption of constant returns to scale in production, given by the difference between the rate of change of real output and the weighted average of the rates of change of capital and labor.

13. The Gini coefficient is a standard measure of the degree of equality of an income distribution. The higher the value of the Gini coefficient, the more unequal the income distribution.

14. I am grateful to Eric T. Wu for providing valuable information on the Taiwan Stock Exchange.

15. The diversion came first from Japan because of the appreciation of the yen, then from South Korea because of the labor strife there, then from mainland China because of the Tiananmen incident on June 4, 1989.

16. For a more general discussion of this problem, see M. Olson, *The Rise and Decline of Nations: Economic Growth, Stagflation, and Social Rigidities* (New Haven, Conn.: Yale University Press, 1982).

17. Of course, if the polluter cannot be easily identified, there may be no choice but to have the government pay the pollution abatement costs.

18. See, for example, the discussions in M. Aoki, *Information, Incentives, and Bargaining in the Japanese Economy* (New York: Cambridge University Press, 1988); and H. Shimada, "The Perception and the Reality of Japanese Industrial Relations," in L. Thurow (ed.), *The Management Challenge* (Cambridge, Mass.: MIT Press, 1988).

7. Lawrence J. Lau: "Conclusion"

1. The actual figures for Taiwan are US$217 and US$6,105; for South Korea, US$107 and US$3,208. Taiwanese GNP per capita data from Council for Economic Planning and Development, Republic of China, *Taiwan Statistical Data Book 1989* (Taipei: Council for Economic Planning and Development, July 1989), p. 29. Exchange rates used are the annual averages of the buying and selling rates, *ibid.*, p. 199. South Korean data from International Monetary Fund, *International Financial Statistics Yearbook 1989* (Washington, D.C.: International Monetary Fund, 1989), pp. 456–459. If one uses the exchange rate at year-end 1988, the GNP per capita of South Korea is in excess of US$4,000.

2. See the sources in note 1.

3. See M. Abramovitz and P. A. David, "Reinterpreting Economic Growth: Parables and Realities," *American Economic Review*, Vol. 63 (1973), p. 431, table 2.

4. This calculation is based on data from International Monetary Fund, *International Financial Statistics Yearbook 1987*, pp. 426–427.

5. Imports are measured f.o.b. in accordance with the convention used in *International Financial Statistics*. The 1965 figures for Taiwan are taken from International Monetary Fund, *International Financial Statistics, 1978 Supplement: Annual Data, 1953–1977*, Vol. 31 (May 1978), pp. 114–17. The 1988 figures for Taiwan are taken from Central Bank of China, *Financial Statistics: Taiwan District*,

the Republic of China (Compiled in Accordance with IFS Format) (Taipei: Central Bank of China, 1989).

6. International Monetary Fund, *International Financial Statistics Yearbook 1989*, pp. 456–59.

7. An alternative estimate of the growth rate of the net capital stock of South Korea between 1965 and 1986 is 12.0 percent. H. K. Pyo, "Estimates of Capital Stock and Capital/Output Coefficients by Industries for the Republic of Korea (1953–1986)," Working Paper No. 8810 (Korea Development Institute, Seoul, September 1988).

8. Using Pyo's estimates of net capital stock of South Korea, H. K. Pyo and H. Y. Kwon estimated the growth rate of total factor productivity in South Korea to be 2.4 percent per year between 1965 and 1985. H. K. Pyo and H. Y. Kwon, "The Measurement of Real Product and Real Factor Input in the Republic of Korea, 1960–1985," typescript, 1989.

9. See D. W. Jorgenson, F. M. Gollop, and B. M. Fraumeni, *Productivity and U.S. Economic Growth* (Cambridge, Mass.: Harvard University Press, 1987).

10. South Korea was not as faithful an adherent to the latter policy as Taiwan. See the discussions in S. C. Tsiang, "Taiwan's Economic Miracle: Lessons in Economic Development," in A. C. Harberger (ed.), *World Economic Growth* (San Francisco: ICS Press, 1984), pp. 301–25; and A. O. Krueger, *The Developmental Role of the Foreign Sector and Aid: Studies in the Modernization of the Republic of Korea, 1945–1975* (Cambridge, Mass.: Harvard University Press, 1979).

11. Among the proponents of this theory of "new authoritarianism" are some of the advocates of economic reform in mainland China, who used it to justify the centralization (and recentralization) of economic and political power there.

12. See K. T. Li, *The Evolution of Policy Behind Taiwan's Development Success* (New Haven: Yale University Press, 1988) for a description of the policy planning, decision, and implementation process in Taiwan.

13. At a later stage, when the family firms have expanded so much that they require non–family members as executives, there may be an incentive incompatibility problem to the extent that the objectives of the owners and the non-owner–managers do not coincide. Unavoidable economic inefficiency may result from such incentive incompatibility, generally referred to in the literature as the principal-agent problem.

14. See T. Scitovsky, "Economic Development in Taiwan and South Korea, 1965–1981," chapter 4, this volume.

15. On the importance of competition, see, for example, the discussion in L. J. Lau, "A Comparative Analysis of Economic Development Experiences in Chinese Societies," in Y. C. Jao, V. Mok, and L. S. Ho (eds.), *Economic Development in Chinese Societies: Models and Experiences* (Hong Kong: Hong Kong University Press, 1989), pp. 9–23.

16. Both Taiwan and South Korea, especially the latter, have some of the highest enrollment rates at the tertiary (postsecondary) level in the world.

Contributors

LAWRENCE R. KLEIN, Nobel laureate in economics, is professor of economics at the University of Pennsylvania. The author of numerous seminal texts on econometrics, economic forecasting, prediction, and macroeconomics, he has also edited scholarly journals and served as adviser or consultant to many research institutes and governmental task forces. He is the founder of Project LINK and Wharton Econometric Forecasting Associates, Inc.

SUNG YEUNG KWACK is professor of economics at Howard University. His previous positions include deputy director of the Office of Econometric Balance of Payments, U.S. Department of the Treasury; economist with the Federal Reserve Board; senior research fellow and research director at SRI International, Arlington, Virginia; and senior economist and director at the Center for Pacific Basin Studies, Wharton Econometric Forecasting Associates, Inc. In addition to teaching at the graduate level, publishing many articles, and speaking at seminars and conferences, he is the principal investigator for the Financial Intermediation Project.

LAWRENCE J. LAU is professor of economics at Stanford University. He has received numerous honors, awards, and grants; been a consultant on economics and management to many organizations; and edited several books and academic journals. Among his extensive publications in economic theory, economic development, econometrics, East Asian studies, and agricultural economics, is *Farmer Education and Farm Efficiency* (with D. T. Jamison, 1982).

RAMON H. MYERS is curator-scholar of the East Asian collection and senior fellow at the Hoover Institution, Stanford University. Author of many articles and reviews on the East Asian international order, its security, economic development, and political-social modernization, his recent publications include *The Japanese Colonial Empire, 1895–1945* (coedited with M. Peattie, 1984); *The Japanese Informal Empire in China, 1895–1937* (coedited with P. Duus and M. Peattie, 1989); *Defending an Economic Superpower: Reassessing the U.S.–Japan Security Alliance* (with T. Kataoka, 1989); and *Last Chance in Manchuria: The Diary of Chang Kia-Ngau* (coedited with D. Gillin, 1989).

TIBOR SCITOVSKY is emeritus professor of economics at Stanford University and the University of California at Santa Cruz. Formerly he was professor of economics at the University of California at Berkeley, Yale University, and the London School of Economics. He also served as an economist with the U.S. Department of Commerce and a research fellow at the Development Center of the Organization for Economic Cooperation and Development (OECD) in Paris. In addition to publishing many articles, his books include *Money and the Balance of Payments* (1969); *Industry and Trade in Some Developing Countries* (with I. Little and M. Scott, 1970); and *The Joyless Economy* (1976).

Index

ICEG Academic Advisory Board